100
Cross-curricular
Maths
Lessons

David & Penny Glover

Years 3 & 4

Scottish Primary 4–5

Authors
David Glover and Penny Glover

Editor
Joel Lane

Assistant Editor
David Sandford

Series Designer
Heather C Sanneh

Illustrations
Shirley Walker

Cover photography
© Photodisc, Inc

Text © Penny Glover and David Glover
© 2002 Scholastic Ltd

Designed using Adobe Pagemaker

Published by Scholastic Ltd, Villiers House,
Clarendon Avenue, Leamington Spa, Warwickshire CV32 5PR

Visit our website at www.scholastic.co.uk

Printed by Cromwell Press Ltd, Trowbridge

1 2 3 4 5 6 7 8 9 0   2 3 4 5 6 7 8 9 0 1

British Library Cataloguing-in-Publication Data A catalogue
record for this book is available from the British Library.

ISBN 0-439-98345-2

Acknowledgement
Extracts from the National Curriculum for England © Crown copyright
material is reproduced with the permission of the Controller of HMSO
and the Queen's Printer for Scotland.
Extracts from the National Numeracy Strategy *Framework For Teaching
Mathematics* © Crown copyright. Reproduced under the terms of HMSO
Guidance Note 8.

Contents

Year 4

Introduction

Few of us are pure mathematicians. Our mathematical skills are practical, not abstract. We use mathematics to compare prices as we shop, to make measurements for DIY projects and to follow recipes in the kitchen. Often, we are hardly aware of the maths skills we are using. However, children need to have the value and application of their mathematics in other school subjects, as well as in everyday life, made clear. Such realistic contexts broaden and develop their mathematical understanding and skills. For this reason, the National Numeracy Strategy and National Curriculum, and the Scottish National Guidelines on Mathematics 5–14, emphasise the importance of looking for links between mathematics and other curriculum areas.

The *100 Cross-curricular Maths Lessons* series presents lesson plans linking objectives from the National Numeracy Strategy to objectives in other subjects. The lessons are intended to take place during your numeracy time, but the mathematics is set in a cross-curricular context.

Each book in this series provides content for the daily maths lessons of two year-groups. This book supports Years 3 and 4. The materials presented here can be used to substitute or supplement your daily maths lessons. The organisation of the mathematical objectives covered by the lesson plans follows the term-by-term sequence of topics set out in the National Numeracy Strategy's *Framework for Teaching Mathematics* (March 1999). Their content is also appropriate for, and adaptable to, the requirements of Primary 4–5 in Scottish schools. In Scotland, and in schools elsewhere that have decided not to adopt the National Numeracy Strategy, it will be necessary to choose activities to match your planning. To help you with this, reference grids listing the lessons' objectives are provided for each year group (see pages 10–12 and 94–96), together with a comprehensive index of maths topics and cross-curricular content on pages 175 and 176.

These lesson plans offer ideal additional or alternative activities to the main teaching activities given in the lesson plans of *100 Maths Lessons: Year 3* or *Year 4*, also published by Scholastic.

In Year 3 (Primary 4), children should be counting, reading, writing and ordering numbers to 1000. They should know by heart all of the addition and subtraction facts of numbers to 20. They should recognise and be able to use unit fractions. They should know by heart the 2, 5 and 10 times tables. They should understand division. They should be able to use the £.p notation, as well as use all four operations to solve word problems. They should also be able to identify right angles and lines of symmetry in simple shapes, and to organise and interpret numerical data in tables and graphs. In Year 4 (Primary 5), children should extend their knowledge of numbers beyond 1000. They should be able to round positive integers to the nearest 10 or 100. They should recognise fractions that are several parts of a whole. They should begin to carry out column addition and subtraction. They should extend their knowledge of tables to include the 3 and 4 times tables and be able to use tables to derive division facts. They should know and be able to use and convert between familiar units of length, mass and capacity. They should also be able to classify polygons, and should develop their problem-solving skills.

The lessons in this book are planned to support this progression of mathematical knowledge and skills with activities designed to match the children's developing abilities. Each lesson presents a mathematical challenge in the context of work in another subject, thus developing the child's knowledge and skills in that area also.

Using this book

The materials

This book provides 50 cross-curricular maths lessons for Year 3 and 50 for Year 4. Each lesson plan sets out its objectives for numeracy and another curriculum subject or subjects. The intention is to develop the mathematics in a context that links strongly to another subject area, so fulfilling the linked subject objectives. Photocopiable activity sheets and assessment activities support the lesson plans for each term.

Organisation

This book follows the Year 3 and Year 4 topic plans given in the National Numeracy Strategy's *Framework for Teaching Mathematics*. Complete planning grids are set out on pages 10–12 for Year 3 and 94–96 for Year 4.

An extract from the planning grid for Year 3 is reproduced on page 6. Columns one and two list the National Numeracy Strategy unit numbers and topics. Column three gives the numeracy objective(s) met by each lesson plan.

Planning Grid

Term 1	Topics	Maths objectives	Cross-curricular objectives	Activities
Unit 1	Place value, ordering, estimating, rounding	Read and write whole numbers to at least 1000 in figures and words.	**Literacy** Read and spell correctly high-frequency words. Notice differences in the style and structure of fiction and non-fiction writing.	p13: **Number words** Read and write whole numbers to at least 1000 in figures and words.
	Reading numbers from scales	Order whole numbers to at least 1000, and position them on a number line.	**History** Place events in chronological order. Use dates and vocabulary relating to the passing of time. Links to QCA History Units 6A, 6B, 6C.	p14: **Order the years** Place events in order on a 1000-year timeline.
2–3	Understanding + and –	Read and begin to write vocabulary related to time. Read and begin to write vocabulary related to length. Measure and compare using standard units. Read scales to the nearest division. Record estimates and measurements to the nearest whole or half unit.	**Physical education** Measure and record athletic activity. Links to QCA PE – Athletic activities Units 1 and 2.	p15: **How far can you jump?** Use measuring scales in PE to find a distance jumped, hopped...
	Mental calculation strategies (+ and –)			
	Money and 'real-life' problems	Explain methods and reasoning orally.	**English** Speak with confidence in a range of contexts, adapting their speech for a range of purposes. Listen, understand and respond appropriately to others.	p16: **I'm looking at a number** Oral mental calculations.
	Making decisions and checking results			
4–6	Measures – including problems	Add three or more two-digit numbers with the help of apparatus or pencil and paper.	**Geography** Identify and describe what places are like. Could be linked to QCA Geography Unit 8. **History** Study aspects of everyday life in a past world society, including technology.	p17: **Abacus** Use an abacus to add two and three numbers up to 100.
	Shape and space			
	Reasoning about shapes	Solve word problems involving numbers in 'real life' and money... including finding totals and giving change, and working out which coins to pay.	**Geography** Use maps and plans at a range of scales. Links to QCA Geography Unit 6. **English** Speak with confidence in a range of contexts, adapting their speech for a range of purposes. Listen, understand and respond appropriately to others.	p18: **Buy a ticket** Role-play purchasing a bus ticket, giving and receiving change.

The cross-curricular objectives are set out in column four, together with links to relevant units in the QCA's primary schemes of work. The individual lesson titles, with brief descriptions of their content, are listed in column five.

Lesson plans

Each lesson plan contains the following sections:

Objectives
The numeracy and cross-curricular subject objectives are stated, together with links to relevant QCA schemes of work.

Resources
Resources required for the lesson are listed.

Vocabulary
The vocabulary sections have drawn on the National Numeracy Strategy's *Mathematical Vocabulary* booklet. New or specific maths vocabulary to be used during the lesson is listed. Use this vocabulary with the whole class, so that all the children have a chance to hear it in context and understand it. Encourage children to use the vocabulary orally when asking or answering questions, so that they develop understanding of its mathematical meaning.

Background
Key maths strategies, skills or operations relevant to the specific lesson are outlined

and the cross-curricular context is introduced. This section may provide useful background for the lesson, such as historical facts or science explanations.

Preparation
Preparation needed in advance of the lesson is highlighted – for example, assembling materials, making resources and photocopying activity sheets.

Main teaching activity
This explains what the teacher should do in the whole-class teaching session, lasting about 30 minutes. In some lessons, much of the time will be spent in whole-class, interactive teaching. In others, the whole-class session will be shorter, with practical or paper-based activities provided for groups, pairs or individuals.

Differentiation
This section suggests adaptations and extensions to the main teaching activity in order to meet the needs of less able and more able children within your class.

Plenary
This section is a chance to bring the children together again for a concluding whole-class session. The plenary session provides opportunities to review and reinforce key ideas, compare strategies and outcomes, develop the cross-curricular links and assess the children's progress.

Planning and organisation

These lesson plans do *not* form a self-contained mathematics course. Rather, they are designed to be integrated into your overall scheme of work for mathematics and, more generally, to be linked to your plans for other subject areas. The planning grids on pages 10–12 and 74–76 are the best starting point for deciding how these lessons can be incorporated into your teaching.

Assessment

Three termly assessment activity sheets, together with supporting notes (including practical assessment opportunities) are included with each year's lesson plans. These can be incorporated into your overall assessment strategy for mathematics.

The assessment activity sheets are designed to introduce children to the style of questions found in the national tests. They are set in cross-curricular contexts drawn from the preceding term's lessons. Three activities have been included on each assessment sheet. It is not essential for the children to have had experience of these particular contexts; but it is important that they are comfortable using their maths in a variety of less obviously mathematical situations. More able children will probably complete the exercises with minimal guidance. Most children, however, will need considerable support the first few times they tackle this type of activity.

Practical assessment tasks are also of great value in making a judgement of a child's progress, particularly for less able children who find formal paper-and-pencil activities demanding. A suggestion for a practical assessment task has been included in each assessment lesson. Set selected children to complete the practical task while the rest of the class work on the paper-based activities. Review the answers as a class. Collect the completed activity sheets and make notes on your observations of the practical work. Use these as an aid to judging individual children's progress, and include them in your records.

Resources

Photocopiable sheets

These sheets support individual lessons and may be copied for distribution to your class.

Classroom equipment

All the equipment used in this book will normally be found within any primary school. The following list gives items that will be needed on a regular basis.

● A flip chart and marker pens (and/or a whiteboard or chalkboard).
● Sets of numeral flash cards 0–1000.
● Abacuses.
● Counting apparatus (such as counters, sorting toys, wooden cubes, beads and laces).
● Measuring apparatus including centimetre rulers, tape measures, measuring jugs and a classroom balance.
● Craft or technology materials and tools – scissors, glue, adhesive tape, card, dowel, modelling clay, construction kits and so on.
● Shape apparatus including shape tiles and 3-D shapes.
● Safety mirrors.
● Art materials.
● Coins, real or plastic.
● Dice.
● Demonstration analogue and digital clock faces.
● A programmable robot such as Roamer or PIP.
● Recyclable materials, including cardboard boxes and plastic containers.
● PE apparatus, including stop watches, bean bags, hoops and balls.
● Wall maps of the world, the UK and the local environment.
● Musical instruments.

ICT

A number of the activities are computer-based. These activities require a computer program with text, table and drawing capabilities such as *Textease* (Softease Ltd) or *Microsoft Word*. There are many equivalent programs in use that allow children to enter and edit text, and to create and manipulate geometrical shapes on the same page. Use a program with which you are familiar and check that you can produce the desired outcome with confidence before setting children to work on the activity. These activities will be greatly enhanced if the computer is connected to a printer on which children can print their work for subsequent discussion and display.

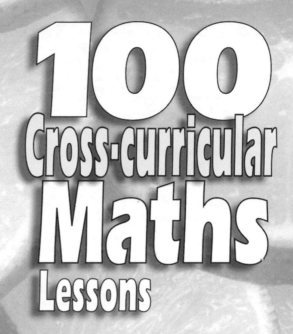

100
Cross-curricular
Maths
Lessons

Lesson plans and photocopiable activity pages

Year
3

Planning Grid

Term 1	Topics	Maths objectives	Cross-curricular objectives	Activities
Unit 1	Place value, ordering, estimating, rounding	Read and write whole numbers to at least 1000 in figures and words.	**Literacy** Read and spell correctly high-frequency words. Notice differences in the style and structure of fiction and non-fiction writing.	**p13: Number words** Read and write whole numbers to at least 1000 in figures and words.
	Reading numbers from scales	Order whole numbers to at least 1000, and position them on a number line.	**History** Place events in chronological order. Use dates and vocabulary relating to the passing of time. Links to QCA History Units 6A, 6B, 6C.	**p14: Order the years** Place events in order on a 1000-year timeline.
2–3	Understanding + and –

Mental calculation strategies (+ and –) | Read and begin to write vocabulary related to time. Read and begin to write vocabulary related to length. Measure and compare using standard units. Read scales to the nearest division. Record estimates and measurements to the nearest whole or half unit. | **Physical education** Measure and record athletic activity. Links to QCA PE – Athletic activities Units 1 and 2. | **p15: How far can you jump?** Use measuring scales in PE to find a distance jumped, hopped... |
| | Money and 'real-life' problems

Making decisions and checking results | Explain methods and reasoning orally. | **English** Speak with confidence in a range of contexts, adapting their speech for a range of purposes. Listen, understand and respond appropriately to others. | **p16: I'm looking at a number** Oral mental calculations. |
| 4–6 | Measures – including problems

Shape and space

Reasoning about shapes | Add three or more two-digit numbers with the help of apparatus or pencil and paper. | **Geography** Identify and describe what places are like. Could be linked to QCA Geography Unit 8. **History** Study aspects of everyday life in a past world society, including technology. | **p17: Abacus** Use an abacus to add two and three numbers up to 100. |
		Solve word problems involving numbers in 'real life' and money... including finding totals and giving change, and working out which coins to pay.	**Geography** Use maps and plans at a range of scales. Links to QCA Geography Unit 6. **English** Speak with confidence in a range of contexts, adapting their speech for a range of purposes. Listen, understand and respond appropriately to others.	**p18: Buy a ticket** Role-play purchasing a bus ticket, giving and receiving change.
		Read and begin to write vocabulary related to capacity. Measure and compare using standard units. Know the relationship between litres and millilitres.	**Science** Measure volumes of liquids using appropriate apparatus. Links to QCA Science Unit 3D	**p19: Which holds most?** Measure the capacities of various containers.
		Classify and describe 3-D shapes. Relate solid shapes to pictures of them.	**History** Study the characteristic features of periods and societies, for example Ancient Egypt. Links to QCA History Unit 10.	**p20: Shape words** Classify 3-D shapes and relate to Egyptian pyramid and other structures.
		Classify 2-D shapes. Make and describe shapes and patterns.	**Art** Investigate shape, colour and pattern. Links to QCA Art Unit 3B. **History** Study Roman settlement in Britain. Links to QCA History Unit 6A.	**p21: Tessellations** Investigate two-dimensional tiling patterns.
7	Assess and review			see p29
8	Counting and the properties of numbers

Reasoning about numbers

Understanding × and ÷ | Read and begin to write vocabulary of comparing and ordering numbers, including ordinal numbers to at least 100. Order whole numbers to at least 1000, and position them on a number line. Read and begin to write vocabulary related to time. | **History** Place events in chronological order. Use dates and vocabulary relating to the passing of time. | **p22: Which century?** Place years in centuries. |
| | | Explain methods and reasoning orally. Extend understanding of the operations of addition, subtraction, multiplication and division. | **English** Speak with confidence in a range of contexts, adapting their speech for a range of purposes. Listen, understand and respond appropriately to others. | **p23: Talking numbers** Work in pairs to explain orally mental calculation strategies. |
| 9–10 | Mental calculation strategies (× and ÷)

Money and 'real-life' problems | Know by heart multiplication facts for the 2, 5 and 10 times tables. Begin to know the 3 and 4 times tables. | **ICT** Create and organise text and tables. Links to QCA Information Technology Unit 3A. | **p24: Multiple grids** Use a number grid computer program to display multiples of 2, 5, 10... of a 10 × 10 grid. Describe the patterns made. |
| | Making decisions and checking results

11 Fractions | Derive quickly: doubles of all whole numbers to at least 20, doubles of multiples of 5 to 100, doubles of multiples of 50 to 500; and all corresponding halves. | **PE** Remember and repeat simple skills and actions with increasing control and co-ordination. Can be linked to QCA PE Athletic activities – Unit 1 and Gymnastic activities – Unit 3. | **p25: Double and halve** Mental doubling and halving problems set in the context of repetitions in a PE lesson. |
| | Understanding + and –

Mental calculation strategies (+ and –)

12 Time, including problems | Solve word problems involving numbers in 'real life', money and measures, using one or more steps, including finding totals and giving change, and working out which coins to pay. Recognise all coins and notes. Understand and use £.p notation (for example, know that £3.06 is £3 and 6p). | **History** Study the lives of significant men, women and children drawn from the history of Britain and the wider world (for example, artists, engineers, explorers, inventors, pioneers, rulers, saints, scientists). | **p26: Coins and notes** Relate coins and notes to the £.p notation, changing pounds for pence and vice versa. |
	Making decisions and checking results	Recognise unit fractions such as 1/2, 1/3, 1/4... and use them to find fractions of shapes. Begin to recognise simple fractions that are several parts of a whole, such as 3/4, 2/3 or 3/10.	**Geography** Study a range of places in different parts of the world. **Art** Study visual elements in design. Could be linked to QCA Art Unit 3B.	**p27: Fraction flags** Shade given fractions of patterns to produce flag designs.
13	Handling data	Add three or four single-digit numbers mentally.	**Geography** Use maps and plans at a range of scales. Be taught the locations of places in their local environment. Links to QCA Geography Unit 6.	**p28 How far?** Addition and subtraction problems set in the context of a local bus/train route.
14	Assess and review			**p29: Assessment activity 1**

YEAR 3

Term 2	Topics	Maths objectives	Cross-curricular objectives	Activities
1	Place value, ordering, estimating, rounding	Use patterns of similar calculations. Recognise and use the pattern in an addition table.	Work with others to explore a variety of ICT tools. Organise and reorganise text and tables.	**p30: Addition tables** Use a computer to create and investigate addition tables.
	Reading numbers from scales	Read and begin to write vocabulary related to time. Use units of time and know the relationships between them (second, minute, hour, day, week, month, year).	**Literacy** Experiment with recounting events in different ways. **History** Place events and changes in the correct periods of time.	**p31: How long ago?** Write their own personal history, exploring the relationships between different measures of time.
2–3	Understanding + and −	Solve a given problem by organising and interpreting numerical data in simple lists, tables and graphs, for example: simple frequency tables and bar charts.	**Design and technology** Investigate and evaluate a range of familiar products, thinking about the views of people who use them. Links to QCA Design and Technology Unit 3B.	**p32: Take a vote** Compile frequency tables of favourite sandwiches, groups, TV shows...
	Mental calculation strategies (+ and −)			
	Money and real-life problems	Solve problems in real life involving measures. Round any two-digit number to the nearest 10 and any three-digit number to the nearest 100. Find the position of a square on a grid of squares with the rows and columns labelled.	**Geography** Use appropriate geographical vocabulary. Use maps and plans at a range of scales. Study a range of places including the United Kingdom. Links to QCA Geography Unit 6.	**p33: Distance table** Read distances between cities in UK from a table, order and round to the nearest 10 or 100 kilometres.
	Making decisions and checking results			
4–6	Shape and space	Measure and compare using standard units, including using a ruler to draw and measure lines to the nearest half cm.	**Science** Make systematic observations and measurements. Make comparisons and identify simple patterns or associations.	**p34: Hand measures** Measure and compare dimensions of fingers and hand to the nearest half cm.
	Reasoning about shapes			
	Measures, and time, including problems	Choose and use appropriate operations to solve word problems, and appropriate ways of calculating: mental, mental with jottings, pencil and paper. Solve word problems involving numbers in real life using one or more steps.	**Design and technology** Evaluate a range of familiar products, thinking about how they are used. Links to QCA Design and Technology Unit 3A.	**p35: Number sentences** Orally translate addition and subtraction problems into number sentences to explain mental calculations.
		Solve word problems involving money in 'real life'. Recognise all coins and notes. Understand and use £.p notation.	**English** Speak audibly and clearly, using spoken standard English in formal contexts. **Design and technology** Think about how familiar products are used. Links to QCA Design and Technology Unit 3B.	**p36: Buy a sandwich** Solve money problems involving addition and subtraction set in the context of a sandwich snack bar.
		Recognise and use the four compass directions: N, S, E, W.	**Geography** Use appropriate geographical vocabulary. Use maps and plans. Links to QCA Geography Unit 6.	**p37: Points of the compass** Follow a trail based on points of the compass.
		Use units of time and know the relationships between them. Use a calendar. Know their date of birth in the form day, month, year.	**History** Use dates and vocabulary relating to the passing of time. Study significant events and individuals.	**p38: Dates of birth** Mark own date of birth and those of famous people from history on a calendar.
7	Assess and review			**see p46**
8	Counting and the properties of numbers	Count larger collections by grouping them: for example, in tens, then other numbers. Count on in tens and hundreds.	**Design and technology** Evaluate a range of familiar products, thinking about how they are used. Links to QCA Design and Technology Unit 3A.	**p39: How many in a box?** Devise efficient methods for counting the number of similar small objects in various boxes.
	Reasoning about numbers			
	Understanding + and −	Solve mathematical problems and puzzles, recognise simple patterns and relationships.	**ICT** Organise and reorganise images. Identify patterns and relationships. Create, test and improve sequences of instructions to make things happen. Links to QCA Information Technology Unit 3C.	**p40: Swap the frogs!** Use a computer program (or cut-out photocopiable) to develop a strategy for rearranging the order of objects.
9–10	Mental calculation strategies (+ and −)			
	Understanding × and ÷	Add three or four single-digit numbers mentally. Derive quickly doubles of whole numbers to at least 20.	**PE** Take part in and design challenges that require precision.	**p41: Bean bag darts** In PE, play a 'bean bag darts' game or similar target game involving addition and doubling to keep score.
	Mental calculation strategies (× and ÷)	Measure and compare using a ruler. Know the relationship between centimetres and metres. To multiply by 10 (or 100), shift the digits 1 (or 2) places to the left.	**Design and technology** Communicate designs and ideas in various ways. **Geography** Use maps and plans at a range of scales.	**p42: Times 10, times 100** Relate distances on 1/10 and 1/100 scale diagrams and maps.
	Money and 'real-life' problems			
	Making decisions and checking results	Understand multiplication as describing an array. Extend understanding that multiplication can be done in any order. Know by heart multiplication facts for the 2, 5 and 10 times tables. Begin to know the 3 and 4 times tables.	**Design and technology** Evaluate a range of familiar products, thinking about how they are used. Links to QCA Design and Technology Unit 3A.	**p43: How many in a pack?** Investigate packing cans and bottles into boxes in rows, interpreted as multiplication problems.
11	Fractions	Recognise unit fractions such as 1/2, 1/3, 1/4, 1/5, 1/10... Begin to recognise simple fractions that are several parts of a whole, such as 3/4, 2/3. Compare familiar fractions: for example, know that on the number line 1/2 lies between 1/4 and 3/4.	**PE** Swim unaided for a sustained period of time. Pace themselves in a floating and swimming challenge related to distance. Links to QCA PE Unit 16.	**p44: How far can you swim?** Subdivide the length of the swimming pool into halves and quarters. Position swimmers appropriately, for example at 1/2 length.
12	Handling data	Solve a given problem by organising and interpreting numerical data in simple lists, tables and graphs. For example: frequency tables and bar charts.	**ICT** Working with others to explore a variety of ICT tools. Links to QCA ICT Unit 3C. **Geography** Links to QCA Geography Unit 6.	**p45: Class data** Use a photocopiable form to collect data about children in class. Enter the data into a computer database.
Unit 13	Assess and review			**p46: Assessment activity 2**

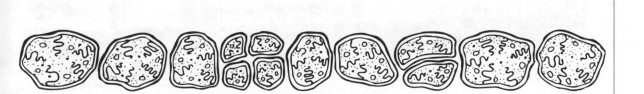

Term 3	Topics	Maths objectives	Cross-curricular objectives	Activities
1	Place value, ordering, estimating, rounding	Describe and extend number sequences. Recognise simple patterns and relationships.	**ICT** Work with others to explore a variety of ICT tools. Organise and reorganise text and tables.	**p47: Number sequences** Use a computer to generate and investigate number sequences.
	Reading numbers from scales	Give a sensible estimate of up to about 100 objects. Round any two-digit number to the nearest 10 and any three-digit number to the nearest 100.	**English** Evaluate fiction and non-fiction texts.	**p48: Making estimates** Estimate the number of words or lines on a page.
2–4	Understanding + and –			
	Mental calculation strategies (+ and –)	Count on or back in tens starting from any two- or three-digit number. Add and subtract mentally a 'near multiple of ten' to or from a two-digit number... by adding or subtracting 10, 20, 30... and adjusting.	**Literacy** Locate information using contents, index, page numbers...	**p49: Find the page** Play a 'find the page' game using a book with more than 100 pages. What page does chapter 3 start on? How many pages are there in chapter 5?
	Money and 'real-life' problems			
	Making decisions and checking results	Begin to use column addition and subtraction for HTU+/–TU where the calculation cannot easily be done mentally.	**History** Study the impact of the Second World War on the lives of children. Links to QCA History Unit 9.	**p50: 'Doing sums'** In the context of children's experience during World War II, use a slate to 'do sums' using a standard method.
5–6	Pencil and paper procedures	Solve word problems involving numbers in 'real life', money and measures.	**Design and technology** Evaluate a range of familiar products.	**p51: How many do we need?** Solve real-life problems set in the context of packaging items.
		Solve a given problem by organising and interpreting numerical data in simple lists, tables and graphs. Read and begin to write the vocabulary related to mass and capacity. Note the relationship between kg and g, l and ml.	**Science** Be taught about the need for food and the importance of an adequate and varied diet for health. **Design and technology** Evaluate a range of familiar products. Links to QCA Design and Technology Unit 3A.	**p52: Read the label** Collect packaging labels and compare the units and measures they display.
	Measures – including problems	Describe and find the position of a square on a grid of squares with the rows and columns labelled.	**History** Study the impact of the Second World War on the lives of children. Links to QCA History Unit 9.	**p53: Battleships** Play 'Battleships' in the context of childhood games of the Second World War.
	Shape and space			
	Reasoning about shapes	Identify and sketch lines of symmetry in simple shapes, and recognise shapes with no lines of symmetry.	**Geography** Recognise and explain human features of the environment. Links to QCA Geography Unit 6.	**p54: Symmetrical shapes** Find symmetrical signs, symbols and other shapes in the local environment.
		Solve a given problem by organising and interpreting data, for example, using Venn and Carroll diagrams (one criterion). Classify and describe the shapes.	**History** Study the impact of significant individuals in Victorian Britain.	**p55: Sorting shapes** Sort plane shapes according to properties using Venn and Carroll diagrams.
		Read and begin to write the vocabulary of mathematics including calculations, estimation and approximation, measures, shape, space and movement.	**Literacy** Have a secure understanding of the purpose and organisation of a dictionary.	**p56: Number words** Create a mathematics dictionary to explore the meanings of number words – even number, odd number, multiple, double, half...
7	Assess and review			see p62
8	Counting and the properties of numbers	Begin to know the 3 and 4 times tables.	**Design and technology** Undertake 'design and make' assignments including mechanical components. Links to QCA Design and Technology Unit 3C.	**p57: Multiplying monster** Make a moving monster that multiplies numbers.
	Reasoning about numbers			
	Understanding × and ÷	Solve mathematical problems, recognise simple patterns and relationships, generalise and predict. Suggest extensions by asking 'what if...?'	**ICT** Use a variety of ICT tools. Links to QCA IT Unit 3A.	**p58: Bigger and smaller** Use word-processing software to investigate changes in text size produced by multiplying or dividing by constant factors.
9–10	Mental calculation strategies (× and ÷)			
	Money and 'real-life' problems	Derive quickly doubles of whole numbers. Solve mathematical problems, recognise simple patterns.	**Science** Know that micro-organisms are living organisms that are often too small to be seen and may be beneficial or harmful. Know that life processes include reproduction.	**p59: Double up** Explore the effect of changing variables in science in relation to the growth of bacteria.
	Making decisions and checking results			
11	Fractions	Read the time to 5 minutes on an analogue clock and a 12-hour digital clock, and use the notation 9:40. Interpret numerical data in simple lists and tables.	**Geography** Identify where places are.	**p60: Departure time** Read time to the nearest 5 minutes from analogue and digital clocks.
12	Understanding + and –			
	Mental calculation strategies (+ and –)	Solve a problem by organising and interpreting numerical data in tables and graphs, for example: pictograms and bar charts.	**Geography** Use appropriate geographical vocabulary. Analyse evidence and draw conclusions.	**p61: What's the weather?** Compare weather data from around the world.
	Time, including problems			
	Making decisions and checking results			
13	Handling data			
14	Assess and review			**p62: Assessment activity 3**

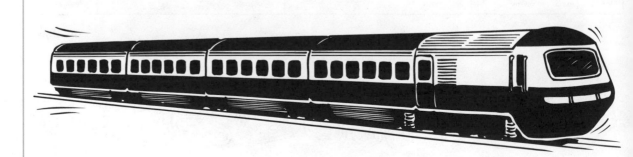

1 Number words

Objectives

Numeracy
Read and write whole numbers to at least 1000 in figures and words.
Literacy
Read and spell correctly high-frequency words.
Notice differences in the style and structure of fiction and non-fiction writing.

Resources

A copy of photocopiable page 63 for each child; counting cubes, wooden Multibase blocks, a flip chart or board; texts in which significant numbers appear (for example, *The Hundred and One Dalmations* by Dodie Smith; *The Hundred Mile an Hour Dog* by Jeremy Strong; *One Thousand and One Arabian Nights* by Geraldine McCaughrean; *Oxford First Book of Maths* by Rose Griffiths; *Kids' Cookbook* by Anne McCord).

Vocabulary

thousands
hundreds
tens
units
digit
one-, two- or three-digit number
place, place value

Background

By the end of Year 3 (Primary 4), the children should be able to read and write numbers to at least 1000. They should understand the significance of the place value of digits in the hundreds, tens and units columns, and appreciate the role of zero as a place holder in numbers such as 503. They should be able to write three-digit numbers in figures and in words. Link this activity to a literacy lesson on the conventions for writing numbers in text. Examine a variety of fiction and non-fiction texts, and discuss how numbers are shown in different circumstances. For example, a common convention is to write numbers up to ten as words but numbers greater than ten as symbols.

Preparation

Make copies of the photocopiable sheet and set them out on tables with the counting blocks ready for individual or group work.

Main teaching activity

Introduce the lesson to the whole class with some counting exercises, counting in ones, tens and hundreds. Line up counting blocks and point to them as you count to give the children visual feedback on the significance of the numbers counted. Write some three-digit numbers on the flip chart and discuss the values of the digits in the hundreds, tens and units places, using the counting blocks to provide visual examples. Discuss the significance of 0 as a place holder. Ask the children to select the correct blocks to represent various three-digit numbers that you say or write in figures or words. When most of the class are working confidently with hundreds, tens and units, set them to complete the exercise on the worksheet.

Develop this by looking at numbers in various texts. How are they written? Are different numbers written in different ways? Do all texts use the same conventions?

Differentiation

Reinforce the less able children's understanding by encouraging them to work with counting blocks to represent the three-digit numbers listed on the sheet.

More able children can be challenged to make the smallest and largest possible three-digit numbers with three digits selected at random. Can they write these numbers in both figures and words?

Plenary

Review the answers to the worksheet. Check that all the children understand that the three digits in a number such as 555 each have a different value: 5 hundreds, 5 tens and 5 units. The answers are:
1. 124 310 870 117 983 506
2. two hundred and ten, two hundred and four, five hundred and sixty, five hundred and eighty-three, eight hundred and six, nine hundred and sixteen, seven hundred and seventy-seven, eight hundred and sixty-eight.

Linked to History

2 Order the years

Objectives

Numeracy
Order whole numbers to at least 1000, and position them on a number line.
Read and begin to write vocabulary related to time.

History
Place events in chronological order.
Use dates and vocabulary relating to the passing of time.
Links to QCA History Units 6A, 6B, 6C.

Resources

A copy of photocopiable page 64 for each child; scissors and adhesive.

Vocabulary

compare
order
before
after
next
between
century

Background

Appreciation of the relative size and sequence of numbers is developed as the children work with numerical quantities in practical contexts in science, geography, technology and other subjects. The sequence of events in the first millennium AD provides an excellent context for sequencing and comparing numbers in the range 0 to 1000. Links to work in history lessons on the Romans in Britain, Vikings and Saxons are readily made.

Preparation

This lesson could be presented as a follow-up to topic work in history. Make copies of the photocopiable sheet and distribute them on tables.

Main teaching activity

Introduce the lesson by discussing the labelling of years. In what year were the children born? What year is it now? What is the starting point for numbering years? Are any other starting points used for alternative calendars? (For example, some children may be aware of the Islamic and Jewish calendars.) What events have the children learned about that took place in the first millennium – the first thousand years after the birth of Christ? For example, when were the Romans in Britain? When did the Vikings come to Britain? Set

the children to complete the worksheet. They should make a 1000-year timeline, cut out the listed events, and place the events in the correct locations on the line.

Differentiation

Less able children could be given some number cards in the range 0 to 100 to sequence before progressing to the main activity.

Most children should be able to sequence the numbers correctly.

Encourage the more able children to space events correctly along the line, using estimation, and to calculate the time periods between different events. Ask them questions such as: *How many years passed between the Romans leaving Britain and the first Viking invasions?*

Plenary

Make sure that all the children can sequence numbers to 1000 correctly. Use questions such as *Which is greater/less?* to compare numbers. As a follow-up exercise, the children could make their own labels to place further events that have been discussed in history lessons on their millennium line.

3 How far can you jump?

Objectives

Numeracy
Read and begin to write vocabulary related to length.
Measure and compare using standard units.
Read scales to the nearest division.
Record estimates and measurements to the nearest whole or half unit.
Physical education
Measure and record athletic activity.
Links to QCA PE: Athletic activities – Units 1 and 2.

Resources

School playground; metric tape measures calibrated and numbered in centimetres; chalk and appropriate PE apparatus for the activities you select; paper and pencils.

Vocabulary

measure
size
compare
measuring scale
division

Background

A measuring scale is a practical application of the number line. Numbered divisions are arranged in sequence and a measurement is taken by reading a number from the scale. There are numerous opportunities for using measurement scales in science, design and technology, geography, physical education and other curriculum areas. In this lesson, the children measure, record and compare distances jumped, thrown, or achieved in other ways during a PE lesson.

Preparation

Collect the tape measures and PE apparatus and prepare the class for a PE lesson according to your normal practice.

Main teaching activity

Take the class out to the playground. Introduce the lesson by asking the children how far they think they can jump. Examine tape measures together, looking carefully at the cm measuring scale. Discuss how to measure the distance of a standing jump.

Mark a chalk line and demonstrate a standing jump from the line, marking the landing place with a second chalk mark. Show the children how to measure the distance between the two marks with the measuring tape. Read off the distance jumped in cm. Set the children to work in pairs to make their own measurements. Ask them to write down their results.

Differentiation

Less able children could make simple comparisons between two marked jumps. Which is longer?

Most children should be able to measure and record their standing jump distances.

Encourage the more able children to devise, make and compare a range of other measurements, for example, the distance they can hop, reach on the floor by bending over, or throw a bean bag.

Plenary

Review the children's results. Ask a series of questions to prompt the children to sequence and compare measurements:
● *Can you reach further than you can jump?*
● *Who can jump the furthest?*
● *Which can you throw further, a beanbag or a ball?*

4 I'm looking at a number

Objectives

Numeracy
Explain methods and reasoning orally.
English
Speak with confidence in a range of
contexts, adapting their speech for a range
of purposes.
Listen, understand and respond
appropriately to others.

Resources

Packs of number cards containing numbers
in the range 0–100 to begin the activity, and
numbers in the range 0–1000 to extend
more able children.

Vocabulary

more than
less than
double
half
equals

Background

The ability to work mentally with numbers, reasoning about calculations both internally and out loud, is a key component of mathematical understanding. Mental calculation skills can be developed with regular group discussion and mental maths exercises. The facility to explain mental processes in words, and to formulate, interpret and answer verbal problems, builds on developing language skills. Verbal games and exercises such as those suggested in this lesson can be linked to oral work in English.

Main teaching activity

Start the lesson by showing the children the pack of number cards and explaining that you are going to play a 'guess the number' game. Draw a card from the pack at random but do not show it to the class. Say: *I'm looking at a number, it is twice as big as 10. What is my number?* Repeat the exercise with a range of questions of different types, including examples such as:

My number is:
ten more than...
five less than...
When I add 25 to my number, the answer is...
If I take away 8 from my number, the answer is...
If I double my number, I get...
and so on.

Ask the children to explain their reasoning as they give their answers. When the children have understood the game, ask them to take it in turns to select a card and pose a question to the rest of the class. Finally, match the children in pairs to play the game, taking it in turns to set and answer problems.

Differentiation

Encourage the more able children to devise a range of more challenging questions, selecting numbers from a pack containing numbers up to 1000.

Less able children can work with numbers to 100, setting simple addition and subtraction problems for their partners to answer.

Plenary

Ask the children to give examples of some of the questions they have devised, and to work out the answers. Confirm that they are both expressing themselves clearly and using appropriate mathematics to solve the mental problems.

Linked to
Geography
History

5 Abacus

Objectives

Numeracy
Add three or more two-digit numbers with the help of apparatus or pencil and paper.
Geography
Identify places and describe what they are like.
Could be linked to QCA Geography Unit 8.
History
Study aspects of everyday life in a society in the past world, including technology.

Resources

A large demonstration abacus; sets of abacuses for the children to use for their own calculations.

Vocabulary

abacus
place value
addition
exchange
units
tens
hundreds

Background

The abacus is one of the earliest calculating machines, and is still used widely today in countries in East Asia. It is a valuable teaching aid in the classroom because of the visual and tactile appeal of the sliding coloured beads, and the clear way they are grouped in place-value order. Work with an abacus could link to studies of other places and cultures in geography and history (for example, by looking at photographs of life in China where street traders can be seen using the abacus to make calculations).

Preparation

Set up the demonstration abacus where all the children can see it.

Main teaching activity

With the whole class, discuss how calculations are made with an abacus. Demonstrate how the abacus can be used to add two numbers up to 100, including the process of regrouping. For example, to calculate 7 + 8, seven unit beads are counted from one end of the rod to the other. The 8 is then added by counting on. When all ten unit beads have been moved (when the

counting on has reached 3), they are returned to their starting place and a ten bead is moved; this is called 'regrouping'. The final five units are then counted and moved to give the result 15. (The figure below illustrates this process.)

Set a number of problems for the children to solve with their own abacuses. After the children have had some practice, explain that street traders in Hong Kong are so skilled with the abacus they can add a price list faster than a person using an electronic calculator. If possible, show the children pictures of Hong Kong street markets.

Proceed to demonstrate the use of the abacus to add three numbers up to 100, setting the children a number of examples to complete.

Differentiation

Less able children may struggle with regrouping. Set them simpler problems at first that do not involve this process.

Challenge more able children to use the abacus to sum lists of numbers up to 1000.

Plenary

Check that the children are using the abacus correctly by asking them to take turns to demonstrate how they add a list of numbers.

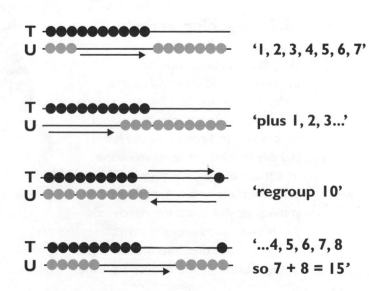

'1, 2, 3, 4, 5, 6, 7'

'plus 1, 2, 3...'

'regroup 10'

'...4, 5, 6, 7, 8
so 7 + 8 = 15'

Buy a ticket

Objectives

Numeracy
Solve word problems involving numbers in 'real life', money... including finding totals and giving change and working out which coins to pay.
Geography
Use maps and plans at a range of scales.
Links to QCA Geography Unit 6.
English
Speak with confidence in a range of contexts, adapting their speech for a range of purposes.
Listen, understand and respond appropriately to others.

Resources

Plastic or real coins; a copy of photocopiable page 65 for each child; scissors.

Vocabulary

money
coin
penny
pound
price
buy
pay
change
total

Background

Real-life money problems involve finding totals, working out which coins to pay and calculating change. Buying tickets for an imaginary journey is an excellent context for role-play that combines numeracy, geography and language skills. The journey must be planned with the aid of a route map. The conventions for using language when purchasing a ticket or in other transactions can be discussed (for example, deciding what you need to say before making the purchase, saying 'good morning' or 'good afternoon', saying 'please' and 'thank you' appropriately.

Preparation

Make copies of the photocopiable sheet and distribute them with the coins and scissors on tables.

Main teaching activity

Introduce the lesson with a discussion of bus, train or underground journeys that the children have made. *How do you plan your journey?* Talk about the use of timetables and route plans. *How do you buy a ticket? How do you know how much the journey costs? Is there a ticket machine or a ticket office, or do you pay as you board the vehicle? Do you have to hand over the correct money, or does the driver/machine give change?* Look at the exercise on the

worksheet together. Discuss the fares listed and how the fare from one destination to another is calculated. Let the children work in pairs to role-play some of the suggested transactions. They should take it in turns to act as passenger and ticket seller.

Differentiation

Less able children should concentrate on purchasing a single ticket for their chosen journey.

Encourage more able children to role-play transactions in which they purchase multiple tickets – for example, a return for two adults and three children. They could also use local route plans and timetables to plan journeys to local destinations.

Plenary

Select pairs of children to role-play ticket purchases that you suggest in front of the whole class. Check that they are speaking clearly and politely and making the money calculations correctly.

The answers to the worksheet are:
1. 20p   2. 60p   3. 40p   4. 90p   5. £1.60

Linked to
Science

7 Which holds most?

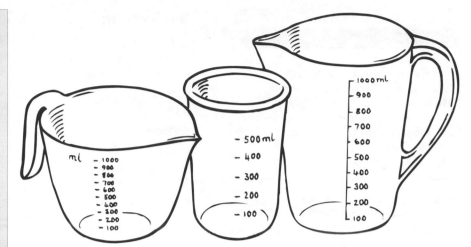

Objectives

Numeracy
Read and begin to write the vocabulary related to capacity.
Measure and compare using standard units.
Know the relationship between litres and millilitres.
Science
Measure volumes of liquids using appropriate apparatus.
Links to QCA Science Unit 3D.

Resources

A selection of plastic cups, beakers, jars and bottles; measuring jugs or cylinders labelled with ml scales; adhesive labels, felt-tipped pens; a plastic water bowl for each group.

Vocabulary

capacity
litre
half-litre
millilitre
holds
contains
container

Background

The capacity of a container is a measure of the volume of fluid that it will hold. The standard units used to label the capacity of cans, bottles and jars are litres (l) and millilitres (ml). One litre is equal to 1000ml. Occasionally you may find bottles and jars labelled in decilitres (dl) and centilitres (cl), but the children are not expected to work with these units at this stage. The ability to use measuring jugs and cylinders to measure liquid volumes is an important skill in science – for example, when making an investigation of the ability of different soil types to absorb water. The container must be placed on a level surface and left until the liquid is stationary. To read the liquid level to the nearest division from the scale, you need to keep your eye at the same height as the surface of the liquid.

Preparation

Set out a selection of different-sized containers on tables ready for group investigation. Provide each group with a measuring cylinder or jug. Each group will need a plastic bowl filled with water and adhesive labels to record their capacity measurements.

Main teaching activity

Introduce the lesson by showing the class two distinctly different-shaped beakers or bottles. Ask the children to judge which holds more. Explain that this judgement can be difficult because of the difference in shape. Ask for suggestions for checking the capacity of the two containers. Demonstrate how to measure the capacity of a container by filling it with water, then pouring the water into an initially empty measuring cylinder or jug. Show the children how to read the volume of the water from the measuring scale. Write the measurement in ml on an adhesive label and attach it to the container.

Explain that the children's task is to measure the capacities of the different containers set out on their tables. Ask them to label each container with its capacity and arrange the containers in order of capacity.

Differentiation

Most children should read scales to the nearest labelled division.

Encourage more able children to use the subdivisions to improve the accuracy of their measurements.

Plenary

Discuss and compare the capacities of familiar items, such as lemonade bottles and drinks cans. Can the children find the figure on the label that gives the capacity?

Linked to
H i s t o r y

8 Shape words

Objectives

Numeracy
Classify and describe 3-D shapes.
Relate solid shapes to pictures of them.
History
Study the characteristic features of periods and societies in the past – for example, Ancient Egypt.
Links to QCA History Unit 10.

Resources

A collection of different-shaped models and boxes for discussion (cuboids, triangular prisms, cylinders, hemispheres etc); a copy of photocopiable page 66 for each child.

Vocabulary

face
edge
vertex
triangular
rectangular
square
cube
cuboid
prism
cross-section
pyramid
cone
cylinder
sphere
dome
hemisphere

Background

Three-dimensional shapes are classified according to features such as: the number of edges, sides and vertices; the shapes of the faces; and the angles between the edges at the vertices. The vocabulary used to describe shapes can be introduced through discussion of shapes observed in the environment, such as sweet boxes and other containers, vehicles and buildings.

   Work on three-dimensional shapes in numeracy could be linked to work in history on the Egyptian pyramids or other ancient structures, such as Stonehenge. The pyramids, for example, were built from cuboids of stone. In a follow-up history lesson, you could ask the children to investigate how cuboids can be arranged to produce a pyramid shape, and discuss how the Egyptians moved massive stone blocks without the use of modern machines. (This could be linked to work on forces in science.)

Preparation

Make and display a collection of different-shaped containers. Make and distribute copies of the photocopiable sheet.

Main teaching activity

Introduce the lesson by discussing the shapes of the various containers and models. Use the correct vocabulary, including *face, edge, vertex, triangular, rectangular, square, cube, cuboid, prism, cross-section, pyramid, cone, cylinder, sphere, dome* and *hemisphere*, to describe the characteristics of the different shapes. Extend the discussion to include the shapes of Egyptian pyramids or other historical structures that the children are currently studying – for example, mounds, monoliths, towers, steps, domes and spires.

   Set the children to work individually to complete the exercise on the worksheet. Encourage them to find examples of the shapes illustrated there among the collection of models and boxes or to look for them in history reference books.

Differentiation

Less able children should be provided with examples of shapes to turn and investigate in order to answer the questions.

   More able children may be able to answer further questions by visualising the shapes without actually handling them.

Plenary

Review the answers to the questions using actual shapes to check the numbers of faces, edges and vertices. Relate the shapes to the shapes observed in historic (and modern) buildings and structures.

   The answers are:
cube 6, 12, 8
hexagonal prism 8, 18, 12
triangular prism 5, 9, 6
triangular-based pyramid 4, 6, 4

Linked to
H i s t o r y
Art & design

9 Tessellations

Objectives

Numeracy
Classify 2-D shapes.
Make and describe shapes and patterns.
Art
Investigate shape, colour and pattern.
Links to QCA Art Unit 3B.
History
To study Roman settlement in Britain.
Links to QCA History Unit 6A.

Resources

Boxes of coloured plastic shapes including squares, rectangles, parallelograms, triangles, pentagons and hexagons.

Vocabulary

tessellation
pattern
surface
triangle
square
rectangle
hexagon
repeating pattern

Background

Bathroom tiles are fitted together in a repeating pattern to cover a surface. An arrangement of two-dimensional shapes that completely covers a surface in this way is called a tessellation. This word derives from the Latin word *tesserae*, which was the name for the small coloured pieces of stone fitted together to make a mosaic.

Mosaics and lots more information about the Romans in Britain can be found on the Internet at http://www.romans-in-britain.org.uk

Mathematical investigations of the patterns that can be created with 2-D shapes can thus be linked to work on decorative patterns in history and art.

Preparation

Set out the boxes of shapes on tables in preparation for group investigations.

Main teaching activity

Introduce the lesson by reviewing the names and properties of the various two-dimensional shapes. Discuss the numbers of sides and angles, and whether or not all the sides and angles are equal. Demonstrate ways in which two identical shapes can be fitted together. Can the children name the shape that is made?

Ask the children to investigate how many different shapes they can make with various pairs of identical shapes; for example, two identical right-angled triangles can be fitted together to make a rectangle, two different isosceles triangles and various other shapes (see figure below). Can the children name and describe their shapes?

Develop the lesson by talking about tessellations and asking the children to investigate the tessellation patterns they can create with the shapes provided. Talk about the mosaic pictures that the Romans made using *tesserae*.

Differentiation

Less able children should discover how to create tessellations with squares, rectangles and triangles.

Challenge the more able children to create tessellations with combinations of two or more shapes.

Plenary

Ask the children to demonstrate some of the shapes and patterns they have created. Check that they are using the vocabulary of shape correctly as they describe their findings.

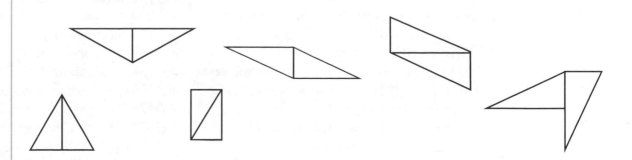

10 Which century?

Objectives

Numeracy
Read and begin to write the vocabulary of comparing and ordering numbers, including ordinal numbers to at least 100.
Order whole numbers to at least 1000, and position them on a number line.
Read and begin to write vocabulary related to time.

History
Place events in chronological order.
Use dates and vocabulary relating to the passing of time.

Resources

A large timeline starting from the year AD1; a copy of photocopiable page 67 for each child; a flip chart or board.

Vocabulary

century
year
order
ordinal number

Background

Many children initially find the difference between the ordinal number that labels a century, and the numbers that label the years in that century, confusing. For example, 1998 was a year in the 20th century. Work on the labelling of centuries with the aid of a timeline will soon clear up this confusion, and will link well to work on timelines in history.

Preparation

Draw up a suitable timeline on the flip chart.

Main teaching activity

Introduce the lesson by discussing the timeline and labelling the sequence of the centuries. The century following the birth of Christ is the 1st century, the next century is the 2nd century and so on. Continue up to the 11th century and beyond. Explain the relationship between the year number and the century number with the aid of some examples, locating the years and centuries on the timeline. For example, the year AD567 is in the 6th century, the year 1066 is in the 11th century, the year 1666 is in the 17th century, and so on. Set the children to complete the exercise on the worksheet.

Differentiation

To help the less able children, write the years 1066, 1166, 1266... 1966 in a column. Write '11th century' next to 1066, then ask the children to continue the pattern.

Ask the more able children to discuss which century a year such as 1900 or 2000 belongs to. Is it the last year of a century or the first year of the next century? (Since it is conventional to label the year following the birth of Christ as AD1, the year 100 was the last year of the 1st century and the year 2000 was strictly the last year of the 20th century – not the first year of the 21st century.)

Plenary

Review the worksheet answers with the whole class. Check the children's understanding of century notation with some oral questions of the form: *In which century was the year 1521?*

The answers are:

AD1423 – fifteenth century
AD2001 – twenty-first century
AD57 – first century
AD163 – second century
AD1542 – sixteenth century
AD1801 – nineteenth century
AD1734 – eighteenth century
AD978 – tenth century
AD1994 – twentieth century
AD1161 – twelfth century

11 Talking numbers

Background

This lesson builds on Lesson 4, 'I'm looking at a number', to develop the children's oral reasoning about numbers and calculations. Working in groups, they take turns to ask each other mental maths problems, give answers and explain their reasoning. This type of exercise should form a regular part of numeracy work. Verbal work in mathematics links closely to work in English, developing speaking and listening skills within a specific context. The children should be encouraged to speak clearly and precisely, organising what they say, and to listen attentively and ask questions to clarify their understanding.

Preparation

Select problems appropriate to the ability levels of your different groups. Make up worksheets, copy them and distribute them on tables.

Main teaching activity

Introduce the lesson with some whole-class mental maths problems. Ask individual children to give answers and then to explain how they solved the problem. Demonstrate with some of your own explanations, such as:

● 23 + 27: *I added 3 and 7 to make 10, two 20s make 40, so altogether the total is 50*
● 46 ÷ 2: *half of 40 is 20, half of 6 is 3, and so half of 46 is 23.*

Ask the children whether they all use the same or different methods to solve the problems. Explain that there are often several ways of solving a mathematical problem, and that all methods that give the correct answer are usually equally valid. Continue the lesson by setting the children to work in their groups, asking each other problems and explaining their methods orally.

Differentiation

Differentiate the children's work with the difficulty of the problems set on the worksheets.

Less able children could work with numbers to 20.

Encourage more able children to tackle more challenging problems, and to discuss and compare different mental methods of solving the same problem.

Plenary

Ask the children to describe some of the methods that they and their friends used to solve the problems. *How did Sophie say that she solved this problem in her head? Who had a good method for solving this problem?* Conclude the lesson with some quick-fire mental maths practice.

12 Multiple grids

Objectives

Numeracy
Know by heart multiplication facts for the 2, 5 and 10 times tables.
Begin to know the 3 and 4 times tables.
ICT
Create and organise text and tables.
Links to QCA Information Technology Unit 3A.

Resources

Computers running *Microsoft Word*, *Textease* or any similar word-processing package with tools for creating tables or grids; a printer and paper; a large 1–100 square (see figure on right).

Vocabulary

times
multiply
multiple of
array
row
column
grid

Background

In Year 3, the children should learn by heart multiplication facts for the 2, 5 and 10 times tables and begin to know the 3 and 4 times tables. Finding and shading multiples of these numbers on hundred squares is a valuable aid to committing these number facts to memory. Number grids can readily be created using various computer software packages, and the children will enjoy creating their own grids as an exercise linking numeracy and ICT skills.

1	2	3	4	5	6	7	8	9	10
11	12	13	14	15	16	17	18	19	20
21	22	23	24	25	26	27	28	29	30
31	32	33	34	35	36	37	38	39	40
41	42	43	44	45	46	47	48	49	50
51	52	53	54	55	56	57	58	59	60
61	62	63	64	65	66	67	68	69	70
71	72	73	74	75	76	77	78	79	80
81	82	83	84	85	86	87	88	89	90
91	92	93	94	95	96	97	98	99	100

Preparation

Use your chosen computer software package to create a table with 10 columns and 10 rows. In *Textease*, select the Create spreadsheet from the Table menu on the toolbar. Drag the cursor to produce a 10 × 10 grid. In *Microsoft Word*, select the Insert table command from the Table menu on the toolbar. Adjust the height and width of the cells, using the options in the menu to create a square grid. Set the font size and formatting appropriately for the cell size. Print some blank grids for children to complete while other children are working at the computer. Check that you know how to enter a number in a cell by pointing, clicking and pressing a number key, and then how to select a cell and change its colour (right mouse click in *Word*, then select the format option).

Main teaching activity

Introduce the lesson with some whole-class work on 2, 3, 4, 5 and 10 times tables. Use a large hundred square to point to the various multiples as the tables are chanted. Explain to the class that they are going to use the computer to create their own versions of the grid for each table. According to the number of computers available, set some children working in pairs to fill in numbers on the grids and to select and highlight given multiples. The children who do not have access to the computer could be set to number and shade the prepared grids.

Differentiation

Less able children should concentrate on numbering the grid correctly and colouring every other square (2 times table).

Challenge more able children to shade 1–100 grids with other multiples, for example 6 or 8.

Plenary

Print and display a selection of the children's grids. Use them to check the answers to a selection of mental multiplication problems based on the 2, 3, 4, 5 and 10 times tables.

13 Double and halve

Objectives

Numeracy
Derive quickly: doubles of all whole numbers to at least 20, doubles of multiples of 5 to 100, doubles of multiples of 50 to 500; and all corresponding halves.

PE
Remember and repeat simple skills and actions with increasing control and co-ordination.
Can be linked to QCA PE Athletic activities Unit 1 and Gymnastic activities Unit 1.

Resources
A copy of photocopiable page 68 for each child; a large 1–100 square.

Vocabulary
double
halve

Background
The ability to find double or half of a number rapidly is an important mental maths skill. In this lesson, the children complete tables of doubles and halves, and develop rapid recall of doubles and halves with some mental exercises. Knowledge of doubles and halves can be reinforced with PE activities in which the children count and time repetitions of actions, doubling and halving the number of repetitions when prompted.

Preparation
Make copies of the photocopiable sheet and distribute them on tables.

Main teaching activity
Introduce the first part of the lesson by discussing the words 'double' and 'halve'. Make sure the children understand that doubling is equivalent to multiplication by 2, while halving equates to division by 2. With examples, demonstrate the relationship between a double and its half: *Double 10 is 20; half 20 is 10.* Orally double all numbers from 1 to 20, and state the corresponding halves: *Double 1 = 2, half 2 = 1; double 2 = 4, half 4 = 2...* Discuss the doubles of multiples of 5, 10 and 50, using a hundred square to investigate the patterns created by doubling and halving. Set the children to complete the double and half tables on the worksheet.

For the second part of the lesson, move outside or into the hall. Select some repetitive actions for the children to perform and count, for example skipping, bouncing a ball, hopping on one leg and walking in a

circle for a given number of paces. Play a game in which you call out a number of repetitions in the range 1 to 20, then say *Double* or *Halve*. The children must perform the doubling or halving appropriately. The activity could be extended to doubles and halves of larger numbers by repeating activities for half or double a given number of seconds, or over a distance measured in cm.

Differentiation
Less able children should concentrate on doubling or halving repetitions to 20.

More able children will soon spot the patterns that enable them to double or halve any number rapidly.

Plenary
Conclude the lesson with some quick-fire mental doubling and halving problems. Ask the children to talk about the strategies they use for mentally doubling and halving.

The answers are:

number	double	number	double	number	double
1	2	11	22	10	20
2	4	12	24	20	40
3	6	13	26	30	60
4	8	14	28	40	80
5	10	15	30	50	100
6	12	16	32	60	120
7	14	17	34	70	140
8	16	18	36	80	160
9	18	19	38	90	180
10	20	20	40	100	200

number	double	number	double	number	double
5	10	50	100	100	200
15	30	100	200	200	400
25	50	150	300	300	600
35	70	200	400	400	800
45	90	250	500	500	1000
55	110	300	600	600	1200
65	130	350	700	700	1400
75	150	400	800	800	1600
85	170	450	900	900	1800
95	190	500	1000	1000	2000

14 Coins and notes

Objectives

Numeracy

Solve word problems involving numbers in 'real life', money and measures, using one or more steps, including finding totals and giving change, and working out which coins to pay.

Recognise all coins and notes.

Understand and use £.p notation (for example, know that £3.06 is £3 and 6p).

History

Study the lives of significant men, women and children drawn from the history of Britain and the wider world (for example, artists, engineers, explorers, inventors, pioneers, rulers, saints, scientists).

Resources

A copy of photocopiable page 69 for each child; scissors, pencils, notebooks, sets of plastic coins; a set of all the coins of the realm plus £5, £10 and £20 notes.

Vocabulary

money
coin
note
penny, pence, pound
price, cost
pay
change
total, amount
value

Background

Working with money is an important practical maths skill, requiring knowledge of addition, subtraction and place value. The mathematics curriculum requires that the children should be familiar with the coins and notes currently in circulation. Coins and notes themselves have intrinsic interest. Many children will be able to bring collections of pennies and other old coins, or coins and notes collected on foreign holidays, to school. These can be used to stimulate work in history and geography. The famous people depicted on current banknotes can be used as the starting point for some historical research.

(£20) was a composer, Dickens (£10) was a writer, and Stephenson (£5) was an engineer and inventor. You could play a sample of Elgar's music or read a short passage from Dickens.

Develop the lesson by considering how the notes should be exchanged fairly – for example, two £5s for a £10 or four £5s for a £20. Set the children to practise selecting the correct notes and coins to make payments quoted in pounds and pence, using plastic coins and notes cut out from the worksheet. Some payments to be made are listed on the worksheet.

In a follow-up history lesson, you could ask the children each to choose one of the individuals depicted on the banknotes and to use research materials to find out some facts about his or her life. They should each write a brief account of their chosen person's life and achievements.

Preparation

Set out the copies of photocopiable page 69, scissors, pencils, notebooks and plastic coins on tables. Make sure the research resources are easily accessible.

Main teaching activity

Introduce the lesson by showing the real coins and notes to the whole class. Ask the children to identify the value of each coin and discuss its features – for example, its shape, its colour and the designs on its two sides. Show the children the banknotes, and discuss the portrait of the Queen on the front of each note and the person and scene depicted on the reverse. Explain that Elgar

Differentiation

Less able children should be able to make up the set sums from the coins and notes provided.

Challenge the more able children to make transactions involving change. For example, what change would you expect to receive from a £20 note when making a payment of £13.57?

Plenary

Review the solutions to the worksheet problems and conclude with some quick-fire mental money problems.

15 Fraction flags

Objectives

Numeracy
Recognise unit fractions such as 1/2, 1/3, 1/4... and use them to find fractions of shapes.
Begin to recognise simple fractions that are several parts of a whole, such as 3/4, 2/3 or 3/10.
Geography
Study a range of places in different parts of the world.
Art
Study visual elements in design
Could be linked to QCA Art Unit 3B.

Resources

A copy of photocopiable page 70 for each child; crayons or felt-tipped pens; a display of flags of the world.

Vocabulary

fraction
part
equal parts
one whole
one half, two halves
one quarter, two quarters...
one third, two thirds...

Background

Many flag designs are based on combinations of squares, or vertical and horizontal stripes. A display of flags provides opportunity for discussion of fractions. *What fraction of the French flag is red? What fraction of the chequered flag used at motor races is white?* In this lesson, the children create their own flags based on square grids. They colour the grids with two or more colours and discuss the resulting fractions. Equivalent fractions can be introduced – for example, a simple 2 × 2 grid can be coloured to show that $\frac{1}{2} = \frac{2}{4}$. Work on flag design can be linked to work on pattern in art, and also to study of flags of the world in geography.

Preparation

Make and distribute copies of the photocopiable sheet on tables with the crayons or felt-tipped pens.

Main teaching activity

Introduce the lesson to the class by looking at some flags of the world and discussing

their designs. Where appropriate, talk about the way in which the design divides the flag into fractions.

Explain that the children are to design their own flags. Start with the simple 2 × 2 grid and ask the children to investigate how many different flag designs they can produce using just two colours. For each design they produce, the children should write down what fraction of the flag is a given colour – for example, $\frac{1}{4}$ blue, $\frac{3}{4}$ red. When they have explored the 2 × 2 flag, they should move on to designs based on the 2 × 3 grid. Explain how to calculate the fractions by counting the number of squares of a given colour, and dividing by the total number of squares that make up the whole flag.

Differentiation

Less able children should concentrate on identifying the fractions associated with 2 × 2 grids.

More able children can develop the activity by introducing more colours and drawing up their own grids for flag designs.

Plenary

Display some of the children's designs and discuss the fractions that arise as the grids are coloured in different ways.

16 How far?

Objectives

Numeracy
Add three or four single-digit numbers
mentally.
Geography
Use maps and plans at a range of scales.
Be taught the locations of places in their
local environment.
Links to QCA Geography Unit 6:
Investigating our local area.

Resources

A copy of photocopiable page 71 for each
child; a flip chart or board.

Vocabulary

add, addition, more, plus
make, some, total
altogether
distance apart... between... to... from...
kilometre

Background

Children need regular
practice to develop
their mental addition
skills. Adding three or
four small numbers
mentally involves two
or more steps in
which the result of an
initial calculation must
be temporarily
'stored' and then used
to complete the
addition. Talking
through the
calculation is a great
help in this process.
You should encourage
the children to talk
through their
calculations as they
make them, or to
explain their thought
processes afterwards. Setting mental
calculation exercises in a real context, such
as determining distances from a map, gives
the maths practice a purpose and will help to
maintain motivation. In this lesson, a map
showing the distances between stops on a
bus route is used as a basis for addition
practice. You could compile a similar map for
a bus route or journey in your local area,
linking the lesson to work in geography.

Preparation

Make and distribute copies of the
photocopiable sheet. Research the distances
for a familiar local bus or train journey.
Sketch a route map similar to page 71 in
preparation for locally based work.

Main teaching activity

Introduce the lesson with the worksheet
map. Explain that the distances shown are
between successive stops on the journey.
Use the map for some mental addition
practice. *How far is it from the Library to the
Station?* Demonstrate how the map is used
by adding the distances between successive
stops to find the total distance between the
two stops required. Thus the distance from
the bus station to the airport is 2 + 3 + 7
kilometres. Talk through the calculations: *3
plus 7 is 10, 10 plus 2 is 12. So the total
distance is 12 kilometres.* Highlight the
strategy of finding pairs of numbers that
make 10 or near 10. Point to the distances
on the map as you say them. Ask the
children a series of questions based on the
map and encourage them to talk through
their answers in the same way.

Develop the geography link by compiling
a similar map on the board, based on a local
route. Select distances as one-digit or two-
digit numbers, according to your judgement
of the children's current mental addition
skills. (Distances could be replaced by
journey times in minutes to extend the
range of numbers used.) Compile a list of
questions on the board for the children to
answer using the map, and set them to work
in pairs to answer the questions orally.

Differentiation

Less able children could be set problems
involving two single-digit numbers.

Challenge more able children with map-
based calculations involving four or more
numbers.

Plenary

Review the children's answers to your local
distance questions. Conclude the lesson
with more quick-fire addition problems
based on the map distances.

Assessment 1

Preparation

Make copies of the assessment sheet. If you feel that the sheet is too 'busy', the three activities could be separated and enlarged on individual sheets.

Lesson introduction

Begin the assessment lesson by reviewing the relevant cross-curricular topics covered during the term. Remind the children of some of the projects and investigations they have undertaken, and ask them to recall and recount their work. Emphasise the mathematical content – for example, *Do you remember how we used flags to calculate fractions?*

Main assessment activity

Distribute the sheets and ask the children to work on them individually. Guide the whole class through the questions one at a time, reading the text with them and prompting them to work out and fill in their answers. Try to make the whole activity enjoyable!

Practical activity

Write this price list on the board. Ask the children to select coins to match each price exactly.

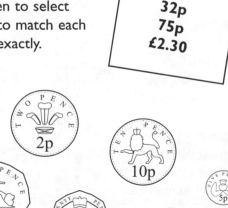

8p
16p
32p
75p
£2.30

Plenary

Review the answers to the questions as a class. Collect the completed question sheets to use as an aid to judging individual children's progress, and to include in your records.

The answers are:

1. 75, 57, 575, 705, 17, 557

2
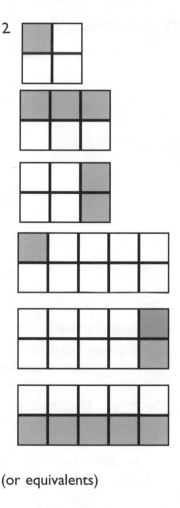

(or equivalents)

3.

full price	half price
20p	10p
10p	5p
12p	6p
60p	30p
£1.00	50p
£1.20	60p

Linked to
I C T

18 Addition tables

Objectives

Numeracy
Use patterns of similar calculations.
Recognise and use the pattern in an
addition table.
ICT
Work with others to explore a variety of
ICT tools.
Organise and reorganise text and tables.

Resources

A copy of photocopiable page 73 for each
child; computers running software with
table or spreadsheet capabilities, for
example *Microsoft Word* or *Textease*; a flip
chart or board.

Vocabulary

addition
table
column
row
pattern

Background

Addition tables
are a powerful
way of visualising
the number
patterns created,
for example, by
the addition of
successive units,
tens or hundreds.
The best way to
appreciate this is to
create the tables for
yourself and see the
patterns emerge.
Addition tables can be
filled in on prepared
grids or generated
using ICT tools.
Creating and
completing tables on
the computer is a
valuable ICT skill and
forms the basis for
later work with spreadsheets.

Preparation

Make and distribute copies of the
photocopiable sheet. Set up computers
running suitable software with which you are
familiar. Check that you can create tables or
spreadsheets confidently. Prepare a table
similar to the one shown below for
completion on the computer. Draw up a
blank addition table on the flip chart.

Main teaching activity

Introduce the lesson by completing the blank
addition table with the whole class. Point out
the diagonal patterns that appear. Ask the
children to explain them. (Moving down a
diagonal from top left to bottom right,
numbers increase by 2 per square – you are
adding 1 as you change column, and 1 as you
change row. But moving along a diagonal
from top right to bottom left, the numbers
stay constant – you are subtracting 1 as you
change column, but adding 1 as you change
row.)

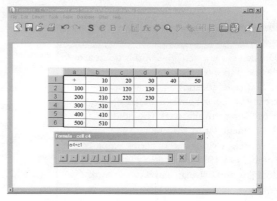

Details of *Textease* are available from www.textease.com

Set the children to work in twos or
threes on the computers to complete their
own addition tables. If insufficient computers
are available for all the children, some
children can complete tables in pencil on the
worksheets. Print the computer-produced
tables for later discussion and display.

Differentiation

Less able children could complete an
addition table for the numbers 1–10.

More able children can be challenged to
make addition tables for multiples of 5, 10,
50 and 100. Challenge children with
exceptional ICT skills to generate tables
automatically, using *Textease*: they need to
insert appropriate addition functions in
spreadsheet cells, as illustrated above.

Plenary

Ask some children to show their tables to
the class and explain the patterns.

+	0	1	2	3	4	5	6	7	8	9	10
0	0	1	2	3	4	5	6	7	8	9	10
1	1	2	3	4	5	6	7	8	9	10	11
2	2	3	4	5	6	7	8	9	10	11	12
3	3	4	5	6	7	8	9	10	11	12	13
4	4	5	6	7	8	9	10	11	12	13	14
5	5	6	7	8	9	10	11	12	13	14	15
6	6	7	8	9	10	11	12	13	14	15	16
7	7	8	9	10	11	12	13	14	15	16	17
8	8	9	10	11	12	13	14	15	16	17	18
9	9	10	11	12	13	14	15	16	17	18	19
10	10	11	12	13	14	15	16	17	18	19	20

Linked to
L i t e r a c y
H i s t o r y

19 How long ago?

Objectives

Numeracy
Read and begin to write vocabulary related to time.
Use units of time and know the relationships between them (second, minute, hour, day, week, month, year).
Literacy
Experiment with recounting events in different ways.
History
Place events and changes in the correct periods of time.

Resources

A clock with a moving second hand or digital second display; a copy of photocopiable page 74 for each child; a flip chart or board.

Vocabulary

time
second
minute
hour
day
week
month
year

Background

The division of an hour into 60 minutes and a minute into 60 seconds probably derives from the ancient Babylonians. They used a base 60 counting system, not the base 10 system we use today. A year is the time taken for the Earth to complete one orbit of the Sun. A month is roughly the time taken for the Moon to orbit the Earth. A day is the time taken for the Earth to rotate once about its own axis. Weeks, hours, minutes and seconds do not have a 'natural' basis in this way, but are 'man-made' units. The children need to learn the relationships between seconds, minutes, hours and longer time units explicitly. Appreciating the relative scale of the different time units is difficult, especially for young children. In this lesson, the children undertake an exercise in their personal history: considering what they were doing one second ago, one minute ago, one hour ago and so on. This also practises writing based on an organised structure.

Preparation

Make and distribute copies of the photocopiable sheet. Set up the clock where it can be seen by the whole class.

Main teaching activity

Introduce the lesson by looking at the passing seconds on the clock and discussing the passing of time. Count the seconds in one minute. Ask the children to close their eyes, wait until they think a minute has passed, then raise their hand and open their eyes to look at the clock. Who was the closest?

Consider longer time units. Write a list of units and conversions on the flip chart:

one year = 365 days
= 52 weeks = 12 months
one month = 28, 29, 30 or 31 days,
depending on the month of the year
one week = 7 days
one day = 24 hours
one hour = 60 minutes
one minute = 60 seconds

Talk through the worksheet exercise with the children, giving examples of answers:

One second ago I took a breath.
One minute ago I picked up a pencil.
One hour ago I was having a coffee in the staff room.
One day ago I was reading the Sunday paper.
One week ago I was teaching this class about addition tables.

Set the children to complete the exercise in groups. They should discuss what they were doing at the various times, then complete their personal histories individually.

Differentiation

Less able children should record simple events they can recall from appropriate intervals in the past.

Encourage the more able children to produce more extended and imaginative writing about the passage of time, perhaps in the form of a poem.

Plenary

Ask selected children to read out their work. Discuss their perceptions of the passage of time. Do some hours seem to pass more quickly than others? Can they remember events a year ago as well as they remember things that happened last week?

Linked to
D & T

20 Take a vote

Objectives

Numeracy
Solve a given problem by organising and interpreting numerical data in simple lists, tables and graphs, for example: simple frequency tables and bar charts.

Design and technology
Investigate and evaluate a range of familiar products, thinking about the views of people who use them.

Links to QCA Design and Technology Unit 3B: Sandwich snacks.

Resources

A copy of photocopiable page 75 for each child; pencils; a flip chart or board.

Vocabulary

count
tally
sort
vote
block graph
bar chart
frequency table
label
axis
most popular
least popular

Background
In this lesson, the children conduct a survey of favourite sandwich fillings. They record their original data in a frequency table. They then translate the table into a bar chart. They should see that the bar chart makes it easier to compare the data visually.

The activity links to the QCA Design and Technology unit 'Sandwich snacks', but could be adapted for simple surveys in science, geography and other curriculum areas.

Preparation
Make and distribute copies of the photocopiable sheet in advance of the lesson.

Main teaching activity
Introduce the lesson by talking generally about sandwiches and sandwich fillings. You could mention the history of the sandwich. (The Earl of Sandwich wanted a convenient portable snack. He placed a slice of meat between two slices of bread: the first sandwich!) Ask the children to list sandwich fillings they like. Compile a list on the flip chart. Convert the list into a frequency table similar to that on the worksheet. Explain that you are going to take a vote to find out which sandwich is the most popular by asking for a show of hands. Show the

children how to count and record a vote as a tally, and how to fill in the totals in the appropriate columns of the table. Explain that it is called a frequency table because it shows the number of times (the 'frequency') with which a particular item is selected.

Set the children to work in small groups to complete the frequency table on the worksheet, then to convert it into an appropriate bar chart. They should label the axes on the chart and draw appropriate bars.

Differentiation
Less able children may need considerable guidance in constructing their bar charts.

More able children could produce their tables and charts on the computer using the spreadsheet and charting facilities of a program such as *Textease*.

Plenary
Ask selected groups to show the charts they have produced to the class. Use the charts as the basis for some maths questions, such as: *Which was the favourite filling? How many children chose peanut butter? How many children were surveyed altogether?* Make a display of the children's work.

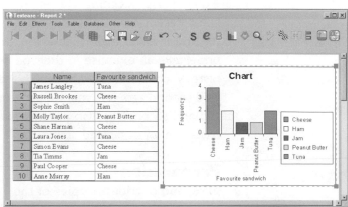

Details of *Textease* are available from www.textease.com

Linked to
Geography

21 Distance table

Background

Distance tables, giving the distances by road between the major towns and cities in the UK, are frequently included in books of road maps. Reading a distance table requires the child to identify the start and finish locations in the leftmost grid column and the top grid row. The distance is found in the cell where the corresponding column and row intersect. This is the same skill as using an addition or multiplication grid. In this lesson, the children practise reading a distance table and develop their rounding skills by rounding distances to the nearest 10 or 100 miles. The activity links to geography work on locations in the UK.

along the top of the table, then reading the distance between them from the cell where the corresponding column and row intersect. Ask the children to find the distances between various towns and cities using the table.

Develop the lesson by reminding the children about rounding to the nearest 10 and the nearest 100. Ask them some further questions in which they must round the distances to the nearest 10 or 100 miles as specified. *What is the distance, to the nearest 10 miles, from Edinburgh to London? Which cities in the UK are, to the nearest 100 miles, 200 miles from London?* (In other words, between 150 and 249 miles from London.) Write some similar questions on the board and set the children to work in groups to answer them with the aid of the table.

Objectives

Numeracy
Solve problems in 'real life' involving measures.
Round any two-digit number to the nearest 10 and any three-digit number to the nearest 100.
Find the position of a square on a grid of squares with the rows and columns labelled.

Geography
Use appropriate geographical vocabulary.
Use maps and plans at a range of scales.
Study a range of places including the United Kingdom.
Links to QCA Geography Unit 6: Investigating our local area.

Resources

A display map of the UK, showing major towns, cities and roads; a copy of photocopiable page 76 for each child; a flip chart or board.

Vocabulary

mile
table
column
row
round up/down
nearest 10
nearest 100

Preparation

Make and distribute copies of the photocopiable sheet. Display the road map where all the children can see it. This lesson should follow on from a numeracy lesson in which rounding has been introduced.

Main teaching activity

Introduce the lesson by discussing some road journeys the children have made. Find towns and cities that they have visited on the map. What is the longest journey the children have made? How far was it? How long did it take?

Show the children the distance table. Explain how it is used by locating the starting point and destination down the side and

Differentiation

Less able children should concentrate on using the table correctly without worrying about the rounding process at this stage.

Challenge more able children to use reference books to compile a similar table for cities in Europe. Explain that in continental Europe, distances are usually quoted in kilometres. Suggest that the children use kilometres for their European distance table.

Plenary

Review the children's answers as a class. Discuss the advantages and disadvantages of rounding to different degrees of accuracy when comparing journey distances.

Linked to
S c i e n c e

22 Hand measures

Objectives

Numeracy
Measure and compare using standard units, including using a ruler to draw and measure lines to the nearest half cm.
Science
To make systematic observations and measurements.
To make comparisons and identify simple patterns or associations.

Resources

A copy of photocopiable page 77 for each child; rulers with cm and half cm divisions.

Vocabulary

measure
size
compare
measuring scale
division
length
ruler
centimetre

Background

This lesson develops the children's measurement skills through an exercise in which they measure dimensions of their hand. It links work in mathematics on standard and non-standard units to work in science on variation in hand size as a measure of similarities and differences between humans. The disadvantage of the hand as a measure is that human hands differ in size!

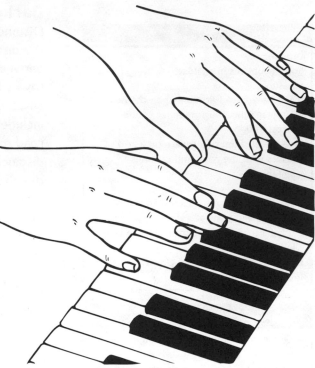

Preparation

Make and distribute copies of the photocopiable sheet, with rulers and pencils.

Main teaching activity

Introduce the lesson by talking about hands. Consider the marvellous ability of the human hand to grip and manipulate pencils, tools and other objects. Look at the hand and observe how the fingers and thumb move. Discuss the relative size of hands. Who might benefit from having big hands? (Goalkeepers and pianists?) Who might benefit from having small hands? (Vets and dentists?)

Set the children to work in pairs on the measurement exercise on the worksheet. Discuss and demonstrate how a ruler is used to measure the indicated lengths to the nearest half cm. The children should measure and record the dimensions of the hand drawing, then proceeded to measure, record and draw lines equal in length to the dimensions of their own hand.

Differentiation

Less able children should concentrate on measuring the hand drawing as accurately as possible.

Challenge the more able children to compile a table of hand lengths and heights for several members of the class. Do taller children have longer hands?

Plenary

Review the children's results. Who has the longest hands? Who has the longest fingers? Who has the smallest hands? Discuss the advantages and disadvantages of fingers and hands as measures.

The answers to the worksheet are:
length = 11cm
width = $5\frac{1}{2}$ cm
first finger = 5cm
thumb = 4cm
little finger = $3\frac{1}{2}$ cm

23 Number sentences

Objectives

Numeracy
Choose and use appropriate operations to solve word problems, and appropriate ways of calculating: mental, mental with jottings, pencil and paper.
Solve word problems involving numbers in 'real life', using one or more steps.
Design and technology
Evaluate a range of familiar products, thinking about how they are used.
Links to QCA Design and Technology Unit 3A: Packaging.

Resources

Samples of packaged materials from the supermarket, for example: a four-pack of 500ml mineral water bottles, a variety pack of mini-cereal boxes, a package of 12 biscuits; pencils and paper.

Vocabulary

word problem
number sentence
jotting
explain
explain your method
show how you...
write in figures

Background

Solving practical problems often involves translating a problem expressed in words into a mathematical calculation expressed as a number sentence. In this lesson, the children tackle a series of word problems based on the packaging of familiar items, such as mineral water bottles, cans and cereal boxes. The activity links to work on packaging in technology where the children investigate different packaging materials, systems and container shapes.

Preparation

Prepare a series of word problems based on the packaged items you have collected (see the example illustrated).
  Write the questions on the board or reproduce them on the computer for distribution in advance of the lesson.

Main teaching activity

Introduce the lesson by looking at the packaged items. Discuss the packaging materials used and the shape and design of the containers. Read the labels, discussing the various numbers listed – for example, quantities, weights and volumes. Ask the children some simple oral word

problems based on the number quantities. Encourage them to explain their reasoning as they give their answers – for example: *If there are 12 biscuits in a box, we need double that to give a biscuit each to 24 children, so that is two boxes. If each child is given 2 biscuits we must double again, so we need 4 boxes.* Summarise the explanations as they are given by jotting number sentences on the board.

$$2 \times 12 = 24$$
$$2 \times 2 = 4$$

Continue the lesson by setting the children to answer your prepared questions. They should work in small groups, discussing their reasoning and making jottings to summarise their calculations.

Differentiation

Prepare a range of questions, including some suitable for your less able and more able children to tackle.

Plenary

Review the children's answers to the word problems as a class. Encourage the children to explain their reasoning and reproduce their jottings on the board as they do so.

There are 500 ml in each bottle. How many litres are there altogether in this pack of bottles? How many packs would we need to give each child in the class a bottle? How many would we need for the whole school?

There are 12 biscuits in the box. If they are shared between four children, how many does each child receive? How many boxes must we buy to give 24 children two biscuits each?

24 Buy a sandwich

Objectives

Numeracy
Solve word problems involving money in 'real life'.
Recognise all coins and notes.
Understand and use £.p notation.
English
Speak audibly and clearly, using spoken standard English in formal contexts.
Design and technology
Think about how some familiar products are used.
Links to QCA Design and Technology Unit 3B: Sandwich snacks.

Resources

Paper £5 and £10 'notes' (from photocopiable page 69) and plastic coins for role-playing transactions.

Vocabulary

money
coin
note
penny, pence, pound
price
buy
spend
pay
change
total

Background

The children will be familiar with our money system from general experience of shopping with parents. In earlier years at school, they should have gained experience of working with all coins and started to use the £.p notation. In this lesson, they practise their calculation skills with this notation by role-playing transactions in a sandwich bar. Work on a sandwich bar links to the QCA Design and Technology unit 'Sandwich snacks', in which the children consider good hygiene procedures for preparing sandwiches and the nutritional value of different fillings.

DAISY'S
SANDWICH BAR

SANDWICHES

cheese £1.20
cheese and tomato £1.50
chicken £1.60
tuna and sweetcorn £1.75

DRINKS

cola 80p
tea 60p
coffee 90p
hot chocolate £1.10

Preparation

Reproduce a sandwich bar price list similar to the one shown for display in the classroom. Copy £5 and £10 'notes' from photocopiable page 69. Distribute the notes and plastic coins on tables.

Main teaching activity

Introduce the lesson by showing the class the sandwich bar price list. Discuss the various prices. Do the children think they are good value? Ask individual children to make an order for a single item and select the correct coins to pay the exact price.

Develop the lesson by asking the children to order two or more items to buy. Finally,

consider the process of receiving change. Ask a child to take the role of the sandwich bar owner and to give you change as you buy items with a combination of coins or notes.

Set the children to work in pairs or small groups to role-play some further transactions. The children should take turns to act as sandwich bar owner and customer.

Differentiation

Less able children should concentrate on buying a single item with the exact money.

Challenge more able children to place an order for a selection of items, calculating mentally the total cost and the change from the money offered.

Plenary

Conclude the lesson with some quick-fire mental maths problems, based on the sandwich bar price list – for example, *How much is a cheese sandwich and a coffee? How much change do you get from £5 when you buy two cheese and tomato sandwiches and two cups of tea?*

25 Points of the compass

Objectives

Numeracy
Recognise and use the four compass directions: N, S, E, W.
Geography
Use appropriate geographical vocabulary.
Use maps and plans.
Links to QCA Geography Unit 6: Investigating our local area.

Resources

Copies of photocopiable page 78; magnetic compasses; school playground; playground chalk, a measuring stick, card, plastic PE cones; a fine day!

Vocabulary

compass point
North
South
East
West
N
S
E
W

Background

The four compass directions are used to describe directions and movement over the surface of the Earth. North is the direction of the North Pole, South is the opposite direction, East and West are perpendicular to the line from North to South. If you face North, your left arm is to the West and your right arm is to the East. In the UK, maps are almost always drawn with North at the top and South at the bottom. The orientation of a map is usually indicated by a compass symbol.

The needle of a magnetic compass settles with one end pointing towards the magnetic North Pole and the other end towards the South. If you turn the compass until the arrow labelled N lines up with the needle, the other compass directions are then also aligned correctly. (The magnetic North and South Poles are close enough to the geographical ones for most purposes.)

Preparation

Collect the compasses and check that they work. If possible, try to have at least one compass for every two children. Use the photocopiable sheet to prepare sets of direction cards.

Main teaching activity

Take the children outside onto the playground. Lay your largest compass on the ground and gather the children in a circle around it. Explain how it works. Emphasise the importance of keeping any metallic or magnetic objects away from the needle, or a false reading will be obtained. Orient the compass correctly and look with the children to see what features are to the North, South, East and West of the playground. Use the chalk and measuring stick to draw a large compass symbol on the playground around the compass. Distribute the compasses, cones and direction cards to pairs or small groups of children. The children should use their compasses to help them follow the directions, placing the cones where indicated.

Differentiation

Less able children can be given sequences of two or three instructions.

Challenge more able children with longer sequences, involving more steps and changes of direction.

Plenary

As a class, examine the arrangements of cones the children have set out. Ask representatives to walk through their sequences, reading out the instructions to confirm that they have been followed correctly.

Linked to
History

26 Dates of birth

Objectives

Numeracy
Use units of time and know the relationships between them.
Use a calendar.
Know their date of birth in the form: day, month, year.

History
Use dates and vocabulary relating to the passing of time.
Study significant events and individuals.

Resources

A large single-page calendar; monthly calendar sheets in the format illustrated (these are readily created on the computer by drawing tables, for example, in *Microsoft Word*); a flip chart or board; research materials including encyclopaedias and historical biographies for research on birth dates.

Vocabulary

date of birth
year
month
day
calendar

Background
Dates of birth can be written in various formats – for example: 6 Aug 1995, 6th August 1995, 6/8/95. In this activity, the children are introduced to these formats for writing their own date of birth and the birth dates of friends, celebrities and historical figures.

Preparation
Generate and print monthly calendar sheets. Display a single-page calendar and set out the research materials where they can easily be accessed.

Main teaching activity
Introduce the lesson by asking the children to take turns to identify their birthdays on the calendar. Discuss the format for writing dates of birth by writing some birthdays on the board.

Divide the children into groups by birth month. Distribute the monthly calendar sheets to the appropriate groups and ask the children each to fill in their birth year and name next to the correct day. When all the children have entered their own birth dates, they can add to the calendar by filling in blanks with celebrities or historical figures. This could develop into an ongoing class challenge to find a person born on every day of the year.

Differentiation
Less able children should concentrate on writing in their own date of birth and finding it on a calendar.

APRIL 2003

T 1	W 16
W 2	T 17
T 3	F 18
F 4	S 19
S 5	S 20
S 6	M 21
M 7	T 22
T 8	W 23
W 9	T 24
T 10	F 25
F 11	S 26
S 12	S 27
S 13	M 28
M 14	T 29
T 15	W 30

More able children can develop the historical research, finding the birth dates of famous people in their own birth month and in other months.

Plenary
Collect and display the monthly calendar sheets. Count the number of birth dates that have been completed and calculate the number of blanks still to be filled in. Ask questions based on the sheets – for example: *Who was born on 23rd April 1564? What was Winston Churchill's date of birth?*

Linked to
D & T

27 How many in a box?

Objectives

Numeracy
Count larger collections by grouping them:
for example, in tens, then other numbers.
Count on in tens and hundreds.
Design and technology
Evaluate a range of familiar products,
thinking about how they are used.
**Links to QCA Design and Technology Unit
3A: Packaging.**

Resources

Several nominally 'identical' packs of small
items. If possible, provide one or more
similar boxes of small items per group to
be counted. You could, for example, raid the
school stock cupboard for boxes of paper
clips. (For safety reasons, do not use boxes
of live matches. Monitor the children
carefully if they are counting elastic bands:
they must not be allowed to flick them at
each other or across the room.)

Vocabulary

count
group
exact, exactly
approximate, approximately, approx.
frequency chart

Background

When we buy large
quantities of small
cheap items, such as
paperclips,
matchsticks, cocktail
sticks, beads, nails or
rubber bands, the
packet often has a
label of the form
'contents approx. 200'.
The items are
probably packaged in
the factory by mass,
and numbers may vary
from pack to pack. In
this activity, the
children develop their
counting skills by
checking the contents
of some packs. The
lesson links to work in
the QCA Design and
Technology
unit on
packaging,
which
suggests
that
children investigate and evaluate a
range of commercial packages –
including the information
provided on the box.

Preparation

Collect together the packaged items and
distribute them on tables.

Main teaching activity

Introduce the lesson by examining one of
the packs you have provided. Read the
contents description on the pack and discuss
the significance of the word 'approximately'
with the children. Why do they think this
word is used for this pack of items? How do
they think the items were packaged in the
factory? Did someone count them one at a
time? Develop the lesson by explaining that
the children are going to do a survey of the
actual contents of the packs. Set the children
to work in their groups to count and record
the number of items in one or more packs.
Discuss efficient counting methods with
them – for example, they could count items
in twos into groups of ten, then group the
tens into hundreds.

Differentiation

Less able children should concentrate on
developing their counting skills.
Suggest that more able children compile
a frequency chart of the numbers of items in
the boxes counted by the class (an example
is shown below).

Plenary

Write a list of the numbers counted by the
children on the board. Are they all identical?
Did some boxes contain more than the
number given as the contents? Did some
boxes contain less? What was the least and
the greatest number in any one box?

number of paper clips in a box	frequency
196	1
199	2
200	5
201	1
203	1

500 SEASHELLS   500 SEASHELLS   500 SEASHELLS

Linked to
I C T

28 Swap the frogs!

Objectives

Numeracy
Solve mathematical problems and puzzles, recognise simple patterns and relationships.
ICT
Organise and reorganise images.
Identify patterns and relationships.
Create, test and improve sequences of instructions to make things happen.
Links to QCA Information Technology Unit 3C: Introduction to databases.

Resources

Computers running software suitable for displaying and moving images by clicking and dragging (for example, *Textease* or *Microsoft Word)*; alternatively, photocopied sheets of different-sized frogs, similar to those illustrated below.

Vocabulary

puzzle
problem
explain your method
what could we try next?
arrange
changed over

Background

Sequencing is an important mathematical skill with numerous applications in other areas of the curriculum – for example, putting names in alphabetical order or bean plants in order of height. Sequencing is a common feature of ICT applications such as spreadsheets and databases, and in this activity the children use their problem-solving skills to develop strategies for sequencing items on the computer screen.

Preparation

Set up the computers with a screen displaying a line of different-sized frogs sitting on lily pads. On the screen shown here the frog is clip art that has been copied repeatedly and re-sized. The pads are simple ovals drawn with the drawing tools in *Textease*. If insufficient computers are available for all the children to work on them in reasonable-sized groups, produce a paper version of the activity.

Main teaching activity

Introduce the lesson by showing the children the frogs on the computer screen. Explain that they have a problem to solve. They must rearrange the frogs in order of size, but they must follow these rules as they do so:
1. They can only move one frog at a time.
2. They must place the frog on an empty lily pad before moving another frog.
    Set the children to solve the puzzle.

Differentiation

Less able children will probably need considerable adult guidance to develop an efficient strategy for solving the problem.
    Once the more able children have found a solution, suggest that they try to write a list of instructions to help someone else solve the problem. (For example: Move the frog at the end to the free pad. Move the biggest frog to the end pad. Move the frog next to it to the free pad. Move the second biggest frog next to the biggest frog. Repeat down the line.)

Plenary

Ask representatives from different groups to describe how they set about solving the problem. Can anyone describe a method for solving the problem that always works?

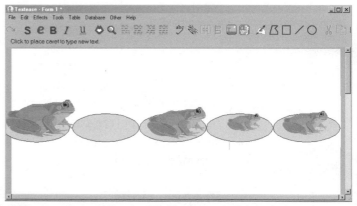

Details of *Textease* are available from www.textease.com

29 Bean bag darts

Objectives

Numeracy
Add three or four single-digit numbers mentally.
Derive quickly doubles of whole numbers to at least 20.
PE
Take part in and design challenges that require precision.

Resources

A dry playground; playground chalk; skipping ropes, bean bags, measuring sticks.

Vocabulary

addition
double
score
circle
semicircle

Background

Keeping score in a game of darts is excellent practice for mental addition skills. For each round, three numbers up to 20 must be added and doubles and triples must be calculated. For safety reasons, metal darts cannot be used in the classroom, though there are now some safe plastic versions of the game available for children's use. A set could be made available for a supervised game in which the children are prompted to add scores correctly. In this lesson, the children set out their own large-scale 'dartboards' in the playground for use in a PE lesson in which they develop their number skills as they practise their throwing skills.

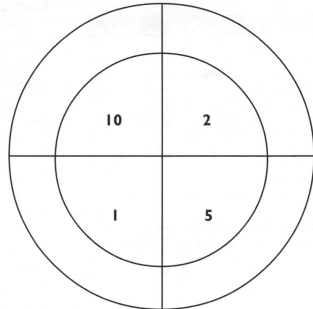

Preparation

Assemble the PE apparatus. Prepare for a PE lesson according to your normal practice.

Main teaching activity

Take the children outside and explain that during the first part of the lesson, they are going to set out 'dartboards' using the chalk ropes and measuring sticks. Demonstrate how two children can draw a large circle with a rope and chalk. One child holds one end of the rope at the centre of the circle, while the other walks around holding the chalk and rope together, keeping the rope taut and pressing the chalk to the ground. Explain that the children should draw two circles with the same centre – one larger than the other. They should then divide their circles in half using the measuring stick as a

straight edge (you could introduce the word 'semicircle' here), and then in quarters by drawing a second line at right angles to the first. The children should produce the dartboard design shown above.

The children should number the sectors in preparation for playing a throwing game. In groups, they take turns to toss three bean bags from behind a line onto their dart board. Bags in the inner ring score the number indicated, bags in the outer ring score double. The children should agree the rules of the game before they start – for example: the first child to reach 50 wins; bags on a line between two numbers score the lower number.

Differentiation

Less able children could label their dartboards with numbers less than 10.

Suggest that more able children use higher numbers and modify their rules correspondingly. Some children may like to subdivide their boards further.

Plenary

Ask representatives from the different groups to demonstrate their throwing skills, with the whole class keeping score as the bean bags land.

30 Times 10, times 100

Objectives

Numeracy
Measure and compare using a ruler.
Know the relationship between centimetres and metres.
To multiply by 10 (or 100), shift the digits 1 (or 2) places to the left.

Design and technology
To communicate designs and ideas in various ways.

Geography
To use maps and plans at a range of scales.

Resources

A copy of photocopiable pages 79 and 80 for each child; rulers and pencils; a scale model (for example, a toy house or car) labelled with its scale; a map of the local environment or a scale drawing of the school.

Vocabulary

metre
centimetre
scale
multiply
ten times
one hundred times

Background

Interpreting plans in technology and maps in geography requires the children to appreciate the concept of a scale drawing. Scaling can be introduced with the aid of models. For example, if the door on a house is 2m high, the door on a $\frac{1}{100}$ scale model of the house is 2cm high. In this leson, the children make measurements of dimensions on scale drawings of a house and a bicycle.

Preparation

Make and distribute copies of the photocopiable sheets.

Main teaching activity

Introduce the lesson with the aid of the scale model and drawings. Discuss the concept of scale, explaining that there is a fixed link between the size of items on a scale model or drawing and the real thing. For example, if the scale is $\frac{1}{10}$, a real length of

10cm is represented by a length of 1cm on the model or plan. Use a metre stick to reinforce the 10 to 1 and 100 to 1 scale relationships.

Show the children the worksheets. The object of the exercise is to measure dimensions on the drawings with a ruler and to complete the tables by listing scale dimensions and actual dimensions. For the bicycle the scale is $\frac{1}{10}$, therefore measurements on the drawing must be multiplied by 10 to give actual measurements. For the house the scale is $\frac{1}{100}$, so measurements must be multiplied by 100. Reinforce the link between cm and m.

Differentiation

Less able children could concentrate on the bicycle, multiplying each of their measurements by 10 to complete the table.

Challenge the more able children to make a scale drawing of their own – for example, of a piece of furniture in the classroom, or of their own body.

Plenary

Review the answers to the worksheets as a class. What scales do the children think would be appropriate for drawing a car, a person or the whole school on a single sheet of paper? The answers are:

bicycle measurements	size on drawing in centimetres	size on real bicycle in centimetres
height	10	100
length	15	150
wheel size	6	60
crossbar	5.5	55
saddle length	2.5	25

house measurements	size on drawing in centimetres	size on real house in centimetres	size on real house in metres
height	4	400	4
roof width	5	500	5
door height	2	200	2
window width	1.5	150	0.15
chimney width	0.5	50	0.05

31 How many in a pack?

Objectives

Numeracy
Understand multiplication as describing an array.
Extend understanding that multiplication can be done in any order.
Know by heart multiplication facts for the 2, 5 and 10 times tables.
Begin to know the 3 and 4 times tables.
Design and technology
Evaluate a range of familiar products, thinking about how they are used.
Links to QCA Design and Technology Unit 3A: Packaging.

Resources

A copy of photocopiable page 81 for each child; examples of items packaged in regular arrays – for example, pencils in a box, boxes of paper clips in a carton, cans in a tray, bottles in a crate; building bricks for setting out regular arrays.

Vocabulary

times table
multiply
array
groups of
repeated addition
row
column

Background

Multiplication can be represented by regular arrays – for example, an array of 5 × 6 milk bottles in a crate. Such an array can be used to demonstrate how multiplication is equivalent to repeated addition by adding the bottle numbers row by row: 5 + 5 + 5 + 5 + 5 + 5 = 30 = 5 × 6 The array can also be used to demonstrate that multiplication can be done in any order: 5 × 6 = 6 × 5

$$6 \times 5 = 30$$

$$5 \times 6 = 30$$

Regularly packed items represent an array. Discussion of the reasons for packaging items in multi-packs (convenience for transportation and stacking, possible increased sales, easier for purchaser to carry) links the mathematics of counting and arrays to the evaluations suggested by the QCA Design and Technology unit 'Packaging'.

Preparation

Make and distribute copies of the photocopiable sheet. Make a collection of regularly packed items.

Main teaching activity

Introduce the lesson with some times table practice as a whole class. Proceed to show the children the packaged items and discuss the properties of the various arrays. Count the rows and columns, and consider how the

same items might be packaged in alternative arrays (3 × 4 = 2 × 6, for example). How would the shape of the package differ? Explain how the quantity in a box can be calculated:

number = number in a row × number of rows

Confirm that this multiplication gives the correct number by counting and repeated addition of the items in rows.

Set the children to work in pairs or small groups on the worksheet activity. They should use their knowledge of times tables to fill in the blanks.

Differentiation

Less able children should concentrate on the worksheet problems. Encourage them to check their answers by counting.

More able children who complete the activity quickly could be challenged to investigate alternative ways of packaging 12, 16, 20 or 24 items in arrays. The alternatives for 12 are shown below.

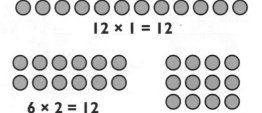

$$12 \times 1 = 12$$

$$6 \times 2 = 12$$

$$4 \times 3 = 12$$

Plenary

Review the worksheet answers (see below) as a class. Make brick arrays to represent the times tables and use them as a basis for some counting in twos, threes, fours, fives and tens. Encourage the children to observe how items are stacked and packaged in regular patterns when they next visit the supermarket.

2 × 3 = 3 × 2 = 6
4 × 2 = 2 × 4 = 8
5 × 3 = 3 × 5 = 15
4 × 5 = 5 × 4 = 20
8 × 5 = 5 × 8 = 40
10 × 3 = 3 × 10 = 30
4 × 10 = 10 × 4 = 40
5 × 10 = 10 × 5 = 50

32 How far can you swim?

Objectives

Numeracy
Recognise unit fractions such as 1/2, 1/3, 1/4, 1/5, 1/10...
Begin to recognise simple fractions that are several parts of a whole, such as 3/4, 2/3.
Compare familiar fractions: for example, know that on the number line 1/2 lies between 1/4 and 3/4.

PE
Swim unaided for a sustained period of time.
Pace themselves in a floating and swimming challenge related to distance.
Links to QCA Physical education Unit 16.

Resources
Laminated coloured cards displaying the fractions 1, 3/4, 2/3, 1/2, 1/3, 1/4, 1/5, 1/10; a sports ground tape measure.

Vocabulary
estimate
fraction
one whole
one half, two halves
one quarter, two... three... four quarters
one third, two thirds
one tenth

Background
Children's swimming ability develops gradually. First they manage a few strokes, then half a width, then half a length and eventually a whole length of the pool. This activity is centred on a swimming lesson in which the children gauge their progress by swimming progressively greater fractions of a length.

Preparation
This lesson should follow on from numeracy lessons in which the children have learned about the fractions considered. Use it as an activity during a swimming lesson.

Main teaching activity
Introduce the activity by asking the children how far they can swim. Explain that you are going to mark out different fractions of the pool length for them to swim. With the help of the children, use the tape to position the fraction cards along one side of the pool. Prompt them with some mental maths as you place the cards: *The pool is 20m long so halfway is at 10m. 20 divided by 4 is 5 so a quarter way is 5m, and three quarters of the way is 15m...*

Having set out the cards, ask the children to swim $\frac{1}{10}$ of the length of the pool and back. Gradually increase the fractions to see who can swim $\frac{1}{2}$ lengths and whole lengths. You could devise various games based on the fractions – for example, mixed swimming ability relay races in which the poor swimmers must swim $\frac{1}{10}$ of a length while better swimmers swim $\frac{1}{2}$ of a length.

Differentiation
Remove the cards and challenge the children to position themselves in the water at various fractions of the pool length.
Less able children should estimate $\frac{1}{2}$ or $\frac{1}{4}$ of a length.
More able children can be challenged to estimate fractions such as $\frac{1}{3}$ or $\frac{3}{5}$.

Plenary
Reposition the cards to check the children's estimates of the fractions.
Follow up the swimming lesson with a discussion of the pool fractions as an introduction to further work on fractions in a maths lesson.

33 Class data

Objectives

Numeracy
Solve a given problem by organising and interpreting numerical data in simple lists, tables and graphs, for example: frequency tables and bar charts.
ICT
Work with others to explore a variety of ICT tools.
Links to QCA IT Unit 3C: Introduction to databases.
Geography
Links to QCA Geography Unit 6:
Investigating our local area.

Resources

A copy of photocopiable pages 82 and 83 for each child; computers running software with simple primary database capabilities – for example, *Textease*.

Vocabulary

bar chart
frequency table
survey
tally
count
most popular
least popular

Background

A survey of the children's modes of transport to school is a good basis for developing data handling skills. The survey links to work in geography on the children's knowledge of their local environment. If computer databases are used to record, sort and present the data, ICT skills are also developed. The children can collect the initial data on photocopied report forms, compile a frequency table, enter the data into a computer database, and display the results graphically.

Preparation

Make and distribute copies of the photocopiable sheets in advance. Set up the computers and make sure that you can use the database facilities of your chosen program with confidence.

Main teaching activity

Introduce the lesson by talking about travelling to school. *Who walks every day? Who comes by car? What are the advantages and disadvantages of the different ways of travelling? Are some means of transport better for the environment than others?* Explain that you are going to make a survey of the children's different methods of transport.

Distribute the report forms to individual children. Explain that the boxes to be completed are sometimes called 'fields'. For example, on this report form the first field is the child's name and the second is his or her mode of transport. There is also a series of

check boxes to indicate the journey distance.

Ask the children to fill in their report forms individually. Some may need help estimating their journey distance. Prompt them to tick an appropriate distance box. (Suggest that they check the distance next time they make the journey by counting their paces if they walk, or looking at the car milometer if they are driven. Help them to make the conversion to km. One child's pace equals approximately $\frac{1}{2}$ m, 1 mile equals approximately $1\frac{1}{2}$ kilometres.) When the forms are complete, collect them in.

The children should then complete the frequency tables individually or in pairs by recording tallies as you read through the pile of forms. When they have completed the frequency tables, they will have suitable data for plotting block graphs or bar charts.

Differentiation

Less able children should concentrate on carrying out the survey on paper.

Suggest that more able children transfer their data to a computer database, using the facilities of the program to display frequency tables and bar charts. A sample screen generated with *Textease* is shown below.

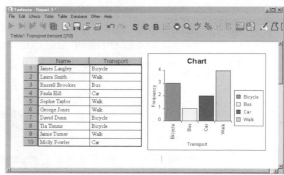

Details of *Textease* are available from www.textease.com

Plenary

Review and discuss the children's tables and graphs as a class. Is there any connection between the distance travelled and the mode of transport chosen? Make a display based on the activity.

34 Assessment 2

Objectives

The assessment activities in this book are designed to introduce Key Stage 2 children to SAT-style questions. They are set in cross-curricular contexts based on the preceding term's lessons. The questions in Assessment 2 test the children's progress in: recall of addition facts to 20 and organising numbers in a table; knowledge of time units and their relationships; interpreting bar charts.

Resources

One copy per child of photocopiable page 84; pencils; abacuses.

Preparation

Make copies of the assessment sheet. If you feel that the sheet is too 'busy', the three activities could be separated and enlarged on individual sheets.

Lesson introduction

Begin the assessment lesson by reviewing the relevant cross-curricular topics covered during the term. Remind the children of some of the projects and investigations they have undertaken, and ask them to recall and recount their work. Emphasise the mathematical content – for example: *Do you remember how we displayed the results of our sandwich survey as a bar chart?*

Main assessment activity

Distribute the sheets and ask the children to work on them individually. Guide the whole class through the questions one at a time, reading the text with them and prompting them to work out and fill in their answers. Try to make the whole activity enjoyable!

Practical activity

Set groups of children to demonstrate how they add two, three and four two-digit numbers with an abacus. Make sure that they can regroup beads to 'carry' from one row to the next when necessary. Can they explain the regrouping process?

Plenary

Review the answers to the questions as a class. Collect the completed question sheets to use as an aid to judging individual children's progress, and to include in your records. The answers are:

1.

+	0	1	2	3	4	5	6	7	8	9	10
5	5	6	7	8	9	10	11	12	13	14	15
6	6	7	8	9	10	11	12	13	14	15	16
7	7	8	9	10	11	12	13	14	15	16	17
8	8	9	10	11	12	13	14	15	16	17	18
9	9	10	11	12	13	14	15	16	17	18	19
10	10	11	12	13	14	15	16	17	18	19	20

2. 60 seconds = 1 minute
   60 minutes = 1 hour
   24 hours = 1 day
   7 days = 1 week
   52 weeks = 1 year
   1 year = 365 days

3. football, 6, 4

35 Number sequences

Objectives

Numeracy
Describe and extend number sequences.
Recognise simple patterns and relationships.
ICT
Work with others to explore a variety of ICT tools.
Organise and reorganise text and tables.

Resources

Computers running *Textease* or a similar program with spreadsheet capabilities, such as *Microsoft Excel*.

Vocabulary

rule
sequence
continue
pattern

Background

The description of a number sequence involves recognising the rule that links one number to the next – for example, 'add 2', 'multiply by 2' or 'add 10'. The sequences below illustrate these rules:

7, 9, 11, 13, 15 (add 2)
1, 2, 8, 16 (multiply by 2)
5, 15, 25, 35, 45 (add 10)

Sequences can be explored with paper and pencil.

Alternatively, a simple spreadsheet, such as the one provided in the program *Textease*, can be used to generate number sequences. Basing the activity on the computer is motivating and develops important ICT skills.

Preparation

Make sure that you are familiar with the spreadsheet functions of your chosen program and can use it to generate number sequences. In *Textease*, select the 'Create new spreadsheet' option from the Table menu. Point, click and drag with the mouse to draw a spreadsheet with a single column and 10 or more rows. Enter the starting number in the first cell. Subsequent cells can then be filled in 'by hand', using the rule you have chosen to calculate the values mentally, or (this is preferable) by using the formula option to enter a rule so that the value is calculated automatically. If you use the formula method, then when the value in the first cell is changed the other cells will automatically be updated according to the rule.

Main teaching activity

Introduce the lesson by writing some number sequences on the board and asking the children to identify the rules used to generate them. Explain that the children are going to use the computers to generate their own number sequences based on rules that they will decide for themselves.

Set the children to work in small groups at the computers (if insufficient computers are available, some groups could work using pencil and paper). Show the children how to create a new spreadsheet on the screen and enter their values into the cells. The children should label each sequence they generate with its rule, and print a hard copy.

Differentiation

Less able groups should enter the values cell by cell, calculating numbers mentally.

Demonstrate to more able children how to use the formula tool, and set them to explore the number sequences generated from rules and starting numbers of their own choice.

Plenary

Review a selection of the children's printouts. Ask representatives to explain the rules they applied to generate their sequences.

36 Making estimates

Objectives

Numeracy
Give a sensible estimate of up to about 100 objects.
Round any two-digit number to the nearest 10 and any three-digit number to the nearest 100.

English
Evaluate fiction and non-fiction texts.

Resources

A selection of books from different levels of a reading scheme, covering Foundation, Year 1, Year 2 and Year 3; a flip chart or board, pencils and paper.

Vocabulary

estimate
roughly
close to
round
nearest (round to the nearest ten)

Background

The children will have observed that, as their reading progresses, the number of words per page in the books they read is increasing. In this activity, the children use their counting and estimation skills to investigate word counts per page in various levels of a reading scheme. The activity links numeracy skills to developing understanding of the features of fiction and non-fiction books.

Preparation

Organise the reading scheme books in levels. Distribute pencils and paper on tables in preparation for group work.

Main teaching activity

Introduce the lesson by discussing the children's reading progress. Ask them to tell you how they have progressed through the reading scheme books. What are the differences between the books at the different levels? Are there different numbers of words on a page? How does the vocabulary differ?

Explain that they are going to investigate how the number of words on a page depends on the reading level. Look at some books with the whole class and ask the children to estimate the numbers of words per page. Check their estimates by counting. Do not be surprised if the children's estimates are wildly out at first – they should improve rapidly with practice. Show the children how to make a good estimate of word count by counting the number of words in a few typical lines, counting the number of lines and multiplying.

Discuss the best way of stating the number of words per page in a book. The exact number varies from page to page, but by comparing several pages a 'typical' number can be stated. This number is probably best rounded to the nearest 10 or 100 words. The children might find that sample Year 1 books have 20–40 words per page; Year 3 books may have 100–200 words per page.

Set the children to work in groups to make and record their estimates of the word counts at the various reading levels.

Differentiation

Less able children could check levels with fewer words per page.

Set the more able children to check the higher-level books and to investigate differences in word counts between fiction and non-fiction, or other genres.

Plenary

Compile the children's findings in a table on the board. Discuss how the word counts increase from level to level. Discuss other features of the text that differ from level to level, and between fiction and non-fiction titles. The table could be converted into a bar chart to produce a classroom display on the topic.

37 Find the page

Objectives

Numeracy
Count on or back in tens, starting from any two- or three-digit number.
Add and subtract mentally a 'near multiple of ten' to or from a two-digit number... by adding or subtracting 10, 20, 30... and adjusting.
Literacy
Locate information using contents, index, page numbers.

Resources

A class set of a book with at least 100 numbered pages (a general encyclopaedia or school dictionary would be suitable); pencils and paper.

Vocabulary

number
calculation
sequence
add
subtract
order

Background

Finding your way around a book using page numbers, chapter numbers and the index is an important literacy skill. It also provides the opportunity for some mental maths practice. In this activity, the children answer maths questions involving counting on, addition and subtraction, based on the numbers found in books.

Preparation

Distribute the class set of books for individual children to use. Prepare a secret message, as described below.

Main teaching activity

Look at the features of your chosen book together. *How many pages are in the book? Are all the pages numbered?* Check to see whether there are a contents list and an index. If you have chosen an encyclopaedia or dictionary, discuss the alphabetical sequence of the entries.

Now explain that you are going to play some number games based on the book. Ask the children to turn to page 35 and find the tenth word on the page. Now ask them to go forwards 21 pages and find the fifth word. Then back 13 pages and find the 21st word. At this stage, discuss how to find the correct pages. *35 plus 21 is equal to 35 plus 20 plus one, which is 55 plus one more, which is 56 – so you should be on page 56.* Issue a series of instructions of the same type, asking the children to make and explain their mental calculations as they work through them. Challenge the children to be the first to find the word you are looking for each time.

When the children are familiar with the process, play a game in which you ask them to find and write down a series of words that will form a 'secret message' (for example: *Meet under the station clock. Carry a red rose.*) Work through the sequence by giving a series of mental calculations to find the pages and words.

Differentiation

Adapt the level of the mental calculations to the abilities of the children. You could work with a group of less able children, while more able children challenge each other with book-based calculations.

Plenary

Ask the children to read out the sentences they produced by following your instructions. Has anyone discovered the secret message?

Linked to History

38 'Doing sums'

Linked to History

Objectives

Numeracy
Begin to use column addition and subtraction for HTU +/– TU where the calculation cannot easily be done mentally.

History
Study the impact of the Second World War on the lives of children.

Links to QCA History Unit 9: What was it like for children in the Second World War?

Resources

A whiteboard or blackboard and chalk; slates (most children can use A4 whiteboards and markers, but try to find some traditional slates and chalks if possible); paper and pencils.

Vocabulary

calculate
addition
total
tens
hundreds
place
place value

Background

During the Second World War, mathematics teaching in the primary school was much more formal than it is today. It was generally based on rote learning and repeated practice of standard calculation methods. Resources were at a premium, so chalks and slates made an ideal medium for doing 'sums'. In this lesson, the children practise standard calculation methods during role play.

Preparation

This lesson should build on numeracy lessons in which you have developed informal pencil and paper methods (jottings) for HTU +/– TU calculations. The history context could be developed by adopting a Second World War school theme for the day or week. Make a display of toys, books, school equipment and other items from the period. Some children may wish to dress in period clothes.

Main teaching activity

Introduce the activity by explaining that you are going to role-play a Second World War 'arithmetic' lesson. The children are going to do their 'sums' on slates. You could arrange the classroom so that the children are sitting in formal rows facing the board, as in a wartime classroom.

Explain your chosen methods formally, using 'chalk and talk'. Demonstrate addition of HTU + TU by showing how to line up tens and units. At this stage, perform the calculation in steps by adding the less and more significant digits in sequence and

completing the calculation mentally. For example:

$$\begin{array}{r} 345 \\ +29 \\ \hline 14 \\ 60 \\ 300 \\ \hline 374 \end{array}$$

Subtraction can be performed by decomposition, with regrouping where necessary:

$$\begin{array}{rcl} 53 & = & 50 + 3 & = & 40 + 13 \\ -27 & = & 20 + 7 & = & 20 + 7 \\ & & & & 20 + 6 & = & 26 \end{array}$$

Practise several examples with the whole class, then write a series of problems on the board for the children to solve on their slates. If you only have a few slates, some children can work with pencil and paper.

Differentiation

Set less able children problems involving tens and units only.

Challenge more able children with addition and subtraction of hundreds, tens and units.

Plenary

Ask selected children to demonstrate their solutions on the board to the rest of the class. Discuss the Second World War teaching style. What would the children think if all their maths work was done on slates? What other resources do we have today to help us learn maths?

Linked to
D & T

39 How many do we need?

Objectives

Numeracy
Solve word problems involving numbers in 'real life', money and measures.
Design and technology
Evaluate a range of familiar products.
Links to QCA Design and Technology Unit 3A: Packaging.

Resources

A copy of photocopiable page 85 for each child; samples of packaged items from the supermarket or school stock cupboard.

Vocabulary

calculate
total
addition
multiplication
division
share
lots of
method
How did you work it out?

Background

Many items in shopping and school situations are packaged in multiples – for example, pencils in boxes of ten, biscuits in packs of six or bags of crisps in packs of 12. Answering the question *How many packs do we need for a family of 4, or a class of 30?* practises mental addition, multiplication and division skills. Discussion of the reasons for packaging items in multi-packs (convenience for transportation and stacking, possible increased sales, easier for purchaser to carry) links to the packaging evaluations suggested by the QCA Design and Technology unit 'Packaging'. (See also Lesson 31.)

Preparation

Make and distribute copies of the photocopiable sheet. Make a collection of suitable packaged materials.

Main teaching activity

Use the samples of packaged materials to introduce the lesson by challenging the class with some mental calculations. For example, look at a pack of 6 biscuits. *How many packs are needed to give each child in the class one biscuit? If there are 24 packets of biscuits in a carton, how many biscuits are there altogether? How many biscuits would each child receive if the class shared the whole carton? If the cost per pack is 72p, what is the cost per biscuit? How much would it cost to give everyone in the class a biscuit? How much does a carton of biscuits cost?*

Set the children to work in pairs or small groups on the worksheet problems.

Differentiation

Less able children should concentrate on answering the first two problems on the worksheet.

The third problem is more challenging and will probably only be completed by the more able children.

Plenary

Review the children's answers to the worksheet. Discuss the different methods they used to solve the problems. How did they use addition? When were multiplication and division required?

The answers are:
1. 10p, 15, 6, £3.00
2. 20p, 3, 24, £4.80
3. 60, 3, £1.00, £6.00

40 Read the label

Objectives

Numeracy
Solve a given problem by organising and interpreting numerical data in simple lists, tables and graphs.
Read and begin to write the vocabulary related to mass and capacity. Note the relationship between kg and g, l and ml.

Science
Be taught about the need for food and the importance of an adequate and varied diet for health.

Design and technology
To evaluate a range of familiar products.
Links to QCA Design and Technology Unit 3A: Packaging.

Resources
A collection of labels from food packages; paper and pencils.

Vocabulary
data
grams
millilitres
bar chart
table

Background
The labels on food containers include much mathematical and scientific data. Typically, a label gives the mass in grams or the volume in millilitres of the contents. It also records information about food value, including energy content, fat content, carbohydrate content, fibre content and sodium (salt) content. An investigation of the numbers on food labels forms the basis for a lesson involving mathematics, science and technology (linking to the QCA Design and Technology unit on packaging).

Preparation
Make a collection of food labels. You could suggest that the children, with their parents' permission and help, cut out the relevant sections of cereal or biscuit packs, or peel off the labels from used tins or jars to bring to school. The information on a typical label is illustrated below. Produce an enlarged version of this to introduce the lesson.

Main teaching activity
With the whole class, look at the 'Baked beans' label and discuss the information it presents. In the context of work on diet in science, talk about the energy content and various components of food. The children should be aware of the importance of a balanced diet with an appropriate combination of carbohydrates, protein, fat, minerals and vitamins.

Set the children to work in groups to record and compare the compositions of a range of foods represented by the labels they have collected. Explain that to be 'fair', they must compare the same quantity of each food. This is why the food label presents typical values for 100g of each foodstuff, and these are the numbers they should use for comparison. Set each group to compile a table comparing the amounts of a particular food component in various foods. For example, one group could look at energy, another at fat, another at carbohydrate and so on. Groups could translate their completed tables into bar charts for presentation to the class and for display. Bar charts could be completed in a second maths lesson if time runs short.

Differentiation
Less able groups should look at components that are represented by whole-number values.

More able children can handle data that sometimes appear with decimal parts. Discuss the significance of decimal notation, relating it to fractions expressed as tenths.

Plenary
Review the children's findings, asking representatives of the groups to present their tables and bar charts. Which kinds of food have the most energy in 100g? Which have the most fat? Which have the most salt? and so on.

Baked Beans
Nutrition information

Typical values	Amount per 100g
Energy	75kcal
Protein	5g
Carbohydrate	14g
Fat	0.2g
Fibre	4g
Sodium	0.5g

41 Battleships

Objectives

Numeracy
Describe and find the position of a square on a grid of squares with the rows and columns labelled.

History
Study the impact of the Second World War on the lives of children.
Links to QCA History Unit 9: What was it like for children in the Second World War?

Resources

A copy of photocopiable page 86 for each child; pencils; a flip chart or board.

Vocabulary

co-ordinates
column
row
grid
cell

Background

'Battleships' was a popular game with children to pass time spent in air raid shelters during the Second World War. The game is based on a grid, with columns and rows identified by letters and numbers. Playing the game can thus link work in history to work on the mathematics of position and direction.

Preparation

Make and distribute copies of the photocopiable sheet.

Main teaching activity

Introduce the lesson by talking about Second World War air raids and shelters. How did people feel when they were in the shelters? How did they pass their time sheltering underground? What games did the children play? Talk about the game of 'Battleships' and explain the rules. Each player should mark his or her ships in the squares on the grid without showing his or her opponent. The ships in each player's fleet are listed on the sheet. A battleship, for example, is marked BBBB, a destroyer DD. The letters are entered one per grid square horizontally, vertically or diagonally. There must be at least one clear grid square between the ships. An example of a grid in play is illustrated on the sheet.

Set the children to play the game in pairs. They decide who goes first by tossing a coin. The first player calls out the co-ordinates of a grid square – for example, C6. The

second player marks a cross in the square and either replies 'miss' or gives the name of the ship hit (for example, 'cruiser'). The second player then takes a turn to call out a square on his or her opponent's grid. The two players continue alternately until one player has found all the grid squares occupied by his or her opponent's ships.

Differentiation

Less able children could work with a 5 × 5 grid initially.

Challenge more able children to think carefully about the tactics they are using. If they hit a battleship, for example, where should they make their next move? It would be sensible to try one square horizontally, vertically or diagonally from their hit to try and hit the rest of the ship. Suggest that they keep track of both their own and their opponent's turns by marking the squares called with crosses and dots.

Plenary

Conclude the lesson with some quick-fire co-ordinates practice, based on a grid drawn up on the board.

42 Symmetrical shapes

Objectives

Numeracy
Identify and sketch lines of symmetry in simple shapes, and recognise shapes with no lines of symmetry.
Geography
Recognise and explain human features of the environment.
Links to QCA Geography Unit 6: Investigating our local area.

Resources

A chart or book of UK road signs, for example the *Highway Code*; a chart of flags of the world; a copy of photocopiable page 87 for each child; safety mirrors.

Vocabulary

symmetry line
mirror line
symmetrical
shape

Background

Many signs, symbols and flags are based on simple symmetrical shapes and patterns. A sign or flag with a symmetry line looks unchanged when it is reflected in an appropriately placed mirror. If a mirror is placed along the line of symmetry, the half shape and its reflection reproduce the complete shape. Identifying the symmetry properties of road signs and flags links work in geography on the local environment and the wider world to work in mathematics on shape and symmetry.

Preparation

Collect together the charts and books. Make copies of the photocopiable sheet and distribute them with the mirrors on tables.

Main teaching activity

Introduce the lesson by reminding the children about lines of symmetry. Explain that a symmetrical object can look unchanged when seen in a mirror. Examine some road signs for symmetry. Use a mirror to demonstrate how to locate lines of symmetry. Which road signs are symmetrical? Which have more than one line of symmetry? Which are not symmetrical?

Set the children to work in small groups on the worksheets. They should use their mirrors to identify and draw the lines of symmetry on the flags.

Differentiation

Less able children should concentrate on completing the worksheet exercise.

More able children, once they have completed the basic exercise, can go on to use the road sign and flag charts. Ask them to find and sketch examples of signs and flags with no symmetry lines, one symmetry line and more than one symmetry line.

Plenary

Review the answers to the worksheet problems with the whole class. Ask representatives to explain their findings and, where appropriate, extend the discussion to the road signs or flag charts the children have been investigating.

The answers are:

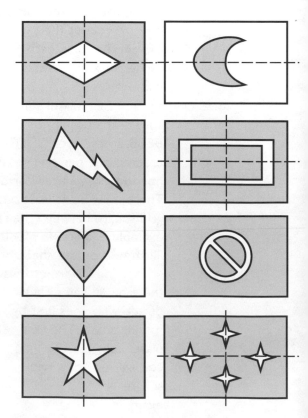

43 Sorting shapes

Objectives

Numeracy
Solve a given problem by organising and interpreting data, for example, using Venn and Carroll diagrams (one criterion). Classify and describe the shapes.

History
Study the impact of significant individuals in Victorian Britain.

Resources

Boxes of shapes for sorting; sorting rings, shoe boxes or similar-sized boxes; cards and felt-tipped pens.

Vocabulary

Carroll diagram
Venn diagram
sort
shape
group
set

Background

John Venn and Lewis Carroll (real name Charles Dodgson) were Victorian mathematicians. They invented diagrams to aid sorting problems. Lewis Carroll was also the author of *Alice in Wonderland*. The two types of diagram are illustrated below. In a Venn diagram, objects with a given characteristic are placed in a set together. In a Carroll diagram, objects are sorted according to whether they have a given property. This lesson can be linked to work in history on famous Victorians and work in literacy on the books and poems of Lewis Carroll.

Preparation

Collect the resources and distribute them on tables in preparation for group work.

Main teaching activity

Introduce the lesson by talking about the Victorian mathematicians Venn and Dodgson. Explain that both of them investigated sorting problems, thinking about ways in which numbers, shapes and other items can be organised. Outline the procedure for sorting according to a Carroll diagram and set the children to sort some shapes into boxes according to a chosen criterion – for example, triangles/not triangles, right angled/not right angled. Emphasise that the criterior must be 'has property/does not have property'. The children should work in groups to sort shapes, labelling their two boxes according to their chosen criterion.

When the children have completed the sorting exercise, review their progress as a whole class. Ask representatives to explain how they have sorted their shapes.

Now explain the Venn diagram. Show how sorting according to two properties can produce overlapping sets. Set the children to work in their groups to sort shapes into a two-set Venn diagram. They should discover that some shapes go in neither set and are left outside.

Differentiation

Less able children will need considerable guidance to select criteria and use them to sort. Challenge more able children to sort using both Carroll and Venn diagrams, according to a variety of criteria.

Plenary

As a class, look at a selection of shapes sorted by the groups. Label the sorting diagrams and arrange a class display.

Venn diagram

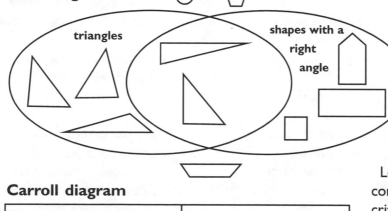

triangles — shapes with a right angle

Carroll diagram

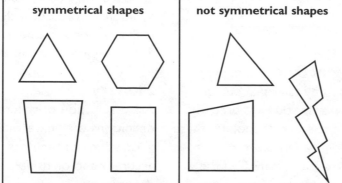

symmetrical shapes | not symmetrical shapes

Linked to
L i t e r a c y

44 Number words

Background
Throughout their work, the children should be encouraged to use the vocabulary of mathematics correctly. Compiling their own maths dictionary will help the children to learn these terms and their meanings. This can be an ongoing activity through the year, linking with work on dictionaries in literacy. As the children encounter new mathematical vocabulary in numeracy lessons, they can add it to their dictionary.

Objectives

Numeracy
Read and begin to write the vocabulary of mathematics including calculations, estimation and approximation, measures, shape, space and movement.
Literacy
Have a secure understanding of the purpose and organisation of a dictionary.

Resources

A notebook with at least 26 pages for each child; pencils; a general school dictionary and/or a mathematics dictionary.

Vocabulary

add
bar chart
Carroll diagram
divide
even number
grid
hexagon

Preparation
Collect the resources and distribute them on tables in preparation for group work. Prepare a preliminary list of mathematical words for the children to enter into their dictionaries. For example:

> **add**
> **bar chart**
> **Carroll diagram**
> **divide**
> **even number**
> **grid**
> **hexagon**

Main teaching activity
Introduce the lesson by talking about the definitions of the words you have prepared in advance. Ask the children to look up these words in the dictionary. Discuss the definitions given. Are they clear? Can the children express them in their own words?

Explain that the children are going to compile their own mathematical dictionary for use in future numeracy lessons. Set the children to work individually, heading the pages of their notebooks alphabetically. Working in pairs or small groups, they should then write a definition of each of the terms you have introduced on the correct page. Suggest that they include an example or illustration to go with each definition.

Differentiation
Less able children should concentrate on the words you have selected, using the dictionaries to help them.

Encourage more able children to define additional words. Can they produce a definition for a mathematical word beginning with each letter of the alphabet?

Plenary
Ask a selection of children to read the definitions they have written and show their illustrations to the class. Discuss the accuracy and/or usefulness of each of the definitions.

Linked to
D & T

45 Multiplying monster

Objectives

Numeracy
Begin to know the 3 and 4 times tables.
Design and technology
Undertake design and make assignments including mechanical components.
Links to QCA Design and Technology Unit 3C: Moving monsters.

Resources

A copy of photocopiable page 88 for each group; craft/technology materials including cards, paper fasteners, scissors, felt-tipped pens, glue; demonstration pneumatic apparatus with a pair of different-sized syringes linked by a plastic tube; cm rulers; a garden cane or long ruler.

Vocabulary

multiplication
multiply
3 times table
4 times table

Background

Simple technology mechanisms such as levers and model pneumatic systems are used to multiply or divide movement. For example, a fishing rod is a long lever that multiplies small movements of the hands at one end into large movements of the rod's tip at the other end. In this activity, the children investigate the multiplying action of levers and pistons, and build a 'multiplying monster' machine.

Preparation

Make and distribute copies of the photocopiable sheet. Gather the craft and technology materials and set them out on tables in preparation for practical work.

Main teaching activity

Introduce the lesson by talking about levers. Use a garden cane to illustrate the principle of the fishing rod. Small movements of the hands at one end are multiplied into large movements of the cane at the other. Explain that arms and legs work as levers to help us move ourselves and other objects. Use the pneumatic demonstration and show that depressing the piston on the larger syringe produces a much greater movement of the piston in the smaller syringe. This machine works like a lever to multiply movement.

Explain that the children are going to use a lever to make a 'multiplying monster'. Look together at the worksheet and discuss how the monster is made. The parts are cut out from card and fastened together with a paper fastener. Discuss how the paper fastener is positioned so that the monster's right arm is three times as long as his left arm. Set the children to make monsters in pairs or small groups. When the monsters are assembled, ask the children to investigate how they multiply. *If you move the right hand by one division on the scale, how many divisions does the left hand move by? How many times has the monster multiplied the movement by?*

Differentiation

Less able children should concentrate on making the basic monster design.

Challenge more able children to produce a monster that multiplies by 4. *How much longer must his left arm be than his right arm?* They could also investigate the pneumatic system further. *What factor does it multiply by? Can you make a multiplying machine using this device?*

Plenary

Look together at the monsters the class have produced. The basic monster multiplies by 3. Have the children produced monsters that multiply by other numbers? Conclude the lesson with some times table practice stimulated by the monster activity.

Linked to
I C T

46 Bigger and smaller

Objectives

Numeracy
Solve mathematical problems, recognise simple patterns and relationships, generalise and predict. Suggest extensions by asking 'what if...?'
ICT
Use a variety of ICT tools.
Links to QCA ICT Unit 3A: Combining text and graphics.

Resources

Computers running a word-processing program such as *Textease* or *Microsoft Word*; printers; rulers.

Vocabulary

measure
size
multiply
sequence
height
cm

Background

As the children work with text and page designs on the computer, they can explore the effects of changing the numbers that determine the size and position of characters and objects. The size of the characters used to display text is generally determined by the point (or font) size and the design of the font. In this activity, the children investigate the effect of changing the point size on the physical height of printed characters.

investigate different font sizes, using their rulers to measure character heights in cm both on screen and on printouts. Times Roman capital letters are approximately 1cm high when the font size is set at 20. What font size should be set to produce 2cm, 3cm, 4cm characters and so on? How does this change when another font is used?

Differentiation

Less able children should concentrate on Times Roman characters, setting the point sizes as multiples of ten: 10, 20, 30, 40...

Challenge more able children to explore character sizes in a range of fonts.

Plenary

Towards the end of the lesson, you could assign a measurement to each group and ask them to produce a printout with characters of that size on a single sheet of paper. Make a wall display with the printouts arranged in size sequence.

Preparation

Set up the computers running your chosen software package, and check that you can select text, change fonts and adjust character size confidently.

Main teaching activity

Explain to the children that you have a computer challenge for them. You want to produce a classroom number display of measurements in which the height of the number character is equal to the measurement it shows. Show them the example below.
Show the children the word-processing software and explain how to change the character size and font. Set them to

1cm **2cm** 3cm

47 Double up

Objectives

Numeracy
Derive quickly doubles of whole numbers.
Solve mathematical problems, recognise
simple patterns.

Science
Know that micro-organisms are living
organisms that are often too small to be
seen and may be beneficial or harmful.
Know that life processes include
reproduction.

Resources

A copy of photocopiable page 89 for each
child; a chessboard; plastic building bricks.

Vocabulary

double
sequence
pattern

Background

In a famous folk story, an emperor was so pleased with his adviser that he offered him any gift he would like. The adviser said he would like a chessboard with one grain of rice on the first square, 2 on the second, 4 on the third, 8 on the fourth and so on – doubling the number of grains until all 64 squares on the board were filled. The emperor was surprised as he thought this was rather a small gift, and agreed readily. A board was brought and the process of filling it with grains of rice started. Very soon, the emperor realised the extent of the gift he had agreed to – as sacks and sacks of rice were delivered. The doubling process grew very rapidly and well before the 64th square was reached the adviser owned all the rice in the empire.

As the story illustrates, repeated doubling produces rapid growth. Bacteria breed by doubling and this is why, if the conditions are right, germs multiply very rapidly. In this lesson, the children investigate germ multiplication in the context of work in science. In the process, they develop their doubling skills.

Preparation

Make and distribute copies of the photocopiable sheet.

Main teaching activity

Introduce the lesson by telling the story of the rice on the chessboard. Reproduce the process with a chessboard and plastic building bricks. Count out the bricks, doubling each time and counting with the children

as you move from square to square. How many squares along can you reach before all the bricks in the box are used up?

Develop the lesson by talking about germs. Germs are microscopic living things. They reproduce by doubling. One germ splits into 2, 2 into 4, 4 into 8 and so on – doubling numbers at each generation. The number of germs grows just like the number of grains of rice on the chessboard. This is why hygiene is so important. In the right conditions, germs may double every 10–20 minutes, so they can breed from one to millions in a day.

Set the children to work in pairs or small groups on the worksheet activity. They should repeatedly double each starting number to find the numbers after the given times.

Differentiation

Less able children can concentrate on completing the first row on the sheet.

More able children can start with various numbers up to 10 and beyond.

Plenary

Review the germ-doubling sheet with the whole class. Develop the science link by discussing the conditions under which germs breed. They need food, warmth and moisture. This is why it is important to keep kitchen surfaces free of food scraps and moisture, and to keep fresh food cold in the refrigerator.

48 Departure time

Numeracy
Read the time to 5 minutes on an analogue clock and a 12-hour digital clock, and use the notation 9:40.
Interpret numerical data in simple lists and tables.
Geography
Identify where places are.

Resources

A copy of photocopiable page 90 for each child; demonstration analogue and digital clocks; a wall map of Europe.

Vocabulary

time
clock
hour
minute
quarter past, half past, quarter to
digital clock
analogue clock

Background

At airports and train stations, departure and arrival times are displayed digitally on monitors and electronic boards. To see whether your train has just left, is about to leave, or will not leave for some time, you must do some mental calculations, perhaps involving comparison between analogue and digital displays. In this activity, the children read times from a departure board. The lesson links to work in geography on the locations of significant places in Europe.

Preparation

Copy and distribute the activity sheets.

Main teaching activity

Introduce the lesson with some whole-class practice in reading times to the nearest five minutes from both analogue and digital clock displays. At this stage, the children are not expected to use a 24-hour digital clock. Work through an hour on an analogue clock, moving the big hand five minutes at a time. Use the conventional language for the time:

**six o'clock, five past six, ten past six,
quarter past six, twenty past six,
twenty-five past six, half past six,
twenty-five to seven, twenty to seven,
quarter to seven, ten to seven,
five to seven, seven o'clock**

Repeat the exercise with the digital clock, giving the alternative expressions for the various times:

**six o'clock, six o'five, six ten,
six fifteen, six twenty, six twenty-five,
six thirty, six thirty-five, six forty,
six forty-five, six fifty,
six fifty-five, seven o'clock**

Develop the lesson by setting times on the analogue clock and selecting children to match them with the digital clock. Ask the class to tell the time using both forms of words shown above.

Introduce the worksheet and discuss the locations of the four cities. Identify them on a wall map of Europe. Set the children to work in small groups on the worksheet activity.

Differentiation

Less able children should concentrate on the first two questions, which involve reading and writing times in different ways.

More able children can progress to the third question, in which they must make time-based calculations.

Plenary

Review the worksheet answers as a class. Conclude the lesson by setting different times on the analogue and digital displays and asking the children to calculate the time difference between them in hours and minutes.

The answers are:
1. six thirty, eleven twenty, nine thirty-five
2.

3. London 55 minutes, Paris 1 hour 50 minutes, Madrid 40 minutes, Rome 5 minutes

49 What's the weather?

Objectives

Numeracy
Solve a problem by organising and interpreting numerical data in tables and graphs, for example: pictograms and bar charts.

Geography
Use appropriate geographical vocabulary. Analyse evidence and draw conclusions.

Resources

A collection of holiday brochures that include weather information in the form of bar charts; a copy of photocopiable page 91 for each child.

Vocabulary

bar chart
temperature
greater than
less than

Background

Many children go abroad on holiday to destinations such as Spain and Greece. Holidays are chosen from brochures in which the weather and the facilities of resorts and hotels can be compared from tables and charts. Interpreting these charts to choose a holiday in the warmest

location is an enjoyable exercise, linking mathematics and geography. Weather information on holiday destinations can be found on many holiday websites – for example, at http://www.weatherguides.com

Preparation

Collect holiday brochures from a local travel agent. Make and distribute copies of the photocopiable sheet.

Main teaching activity

Introduce the lesson by talking about holiday destinations the children have visited. Was it hot? What was the temperature? Where are the best places to go to ensure good weather for your summer holidays? Look together at the holiday brochures, in particular the bar charts showing the monthly temperature ranges in different locations. *Where is it warmest in August? Where is it warmest in January?*

Set the children to work on the worksheet activity. They should answer the questions by interpreting the temperature bar charts.

Differentiation

Less able children should concentrate on the worksheet activity.

Challenge more able children to compile tables of August and January temperatures for resorts around the world from holiday brochures and other resources, such as the Internet.

Plenary

Review the answers to the worksheet as a class. Ask the children who extended their research beyond the worksheets to report their findings. You could make a class display of holiday destinations and temperatures showing the locations on a world map.

The answers are:
1. Sunny Sands
2. Southern Shores
3. Sunny Sands
4. cold
5. warm

Assessment 3

Objectives

The assessment activities in this book are designed to introduce Key Stage 2 children to SAT-style questions. They are set in cross-curricular contexts based on the preceding term's lessons. The questions in Assessment 3 test the children's progress in: recall of 2, 5 and 10 times tables; understanding division; identifying lines of symmetry.

Resources

One copy per child of photocopiable page 92; pencils; a pack of capital letter cards; safety mirrors.

Preparation

Make copies of the assessment sheet. If you feel that the sheet is too 'busy', the three activities could be separated and enlarged on individual sheets.

Lesson introduction

Begin the assessment lesson by reviewing the relevant cross-curricular topics covered during the term. Remind the children of some of the projects and investigations they have undertaken, and ask them to recall and recount their work. Emphasise the mathematical content – for example, *Do you remember how we used a mirror to check the symmetry of shapes?*

Main assessment activity

Distribute the worksheets and ask the children to work on them individually. Guide the whole class through the questions one at a time, reading the text with them and prompting them to work out and fill in their answers. Try to make the whole activity enjoyable!

Practical activity

Ask the children to sort the letter cards into two sets: symmetrical and not symmetrical. They should use a mirror to check whether each letter has a symmetry line.

Plenary

Review the answers to the questions as a class. Collect the completed question sheets to use

as an aid to judging individual children's progress, and to include in your records. The answers are:

×	1	2	3	4	5	6	7	8	9	10
2	2	4	6	8	10	12	14	16	18	20
5	5	10	15	20	25	30	35	40	45	50
10	10	20	30	40	50	60	70	80	90	100

10p, 10p, 20p

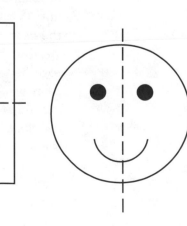

Number words

● Write these numbers in figures.

one hundred and twenty-four

one hundred and seventeen

three hundred and ten

nine hundred and eighty-three

eight hundred and seventy

five hundred and six

● Write these numbers in words.

210

204

560

583

806

916

777

868

Order the years

● Cut out these events. Place them in order on a 1000-year timeline.

AD878 Alfred the Great burns cakes

AD503 King Arthur killed at Battle of Badon

~ AD400 Romans leave Britain

AD61 Boudicca leads revolt against Romans

AD43 Roman army invades Britain

AD122 Hadrian's Wall built

AD793 Vikings raid Britain

AD597 St Augustine brings Christianity to Kent

~ AD449 Anglo-Saxon conquest of Britain begins

Buy a ticket

Single fares from Central Station

	adult	child
Zone 1	40p	20p
Zone 2	60p	30p
Zone 3	80p	40p

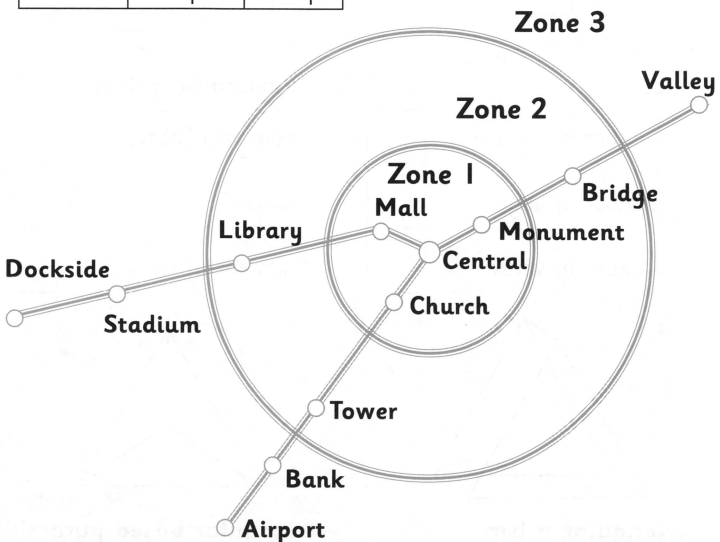

● Find the fares for:
1. A child from Central to Church.
2. An adult from Central to Bridge.
3. A child from Central to Valley.
4. An adult and a child from Central to Tower.
5. An adult and two children from Central to Stadium.

Shape words

● Count the edges, faces and vertices of these solid shapes.

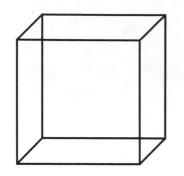

cube

number of faces =

number of edges =

number of vertices =

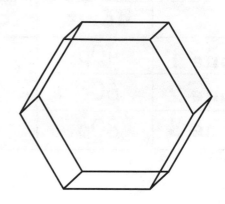

hexagonal prism

number of faces =

number of edges =

number of vertices =

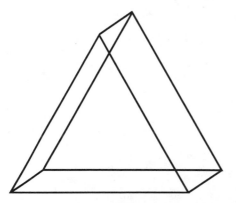

triangular prism

number of faces =

number of edges =

number of vertices =

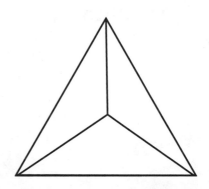

triangular based pyramid

number of faces =

number of edges =

number of vertices =

Which century?

● Match the years to the centuries.

twenty-first century

twentieth century

AD1423

AD2001

tenth century

first century

AD57

AD163

twelfth century

fifteenth century

AD1542

sixteenth century

AD1801

AD1734

AD978

eighteenth century

second century

AD1994

AD1161

nineteenth century

Double and halve

● Complete these doubles tables.

number	double
1	2
2	4
3	
4	
	10
6	
7	
	16
9	
	20

number	double
11	22
	24
13	
14	
	30
16	
	34
	36
19	
20	

number	double
10	
20	
	60
	80
50	
	120
70	
	160
90	
	200

number	double
5	10
15	
25	
35	
45	
55	
65	
75	
85	
95	

number	double
50	
100	
150	
200	
250	
300	
350	
400	
450	
500	

number	double
	200
	400
	600
	800
	1000
	1200
	1400
	1600
	1800
	2000

Coins and notes

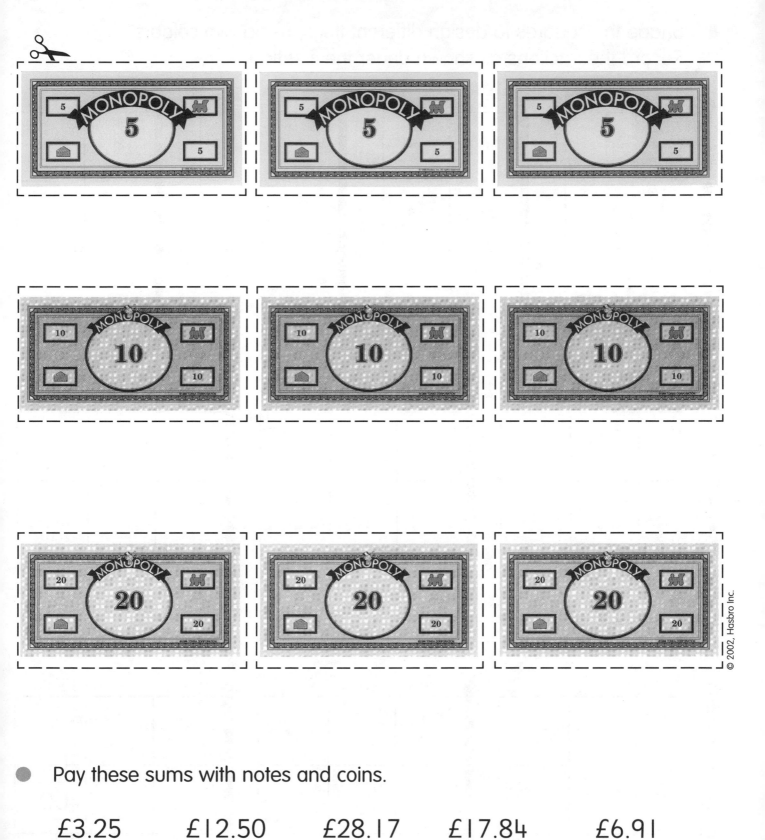

● Pay these sums with notes and coins.

£3.25   £12.50   £28.17   £17.84   £6.91

£34.32   £3.99   £46.49   £8.60   £69.49

Fraction flags

● Shade the squares to design different flags, using two colours.
● Record the fractions as shown under the first flag.

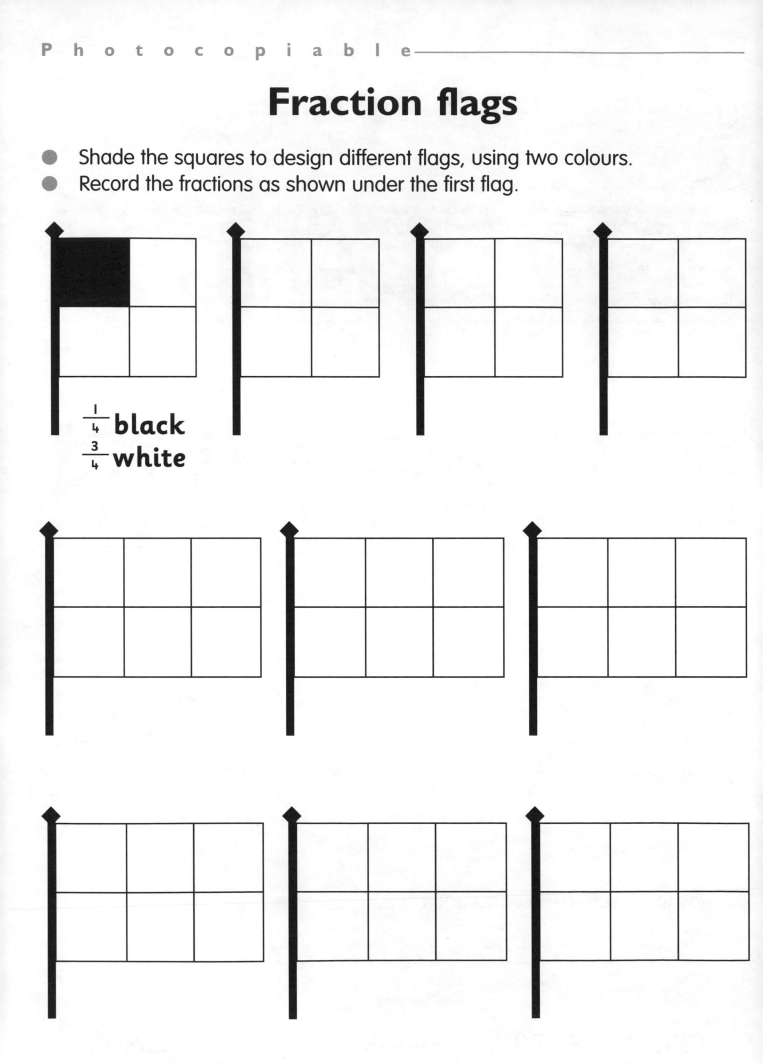

$\frac{1}{4}$ black
$\frac{3}{4}$ white

How far?

This map shows the city bus routes.
The distances are in kilometres.

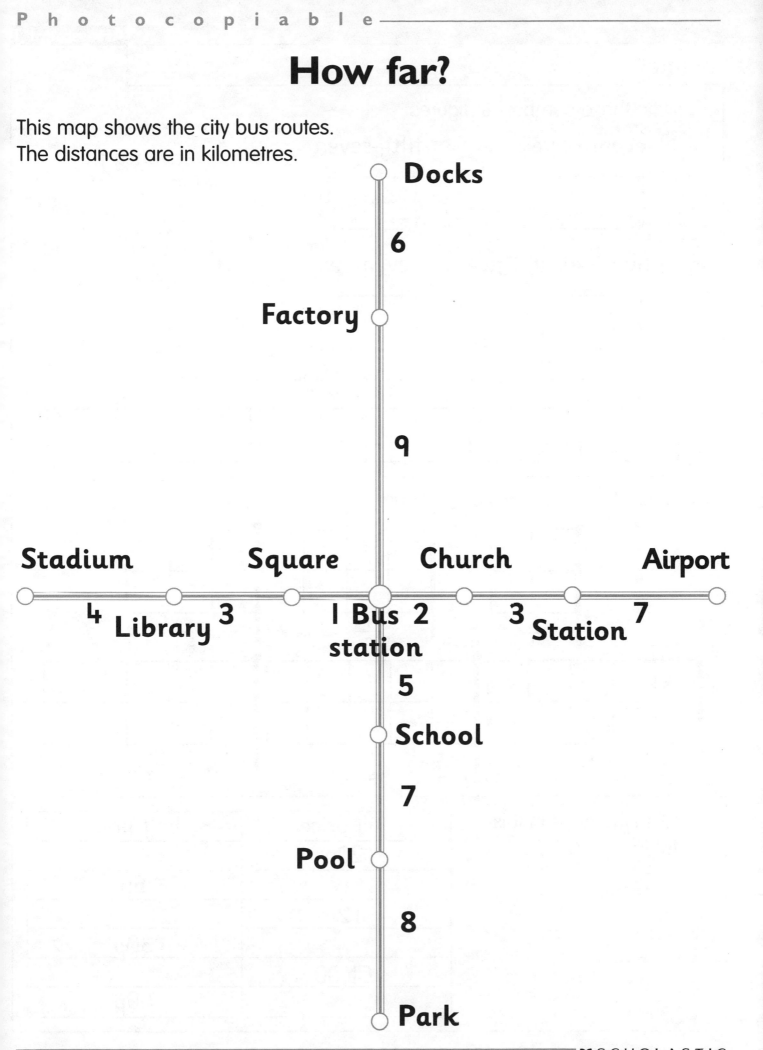

Name

● Write these numbers in figures.

seventy-five

fifty-seven

five hundred and seventy-five

seven hundred and five

seventeen

five hundred and fifty-seven

● Write all the numbers in order, smallest first.

● Colour these fractions of the flags.

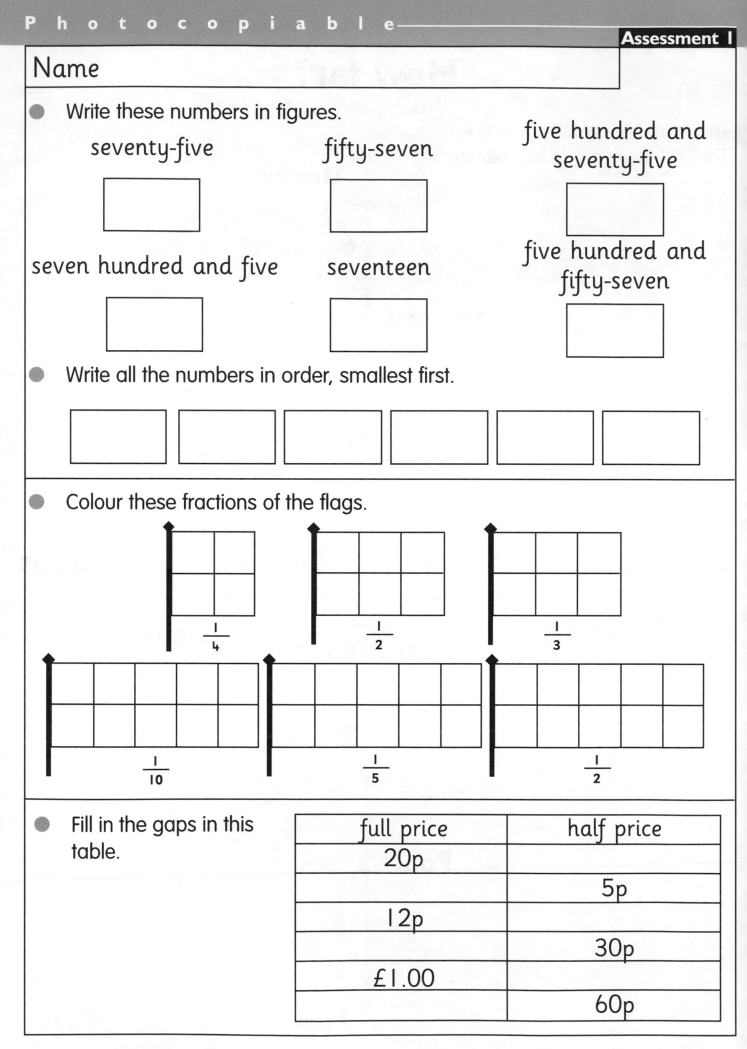

$\frac{1}{4}$

$\frac{1}{2}$

$\frac{1}{3}$

$\frac{1}{10}$

$\frac{1}{5}$

$\frac{1}{2}$

● Fill in the gaps in this table.

full price	half price
20p	
	5p
12p	
	30p
£1.00	
	60p

Addition tables

● Complete this addition table.

+	0	1	2	3	4	5	6	7	8	9	10
0	0										
1	1										
2	2		4								
3				6							
4					8						
5											
6											
7											
8											
9											
10											

● Make your own addition table.

+											
+											

How long ago?

● Write your history.

One second ago

One minute ago

One hour ago

One day ago

One week ago

One month ago

One year ago

Take a vote

● Use this table to make a survey. You could make the survey of favourite sandwich fillings, or choose another topic.

favourite _____	tally	frequency

Distance table

● Use this table to find the distances between some UK cities in miles.

	Birmingham	Bristol	Cardiff	Edinburgh	Glasgow	Leeds	Liverpool	London	Manchester	Newcastle
Birmingham		88	108	296	293	120	99	120	87	210
Bristol	88		48	381	378	219	184	120	172	301
Cardiff	108	48		401	398	239	204	155	191	321
Edinburgh	296	381	401		46	200	224	412	219	108
Glasgow	293	378	398	46		219	221	409	216	152
Leeds	120	219	239	200	219		74	199	44	97
Liverpool	99	184	204	224	221	74		215	35	177
London	120	120	155	412	409	199	215		203	286
Manchester	87	172	191	219	216	44	35	203		147
Newcastle	210	301	321	108	152	97	177	286	147	

Hand measures

● Use a ruler to measure this hand. Write your readings to the nearest half centimetre.

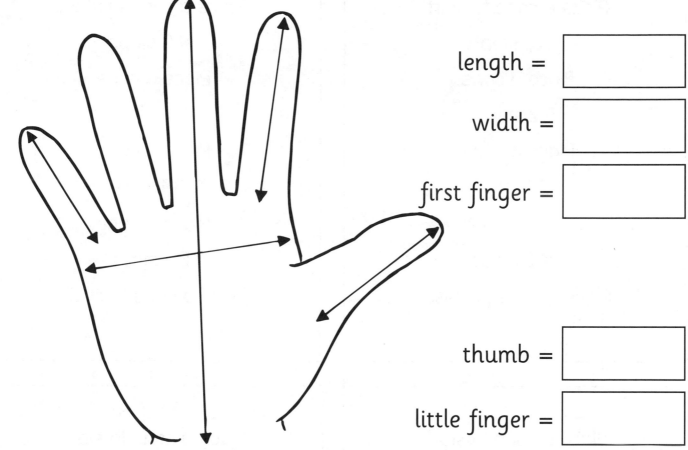

length =

width =

first finger =

thumb =

little finger =

● Measure your hand. Write down the measurements. Draw a line equal to each length.

length =

width =

first finger =

thumb =

little finger =

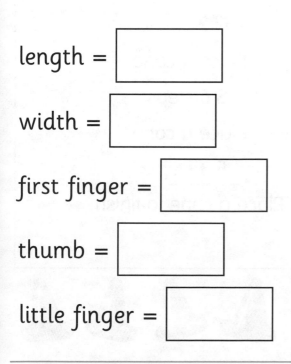

Points of the compass

Place a cone to start.

N 1 step

Place a cone.

E 2 steps

Place a cone.

S 1 step

Place a cone.

W 2 steps

Place a cone to finish.

Place a cone to start.

N 2 steps

Place a cone.

W 3 steps

Place a cone.

S 1 step

Place a cone.

E 4 steps

Place a cone to finish.

Place a cone to start.

W 3 steps

Place a cone.

S 2 steps

Place a cone.

N 5 steps

Place a cone.

E 1 step

Place a cone to finish.

Place a cone to start.

E 4 steps

Place a cone.

N 2 steps

Place a cone.

S 6 steps

Place a cone.

E 3 steps

Place a cone to finish.

Times 10, times 100

This bicycle drawing is $\frac{1}{10}$ scale.

● Use a ruler to measure it and fill in the table.

bicycle measurements	size on drawing in centimetres	size on real bicycle in centimetres
height		
length		
wheel size		
crossbar		
saddle length		

Times 10, times 100

This house drawing is $\frac{1}{100}$ scale.

● Use a ruler to measure it and fill in the table.

house measurements	size on drawing in centimetres	size on real house in centimetres	size on real house in metres
height			
roof width			
door height			
window width			
chimney width			

How many in a pack?

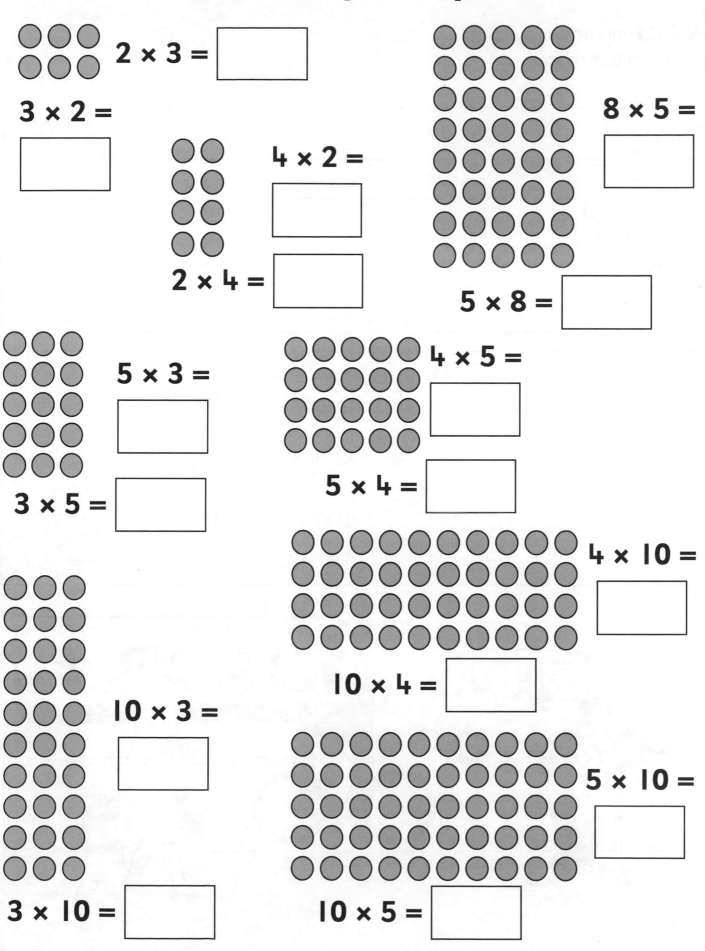

2 × 3 =

3 × 2 =

4 × 2 =

2 × 4 =

8 × 5 =

5 × 8 =

5 × 3 =

3 × 5 =

4 × 5 =

5 × 4 =

4 × 10 =

10 × 4 =

10 × 3 =

5 × 10 =

3 × 10 =

10 × 5 =

■■SCHOLASTIC

Class data

How do you travel to school?
● Fill in this report.

Name

Method of
transport

Distance travelled
(tick one box)

less than 1km	1–2km	2–3km	3–4km	more than 4km
☐	☐	☐	☐	☐

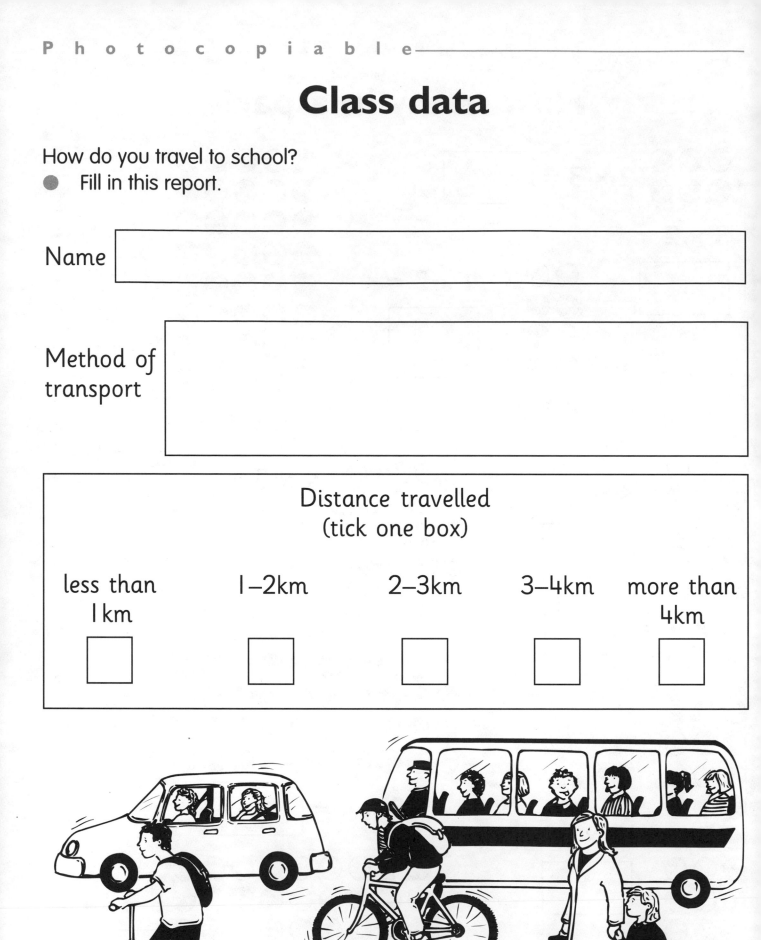

Class data

Transport frequency table

transport	tally	frequency
walk		
bicycle		
bus		
car		
train		

Distance frequency table

distance	tally	frequency
less than 1km		
1–2km		
2–3km		
3–4km		
more than 4km		

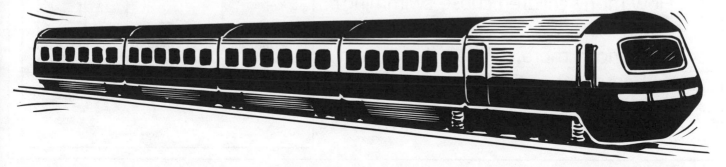

■SCHOLASTIC

Name

● Complete this addition table.

+	0	1	2	3	4	5	6	7	8	9	10
5	5										
6		7									
7			9								
8											
9											
10											

● Fill in the gaps.

60 seconds = ☐ minute

☐ minutes = 1 hour

☐ hours = 1 day

☐ days = 1 week

52 weeks = ☐

1 year = ☐ days

A class did a survey of favourite sports.

● What was the most popular sport?

● How many children chose swimming?

● How many more children chose short tennis than chose netball?

Chart

Frequency

6

4

2

0

football   netball   rounders   short tennis   swimming

Favourite sport

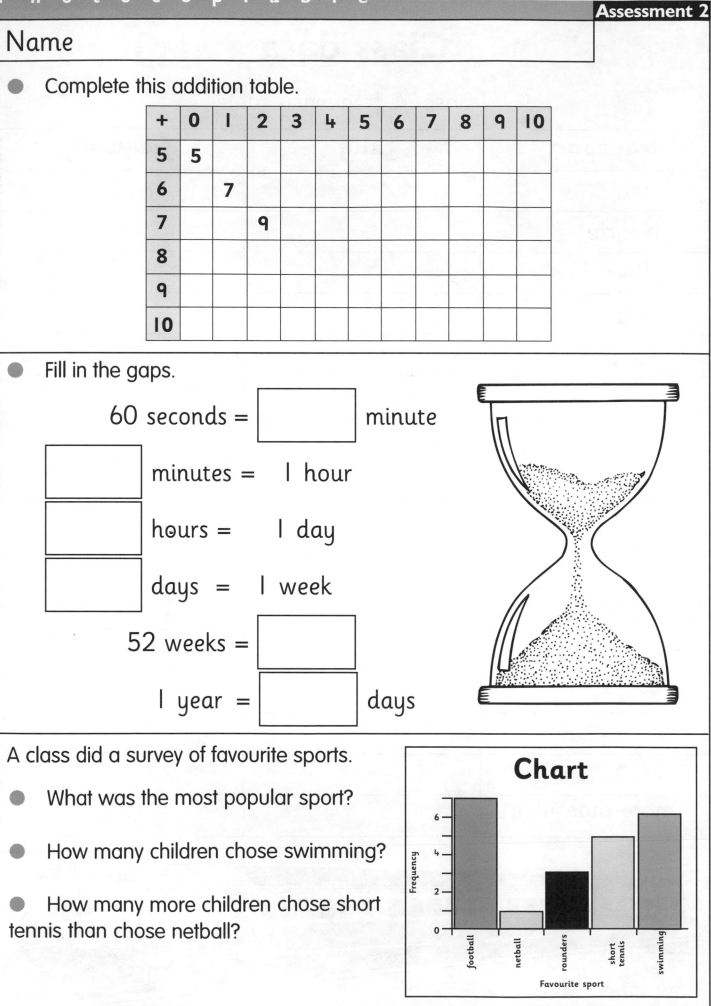

How many do we need?

5 cherry cakes   50p

12 cans   £2.40

How much is each cake? _____

How many cakes are there in 3 packs? _____

How many packs do you need to give one cake each to 30 children? _____

How much would they cost altogether? _____

How much is each can? _____

Four children share a pack. How many cans do they have each? _____

How many cans are there in 2 packs? _____

How much do 2 packs cost? _____

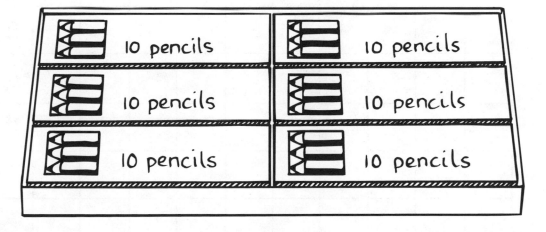

10 pencils   10 pencils

10 pencils   10 pencils

10 pencils   10 pencils

How many pencils are there altogether in the carton? _____

Twenty children share all the pencils between them. How many do they each have? _____

The pencils cost 10p each. How much is a pack of ten? _____

How much is a whole carton? _____

Battleships

- Play with a partner. Use one grid each.
- Mark the positions of your ships. They can be horizontal, vertical or diagonal. The ships must be at least one square apart.
- You have 1 battleship (BBBB), 2 cruisers (CCC), 3 destroyers (DD) and 4 submarines (S).
- Don't let your partner see where you have put your ships!
- Take it in turns to call out squares, for example 'D5'.
- Mark the squares your partner calls with a cross. If there is a ship in the square, call 'hit' and name the ship.
- The first player to hit all the squares occupied by the other player's ships is the winner.

Example grid:

	A	B	C	D	E	F	G	H	I	J
10									D	D
9	X	C	C✗	s				D		D
8	s		X				D	D		
7										
6		B✗		X		B				B
5			X✗					s		
4	s		X		B			s		
3	C									
2	C		X					D	D	
1	C									

Playing grid:

	A	B	C	D	E	F	G	H	I	J
10										
9										
8										
7										
6										
5										
4										
3										
2										
1										

Symmetrical shapes

- Use a mirror to test the symmetry of these flags.
- Draw the mirror lines.

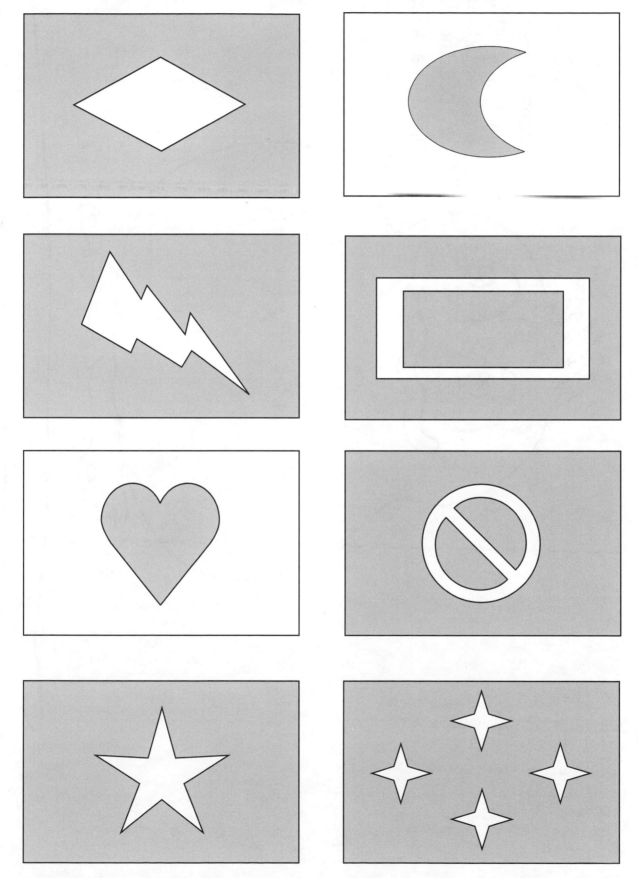

SCHOLASTIC

Multiplying monster

Stick the page onto card.
Cut out the monster's arms. Fix them to his body with a paper fastener. The arms should turn like a lever.
Does the monster know the 3 times table?

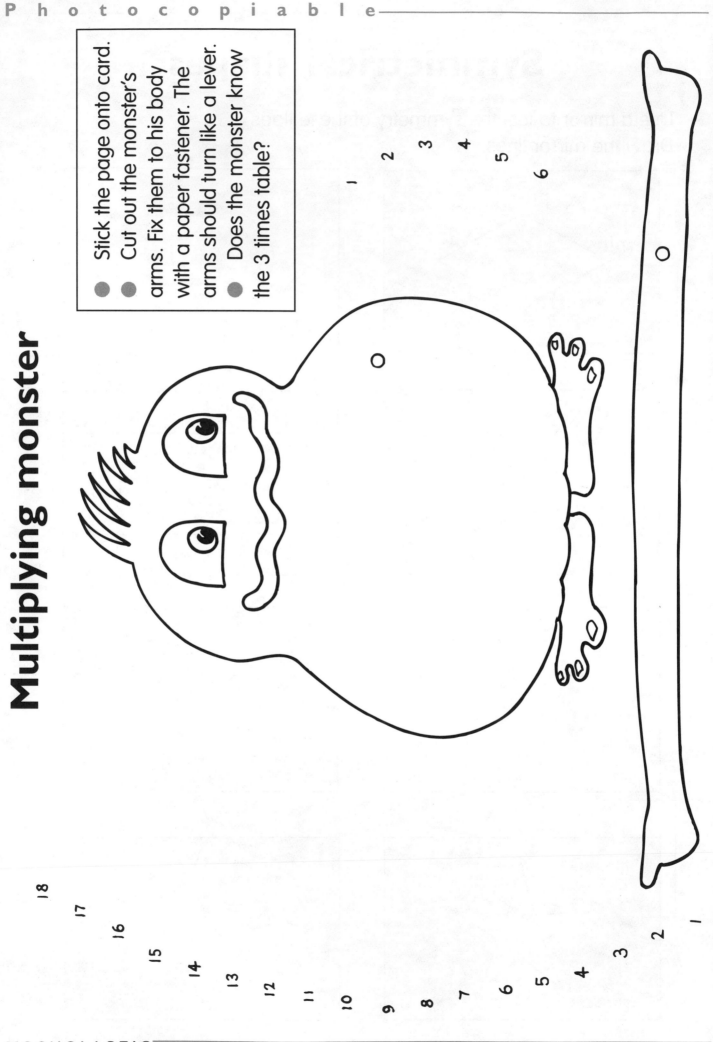

Double up

The bacteria double every 10 minutes.

● Fill in the missing numbers for each set of bateria, and draw the bacteria (if the number is not too big to draw!)

0 mins	10 mins	20 mins	30 mins	40 mins	50 mins
●	● ●	● ● ● ●			
1	2	4	8		

3	6				

5	10				

7					

Departure time

destination	first train	second train	third train
London	6:30	8:45	10:25
Paris	8:00	11:20	12:55
Madrid	4:15	8:40	10:10
Rome	6:50	8:05	9:35

● Write in words the times of:

the first London train

the second Paris train

the third Rome train

● Draw hands on the clocks to show the times of:

the third London train   the second Rome train

● The time is half past nine. How long must you wait for the next train to:

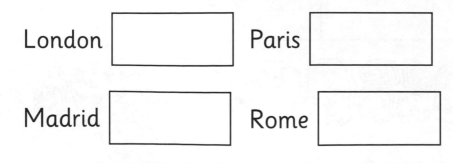

London

Paris

Madrid

Rome

What's the weather?

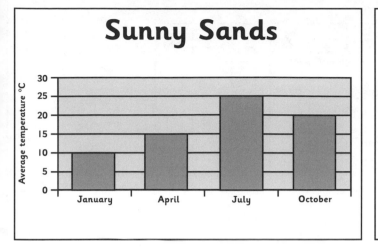

Sunny Sands

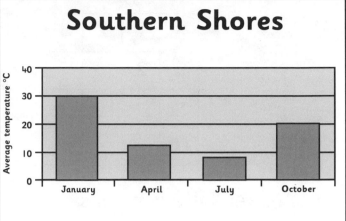

Southern Shores

1. Which holiday resort is warmer in July?

2. Which holiday resort is warmer in January?

3. Which resort has the hottest month at any time of year?

4. Describe the weather in July at Southern Shores.

5. Describe the weather in October at Sunny Sands.

■ SCHOLASTIC

Name

● Complete this multiplication table.

×	1	2	3	4	5	6	7	8	9	10
2	2									
5		10								
10			30							

● Answer these questions.

20p is shared fairly between 2 children.

How much does each receive?

50p is shared fairly between 5 children.

How much does each receive?

£2.00 is shared fairly between 10 children.

How much does each receive?

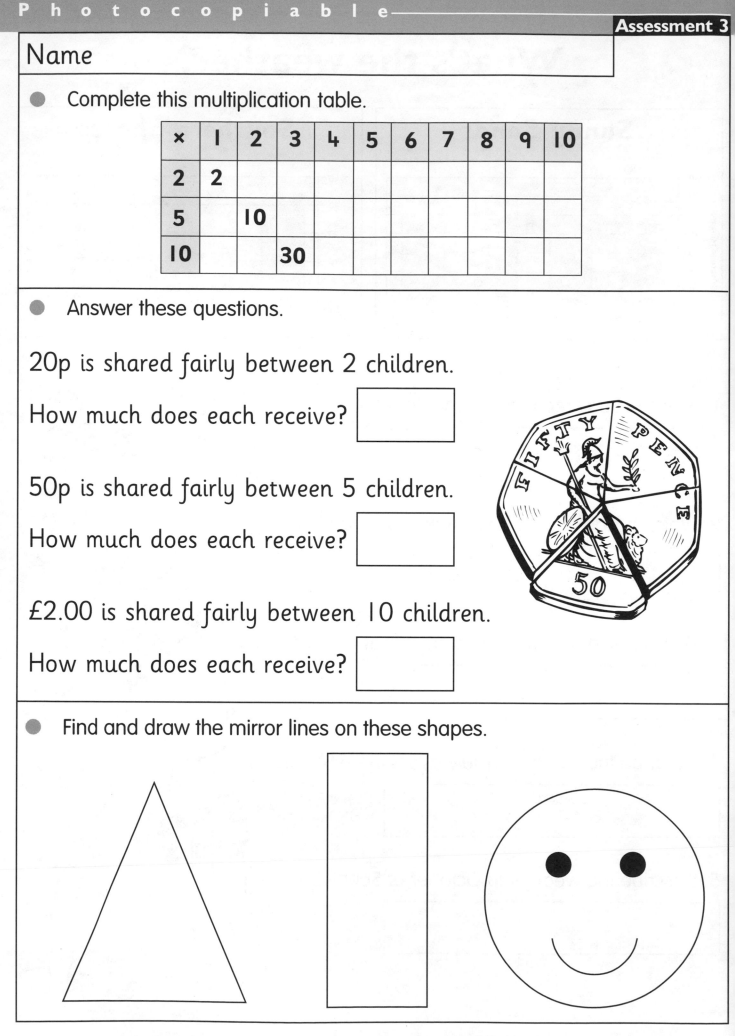

● Find and draw the mirror lines on these shapes.

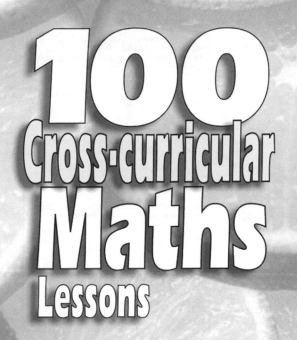

100
Cross-curricular
Maths
Lessons

Lesson plans and photocopiable activity pages

Year 4

Term 1	Topics	Maths objectives	Cross-curricular objectives	Activities
Unit 1	Place value, ordering, estimating, rounding Reading numbers from scales	Read and write whole numbers to at least 10 000 in figures and words, and know what each digit represents. Partition numbers in thousands, hundreds, tens and ones.	**Literacy** Read and spell correctly high-frequency words. **History** Use dates and vocabulary relating to the passing of time, including century and decade.	**p97: Words and numbers** Translate numbers up to 10 000 from figures to words and vice versa.
2–3	Understanding + and – Mental calculation strategies (+ and –)	Use, read and write standard metric units. Suggest suitable units and measuring equipment to measure length and mass. Record readings from scales to a suitable degree of accuracy.	**Science** Make systematic observations and measurements. Make comparisons in their own observations and measurements or other data. Links with work suggested in QCA Science Unit 4A.	**p98: Compare yourself with a gorilla!** Select measuring instruments to make various measurements in science investigations.
	Money and real-life problems Making decisions and checking results	Consolidate knowing by heart addition and subtraction facts for all numbers to 20.	**ICT** Organise text and images using ICT. Links to QCA Information Technology Unit 4B.	**p99: Twenty or bust** Respond rapidly to addition and subtraction questions; play a home-made card game.
		Read and write numbers to at least 10 000 and know what each digit represents. Add/subtract 1, 10, 100 or 1000 to/from any integer.	**Geography** Could be linked to work in QCA Geography Units 6, 9 and 18.	**p100: Milometer** Problems involving the addition and subtraction of tens, hundreds and thousands, based on car milometer readings.
4–6	Measures – including problems Shape and space Reasoning about shapes	Use, read and write the vocabulary related to time. Use the notation 9:53. Read simple timetables and use this year's calendar.	**ICT** Find and interpret information from various sources.	**p101: TV times** Use TV guides to find dates, times and durations of favourite programmes.
		Measure and calculate the perimeters of rectangles and other simple shapes, using counting methods and standard units.	**Geography** Use maps and plans at a range of scales. Use secondary sources of information including aerial photographs. Analyse evidence and draw conclusions. Links to QCA Geography Unit 8.	**p102: Find the perimeter** Use a map to find the perimeters of fields.
		Sketch the reflection of a simple shape in a mirror line parallel to one side (all sides parallel or perpendicular to the mirror line).	**Science** Be taught that light is reflected from surfaces. Make systematic observations. **ICT** Work with a variety of ICT tools. Links to QCA Information Technology Unit 4B.	**p103: Through the looking glass** Explore and sketch the reflections of shapes in a mirror.
		Make and measure clockwise and anticlockwise turns. Begin to know that angles are measured in degrees and that: one whole turn is 360 degrees or 4 right angles; a quarter turn is 90 degrees or 1 right angle; half a right angle is 45 degrees.	**PE** Perform actions and skills with consistent control and quality. Include variations in direction in gymnastic sequences. Links to QCA PE Unit 4.	**p104: Make a turn** In a PE lesson, explore gymnastic sequences using the vocabulary of angles and fractions of a turn.
		Read and write whole numbers to at least 10 000 in figures and words, and know what each digit represents. Order a set of whole numbers less than 10 000.	**History** Place events and objects in chronological order. Use common words and phrases relating to the passing of time.	**p105: Timeline** Make a class timeline from 5000BC to the present day. Locate significant events along the line.
7	Assess and review			see p113
8	Counting and the properties of numbers Reasoning about numbers	Order a set of whole numbers less than 10 000. Use, read and write some imperial units (a mile). Know the relationship between familiar units of length.	**Religious education** Links to QCA Religious Education Unit 4B. **Geography** Use atlases and globes, and maps and plans at a range of scales.	**p106: How far is it to Bethlehem?** Order distances in miles from major world cities to Bethlehem.
	Understanding × and ÷	Recognise and extend number sequences formed by counting on and back in steps of constant size, extending beyond zero when counting back. Recognise multiples of 2, 3, 4, 5 and 10, up to the 10th multiple.	**ICT** Use a variety of ICT tools. Organise and reorganise text and tables.	**p107: Counting grid** Create a computer grid to count in twos, threes, fours and fives to 100 and back.
9–10	Mental calculation strategies (× and ÷) Money and 'real-life' problems	Use all four operations to solve word problems involving numbers in 'real life' and money, using one or more steps including converting pounds to pence and vice versa.	**English** Talk effectively as members of the group. Consider alternatives and draw others into reaching agreement.	**p108: Fair shares** Group discussion of fair strategies for dividing sums of money between a group.
	Making decisions and checking results	Check with the inverse operation. Check the sum of several numbers by adding in reverse order. Check with an equivalent calculation. Estimate and check by approximating (round to the nearest 10 or 100). Use knowledge of sums and differences of odd and even numbers.	**Literacy** Write notes linked to work in other subjects. Write clear instructions.	**p109: Checking results** Compile a checklist of methods to check the results of calculations.
11	Fractions and decimals			
12	Understanding + and – Mental calculation strategies (+ and –) Pencil and paper procedures (+ and –)	Use doubling and halving, starting from known facts. To multiply by 4, double then double again. Find quarters by halving halves.	**Music** Be taught how music is described through established and invented notations. Links to QCA Music Unit 10.	**p110: Half as long, twice as many** Discuss duration in music, in relation to progressive halving – whole notes, half notes, quarter notes, eighth notes...
	Time, including problems	Explain methods and reasoning about numbers orally and in writing. Use informal pencil and paper methods to support, record or explain additions/subtractions/multiplications/divisions.	**English** Speak audibly and clearly, using spoken standard English informal contexts. Use vocabulary and syntax that enables them to communicate more complex meanings.	**p111: Explain yourself – to 100** Play a number quiz using all four operations and explain the strategies used.
13	Handling data	Add or subtract 1, 10, 100 or 1000 to or from any integer. Multiply or divide any integer up to 1000 by 10. Begin to multiply by 100. Use doubling and halving, starting from known facts.	**ICT** Use a variety of ICT tools. **Design and technology** Evaluate a range of familiar products, thinking about how they work and how they are used. Develop ideas and explain them clearly.	**p112: Number games** Make a number game to develop place value concepts and doubling and halving skills.
14	Assess and review			**p113: Assessment activity 1**

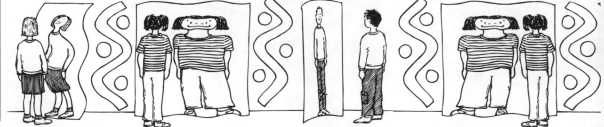

YEAR 4

Term 2	Topics	Maths objectives	Cross-curricular objectives	Activities
1	Place value, ordering, estimating, rounding Reading numbers from scales	Use the vocabulary related to time. Use this year's calendar. Know the number of days in each month. Solve a problem by collecting quickly, organising, representing and interpreting data in tables, charts, graphs and diagrams including those generated by a computer, for example: tally charts and frequency tables, pictograms, bar charts.	**Literacy** Compare and contrast poems on similar themes, particularly their form and language. **Design and technology** Investigate and evaluate a range of familiar products, thinking about how they work, how they are used and the views of the people who use them.	**p114: Through the seasons** Learn the leap year rhyme, and study poetry about time and the seasons. **p115: Shoe styles** Conduct a shoe-style survey, presenting information using tables and bar charts.
2–3	Understanding + and – Mental calculation strategies (+ and –) Pencil and paper procedures (+ and –) Money and 'real-life' problems Making decisions and checking results	Choose and use appropriate number operations. Solve mathematical problems or puzzles and explain patterns and relationships. Recognise negative numbers in context, for example, on a temperature scale. Read and write whole numbers to at least 10 000 in figures and words, and know what each digit represents. Order a set of whole numbers less than 10 000.	**ICT** Use a variety of ICT tools. **Science** Be taught that temperature is a measure of how hot or cold things are. Use simple equipment to make measurements. **ICT** Talk about what information they need and how they can find and use it. Prepare information for development using ICT, including selecting suitable sources, finding information and classifying it. Links to QCA Information Technology Unit 4D.	**p116: Missing digits and signs** Use a computer to create missing number and symbol puzzles for other children to complete. **p117: What temperature?** Read temperatures from a thermometer scale – both positive and negative. **p118: Attendances** Order and compare attendance figures at sports grounds, involving numbers up to 10 000.
4–6	Measures, including problems Shape and space Reasoning about shapes	Measure and calculate the perimeter and area of rectangles and other simple shapes, using counting methods and standard units. Describe and find the position of a point on a grid of squares where the lines are numbered. Recognise simple examples of horizontal and vertical lines. Describe and visualise 3-D and 2-D shapes. Recognise equilateral and isosceles triangles. Classify polygons using criteria such as number of right angles, whether or not they are regular, symmetry properties. Recognise odd and even numbers up to 1000, and some of their properties. Recognise multiples. Make and investigate a general statement about familiar numbers.	**History** Learn about the Romans in Britain and their culture. Links to QCA History Unit 6A. **Geography** Use maps and plans at a range of scales. **History** Study the Anglo-Saxons in Britain. Links to QCA History Unit 6B. **ICT** Know how to prepare information for development using ICT, including classifying information and checking it for accuracy. Links to QCA Information Technology Unit 4C. **Science** Make and use keys. **English/Literacy** Speak with confidence, choosing material that is relevant to the topic and to listeners. Make short notes in list form.	**p119: Roman home** Count squares to find areas and perimeters of rooms in a Roman house. **p120: Give the co-ordinates** Give and find locations on a map, for example of a historical site, by using co-ordinates. **p121: Shape keys** Create and use keys to identify shapes. **p122: Interesting numbers** Identify and explain some of the properties of numbers.
7	Assess and review			see p130
8	Properties of numbers Reasoning about numbers	Solve a problem by collecting, representing and interpreting data in diagrams, for example, a Carroll diagram with two criteria.	**Science** Be taught that some materials are better electrical conductors than others. Construct circuits, incorporating a battery. Links to QCA Science Unit 4F.	**p123: Sorting materials** Test and sort materials according to their properties.
9–10	Understanding × and ÷ Mental calculation strategies (× and ÷) Money and 'real-life' problems Making decisions and checking results	Solve a problem by collecting quickly, organising, representing and interpreting data in tables, charts, graphs and diagrams. Use all four operations to solve word problems involving numbers in 'real life', using one or more steps. Interpret data in tables.	**Geography** Use maps and plans at a range of scales. Collect and record evidence. Study environmental issues. Links to QCA Geography Unit 8. **Science** Compare everyday materials and objects on the basis of their material properties and relate these properties to everyday uses of materials. **Geography** Collect and record evidence. Study environmental issues. Links to QCA Geography Unit 8.	**p124: Litter survey** Conduct a school litter survey. **p125: Recycling sums** Make measurements and calculations set in the context of materials and recycling.
11	Fractions and decimals	Recognise simple fractions that are several parts of a whole. Recognise the equivalence of simple fractions. Know the equivalent of 1/2, 1/4, 3/4 and 1/10 of 1km, 1m, 1kg, 1 litre in m, cm, g, ml. Convert up to 1000cm to m and vice versa. Explain methods and reasoning about numbers orally and in writing. Use informal pencil-and-paper methods to support, record or explain additions/subtractions/multiplications/divisions. Understand decimal notation and place value for tenths and hundredths, and use in context. Record readings from scales to a suitable degree of accuracy.	**Science** Make and compare measurements using standard units. **English** Speak audibly and clearly, using spoken standard English in formal contexts. Use vocabulary and syntax that enables communication of more complex meanings. **Science** Make and compare measurements using standard units.	**p126: Matching measures** Identify equivalent ways of expressing a given measure. **p127: Explain yourself – to 1000** Play a number quiz using all four operations and explain the strategies used. **p128: Decimal scales** Examine measuring scales subdivided into tenths and hundredths. Use corresponding decimal notation.
12	Handling data	Read and write the vocabulary of comparing and ordering numbers. Use symbols correctly, including less than (<) and greater than (>). Understand decimal notation in context. Recognise negative numbers in context.	**Geography** Explain what places are like. Use secondary sources of information. Know the locations of significant places. Builds on QCA Geography Unit 7. **Science** Know that temperature is a measure of how hot or cold things are.	**p129: Highest and lowest** Compare and order temperatures around the world.
Unit 13	Assess and review			**p130: Assessment activity 2**

Term 3	Topics	Maths objectives	Cross-curricular objectives	Activities
1	Place value, ordering and rounding Reading numbers from scales	Understand decimal notation and use it in context, for example, to order amounts of money. Use all four operations to solve problems involving money, including converting pounds to pence and vice versa. Interpret data recorded in tables.	**PSHE and citizenship** Reflect on moral, social and cultural issues. Recognise the role of voluntary and community groups.	**p131: Sponsor me** Make money calculations to complete a sponsorship form.
2–4	Understanding + and − Mental calculation strategies (+ and −) Money and 'real-life' problems Making decisions and checking results	Suggest suitable units and measuring equipment to estimate or measure length. Measure lengths to the nearest half cm. Solve a problem by collecting, organising, representing and interpreting data in tables.	**Design and technology** Evaluate familiar products, thinking about how they are used. **Art and design** Be taught about the materials used in craft and design and how these can be matched to ideas and intentions. Links to QCA Art Unit 4B.	**p132: Choosing chairs** Investigate chair styles and heights for different age groups.
		Describe and find the position of a point on a grid of squares where the lines are numbered. Use the eight compass directions N, S, E, W, NE, NW, SE, SW.	**Geography** Use appropriate geographical vocabulary. Use maps at a range of scales.	**p133: Compass points** Use eight compass directions and co-ordinates to describe locations and directions on a map.
		Begin to know that angles are measured in degrees and start to order angles less than 180°. Classify polygons using criteria such as number of sides and whether or not they are regular. Make shapes.	**ICT** Know how to create, test, improve and refine sequences of instructions to make things happen. Links to QCA Information Technology Unit 4E.	**p134: Turtle time** Use turtle geometry to create shapes and investigate angles of turn.
		Visualise 3-D shapes from 2-D drawings.	**Design and technology** Communicate design ideas in different ways. **Art** Be taught about visual elements including form and space.	**p135: Building blocks** Construct 3-D structures from 2-D diagrams.
5–6	Measures – including problems Shape and space Reasoning about shapes	Use the vocabulary of estimation and approximation; make and justify estimates and approximations of numbers.	**History** Use dates and vocabulary relating to the passing of time. Links to QCA History Unit 9.	**p136: In which year?** Estimate the position of a year on an undivided timeline.
		Read and write whole numbers to at least 10 000 in figures and words. Order a set of whole numbers less than 10 000.	**Geography** Have locational knowledge of the largest mountain ranges and longest rivers in the world, Europe and the United Kingdom. Use atlases and secondary sources, including ICT, to extract geographical information.	**p137: Rivers and mountains** Locate and sequence longest rivers and highest mountains.
		Know by heart multiplication facts for the 2, 3, 4, 5 and 10 times tables. Begin to know multiplication facts for the 6, 7, 8 and 9 times tables.	**ICT** Work with others to explore a variety of ICT tools. Organise and reorganise text and tables.	**p138: Multiplication grids** Make and explore a multiplication grid on a computer.
		Begin to use ideas of simple proportion, for example, 'one for every...' and 'one in every...'.	**ICT** Work with others to use a variety of ICT tools. Develop and refine ideas by organising and reorganising images. Links to QCA Information Technology Unit 4B.	**p139: One in every...** Use the vocabulary 'one in every...' and 'for every...' to describe the proportions of different animals in a group.
		Understand the idea of a remainder, and know when to round up or down after division. Derive quickly division facts corresponding to the 2, 3, 4, 5 and 10 times tables.	**English** Identify the gist of an account and evaluate what they hear. Speak for different purposes.	**p140: Leftovers** Discuss and give answers to word problems involving division and remainders.
7	Assess and review			**see p146**
8	Properties of numbers Reasoning about numbers Understanding × and ÷	Begin to know that angles are measured in degrees. Start to order a set of angles less than 180°.	**Science** Learn about friction as a force that may prevent objects from starting to move. To compare everyday materials and objects on the basis of their material properties. Links to QCA Science Unit 4E.	**p141: Slippery slopes** Compare angles of slope in an experiment to investigate friction.
9–10	Mental calculation strategies (× and ÷) Pencil and paper procedures (× and ÷) Money and 'real-life' problems	Use informal pencil-and-paper methods to support, record and explain money calculations.	**English** Take part in group discussion.	**p142: Choosing presents** Make money calculations in the context of choosing presents.
		Use, read and write the vocabulary related to time. Estimate and check times using minutes and hours. Use the notation 9:30. Read simple timetables.	**Geography** Use secondary sources of information. Use maps and plans. Builds on QCA Geography Unit 6. **ICT** Work with others to explore a variety of information sources.	**p143: Plan a journey** Plan a local rail journey using the Internet.
11	Making decisions and checking results	Use this year's calendar.	**PSHE and citizenship** Respect cultural, ethnic, racial and religious diversity.	**p144: Festivals and holidays** Mark the dates of festivals and holidays on a calendar.
12	Fractions and decimals Understanding + and − Mental calculation strategies (+ and −) Pencil and paper procedures (+ and −) Time, including problems	Solve a problem by collecting quickly, organising, representing and interpreting data in tables, charts, graphs and diagrams, including those generated by a computer.	**Science** Identify locally occurring animals. Links to QCA Science Unit 4B.	**p145: Wildlife survey** Conduct a survey of wildlife around the school. Present data in different ways.
13	Handling data			
14	Assess and review			**p146: Assessment activity 3**

Linked to
Literacy
History

1 Words and numbers

Background

In Year 4, the children should begin to read and write numbers to 10 000 and beyond. They should be able to read four-digit numbers and translate them from figures to words and vice versa. This lesson could be linked to a literacy lesson on the conventions for writing and speaking numbers to do with time. Discuss the different circumstances in which we say the number 1857 as 'one thousand eight hundred and fifty-seven', 'eighteen fifty-seven' or 'eighteen hundred and fifty-seven'. Why do the children think we say 1901 as 'nineteen-o-one' but 2001 as 'two thousand and one', not 'twenty-o-one'? (This is simply a matter of common convention – it's what everyone does!)

Preparation
Make and distribute copies of the activity sheet and number word cards on tables.

Main teaching activity
Introduce the lesson with some whole-class counting practice in tens, hundreds and thousands. Write some four-digit numbers on the board and read them with the class, pointing at the digits as you say their values: *four thousand, eight hundred and twenty-seven.*

Develop the lesson by writing up some four-figure numbers that could be interpreted as dates – for example, 1066,

1812, 1966, 2001. Say to the children: *If I told you this was the number of people at a football match, how would you say the number? If I said it was the year in which something happened, how would you say it then?* Proceed to discuss the conventional ways in which we talk about centuries and decades.

Set the children to work through the exercises on the worksheet.

Differentiation
Translating from words to figures is generally easier than the reverse process. Encourage less able children to set out the numbers using the number word cards before writing them down.

Challenge the more able children with a series of five-, six- and seven-digit numbers to translate between words and figures.

Plenary
Review the answers to the worksheet, checking that the children are both writing and saying numbers correctly.
The answers are:
1. 3200 5360 4876 2183 7606 9018
2. three thousand and one
two thousand and fifty
four thousand seven hundred
five thousand and eighteen
five thousand six hundred and eight
nine thousand three hundred and sixteen
seven thousand eight hundred and fifty-four
nine thousand nine hundred and ninety-nine

2 Compare yourself with a gorilla!

Objectives

Numeracy
Use, read and write standard metric units.
Suggest suitable units and measuring equipment to measure length and mass.
Record readings from scales to a suitable degree of accuracy.

Science
Make systematic observations and measurements.
Make comparisons in their own observations and measurements or other data.

Links with work suggested in QCA Science Unit 4A : Moving and growing.

Resources

A copy of photocopiable page 148 for each child; tape measures labelled in cm; a set of bathroom scales; photographs or a video of gorillas in the wild.

Vocabulary

measure
size
compare
measuring scale
division
length
metre
centimetre
mass
kilogram

Background

The children should read numbers from scales with increasing accuracy as they move through the primary school. By Year 4, they should be using tapes and rules to measure lengths to the nearest 0.5cm, and weighing with scales and balances to the nearest scale division. Measurement skills are required in science and many other curriculum areas. In this lesson, the children measure their body dimensions and mass, and compare themselves with a fully-grown male gorilla.

Preparation

Make copies of the photocopiable sheet and distribute them on tables. Distribute the tape measures, and position the bathroom scales where the children can use them easily.

Main teaching activity

Introduce the lesson by showing a video or photographs of gorillas. Explain that gorillas are closely related to humans. Discuss the size of a fully-grown adult gorilla. How much bigger is it than the children: is it twice as big, ten times as big? Explain that the children are going to make measurements to compare themselves with a gorilla. What is the best measure of 'how big'? Should they compare height, arm span or mass? Discuss how these could be measured. What units would be suitable? Show the children the worksheet and discuss the dimensions listed. Set them to measure their own dimensions and mass, using the tape measures and bathroom scales. Demonstrate and discuss how to read the scales accurately.

Differentiation

Less able children should concentrate on making and recording the measurements.

Ask more able children to calculate the ratios between the gorilla's dimensions and their own.

Plenary

Review the children's findings. How much taller is the gorilla than the children? How much longer are his arms? How much more massive is he?

Linked to
ICT

3 20 or bust

Objectives

Numeracy
Consolidate knowing by heart addition and subtraction facts for all numbers to 20.
ICT
Organise text and images using ICT.
Links to QCA Information Technology Unit 4B.

Resources

Pack of playing cards; a computer and printer; thin card and scissors.

Vocabulary

add
addition
score
total
greater than
less than

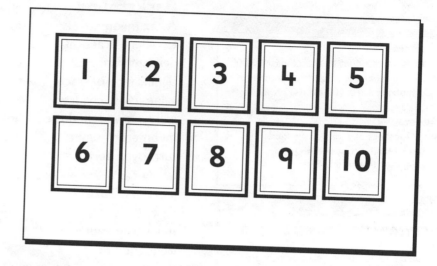

Background

In this lesson, the children play number games based on the card game 'Pontoon' or '21s'. The games are designed to practise rapid recall of addition and subtraction facts to 20. The children can make their own versions of the games using the computer, developing their skills in manipulating and combining text and graphics as they design and print number cards.

Preparation

Run *Microsoft Word* or a similar word-processing/page-making program with a text box facility on the computer. Check that you know how to draw a text box and enter text in it.

Main teaching activity

Introduce the lesson by discussing a pack of playing cards with the children. Name the different suits and discuss the number values usually associated with the different cards. Explain that the children are going to make their own card game. Show them how to create and resize text and enter it into a text box on the computer screen. Demonstrate how to create a page of number cards similar to the one shown above. The children could experiment with borders, choices of font, character size and

use of clip art as they design their cards. They should print four copies of the page on thin card and cut them up to make packs of 40 cards.

The children can play the games in pairs or groups of up to six. The rules of the basic game are:
● shuffle the cards
● turn the pack face down
● take it in turns to take a card from the top of the pack
● add the numbers on the cards you have taken
● if the total is less than 20, you can take another card or 'stick'
● if the total is greater than 20, you have 'bust' and are out
● when everyone has either 'stuck' or 'bust', the person who stuck closest to 20 wins the round.

Differentiation

Less able children should play the basic game.

More able children can play the game with different target numbers, such as 30. They can also practise subtraction by starting from 20 and subtracting the values of the cards drawn towards a target of 0.

Plenary

Conclude the lesson with some quick-fire mental addition and subtraction practice to 20.

4 Milometer

Objectives

Numeracy
Read and write numbers to at least 10 000 and know what each digit represents. Add/subtract 1, 10, 100 or 1000 to/from any integer.
Geography
Study localities at a range of scales.
Could be linked to work in QCA Geography Units 6, 9 or 18.

Resources

A copy of photocopiable page 149 for each child; a cassette recorder with a rotary number counter; a flip chart or board.

Vocabulary

units
tens
hundreds
thousands
place
place value
stands for, represents

Background

A car milometer is an excellent practical demonstration of the significance of place value. Most children will have watched the milometer numbers turn over during family car journeys. Each digit turns ten times as frequently as the next digit to the left. The point at which a milestone such as 10 000 miles is passed, or all the digits are identical (for example, 55555), is a call for comment during a journey. This lesson sets problems involving the addition and subtraction of tens, hundreds and thousands in the context of milometer readings. It could be linked to work on locational knowledge in geography: the children can discuss the distances between locations in the UK and further afield.

Preparation

Make and distribute copies of the photocopiable sheet.

Main teaching activity

Introduce the lesson by showing the children the counter on the cassette recorder. Demonstrate how the numbers turn as the tape is wound fast forward and then rewound. Ask the children to think of similar counters they have seen. Discuss the milometers in cars. Have the children noticed how fast the different numbers turn? Why do the numbers turn at different rates? (Because they count miles, tens of miles,

hundreds of miles and so on.) How many miles have their family cars done? Talk about the distances between well-known locations in the environment around the school. How far is it to the next village/town/city? How far do the children travel when they go on holiday? How far do long-distance lorry drivers travel in a day?

Work through some examples of milometer problems on the board. Discuss which digits have changed following journeys of 1 mile, 10 miles, 100 miles and so on. Set the children to complete the problems on the worksheet.

Differentiation

Let less able children observe the number counter on the cassette player as it turns. They could count the turning numbers in tens or hundreds. Press rewind for some practice counting back.

Tell more able children the milometer reading on your car and challenge them to predict the reading when you have made return journeys to various UK locations. They could refer to charts in a road map to find mileages.

Plenary

Review the worksheet answers and conclude with some quick-fire tens, hundreds and thousands addition problems – for example, 2537 + 1000, 4832 + 100

The answers to the worksheet are:
1. 00546
2. 20470
3. 08442
4. 25751
5. 61000
6. 43356
7. 90000
8. 99999

Linked to
ICT

5 TV times

Objectives

Numeracy
Use, read and write the vocabulary related to time.
Use the notation 9:53.
Read simple timetables.
ICT
Find and interpret information from various sources.

Resources

Copies of the week's television timetables in newspaper supplements and magazines; access to Teletext and/or the Internet – look, for example, at www.bbc.co.uk.

Vocabulary

time
timetables
am
pm
hour
minute
morning
afternoon
evening
night

Background

Television timetables are printed daily in newspapers; they are also available on Teletext and the Internet. Programme times are normally published using a 12-hour clock, and the difference between the morning and afternoon is established by the sequence of programming during the day. Some listings use the 24-hour clock or the 0930 format instead of 9:30. These differences should be discussed with the children. Reading start times and programme durations from programme listings will develop the children's understanding of time and timetables. Extracting information from printed tables, Teletext and the Internet supports the development of the children's ICT information retrieval skills.

Preparation

Make a collection of television timetables for the week.

Main teaching activity

Introduce the lesson by discussing the children's favourite television programmes. *How do you know when they are on? How long do they last? How can you find out what else is on television this evening?* Look at examples of programme listings and discuss the format used for giving the time. Set the children a challenge to find the times and durations of particular programmes during the following week. Ask different groups to use different resources to tackle the challenge. One group could use printed timetables, another Teletext and a third the Internet. Which group can find the information first?

Differentiation

Different levels of ability will need varying degrees of support to complete this task. The children familiar with the Internet, for example, might use a search engine to locate UK TV listings. Others may need direction towards a suitable website such as http://www.bbc.co.uk/whatson/

Plenary

Ask the groups to report back their findings and discuss the efficiency with which information can be located using the different resources.

6 Find the perimeter

Objectives

Numeracy
Measure and calculate the perimeters of rectangles and other simple shapes, using counting methods and standard units.
Geography
Use maps and plans at a range of scales.
Use secondary sources of information including aerial photographs.
Analyse evidence and draw conclusions.
Links to QCA Geography Unit 8: Improving the environment.

Resources

Aerial photographs of the countryside, showing the pattern of fields. Suitable aerial photographs can be downloaded from Internet sites (such as www.multimap.com and www.getmapping.com). On these sites photographs and maps can be viewed at different scales, and this is an opportunity for the children to explore the relationship between scale and the features visible on a map or photograph. A copy of photocopiable page 150 for each child; a flip chart or board; a trundle wheel.

Vocabulary

perimeter
edge
rectangle
shape
side
measure
metre

Background

The term 'perimeter' refers both to the edge or boundary of a shape and to the length or distance all the way round the boundary. If a farmer wants to erect a fence around a field, then the length of fence needed is equal to the perimeter of the field. In this lesson, the children investigate the perimeters of different-shaped fields on a simple map. The lesson would support a geography project on the changing landscape and hedgerow loss, where fences replace shrubs and trees.

Preparation

Make and distribute copies of the photocopiable sheet.

Main teaching activity

Introduce the lesson by drawing some shapes on the board. Explain that the perimeter is the distance all the way around the outside of a shape. Draw a selection of rectangles on the board, label the side lengths and show the children how to calculate perimeters by simple addition. Introduce the terms 'perimeter hedge' and 'perimeter fence', and identify the perimeters of fields on aerial photographs.

Show the children the worksheet. Highlight how hedges are being lost, and how efforts are being made to record and conserve those remaining. Explain that the farmer must use the plan to measure the length of the hedges and fences on his land

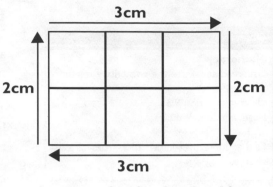

perimeter = 3 + 2 + 3 + 2 = 10cm

for a national hedgerow survey. Discuss how the perimeters can be found by counting squares. Set the children to complete the activity.

Differentiation

Less able children should concentrate on the worksheet activity.

Challenge more able children to think about the differences between perimeter and area. How can they find the areas of the different fields? Is there any connection between perimeter and area? (There is no direct link, though we can say that the rectangle with the maximum area for a given perimeter is a square.) Ask the children to investigate the maximum rectangular area that can be enclosed by a given length of perimeter fence.

Plenary

Review the answers to the worksheet as a class. Ask the children how they would find the perimeter of the school hall, playground and so on. If possible, walk the children around the perimeter of the school field or playground with a trundle wheel to measure and record the side lengths and then calculate the perimeter.

The answers are:
200m 380m 420m 320m 450m

7 Through the looking glass

Objectives

Numeracy
Sketch the reflection of a simple shape in a mirror line parallel to one side (all sides parallel or perpendicular to the mirror line).

Science
Be taught that light is reflected from surfaces.
Make systematic observations.

ICT
Work with a variety of ICT tools.
Links to QCA Information Technology Unit 4B.

Resources
A copy of photocopiable page 151 for each child; safety mirrors; a flip chart or board; a torch.

Vocabulary
symmetry
symmetrical
shape
mirror
mirror line

Background
Sketching the reflection of a shape is a skill that requires understanding of the connection between an object and its mirror image. Corresponding points in the image and the object appear to be on either side of a plane (flat) mirror, at equal distances from it. The line connecting an object point and its image is perpendicular to the mirror. The overall effect of the mirror can be summarised by saying that it 'flips' the shape over the mirror line. This process can be illustrated using a graphics package on a computer. For example, a shape drawn in *Microsoft Word* can be 'flipped' by selecting the appropriate option from the Draw menu.

Work on sketching reflections in mathematics links to work on light, mirrors and reflections in science. The light that illuminates objects and is scattered into our eyes so that we see the objects is also reflected by a mirror. Our eyes see the reflected light as if it were coming from behind the mirror, so we see images or 'reflections' of objects. The fact that a mirror reflects light can be demonstrated with a torch.

Preparation
Copy and distribute the photocopiable sheets together with the safety mirrors.

Main teaching activity
Introduce the lesson by talking about mirrors and reflections. Make the link to work in science by explaining that we see

reflections in mirrors because light bounces from their surface into our eyes. This can be demonstrated by shining a torch at a mirror and reflecting the beam onto a wall. (Take care that bright torch light is not reflected directly into the children's eyes.) What is the relationship between a shape and its reflection in a mirror? Explain that the shape and reflection are on 'opposite sides' of the mirror. Demonstrate this with an actual mirror and some mathematical shapes. Sketch some shapes, the line of a mirror and the shape reflections on the board. Talk about the sketches you make, emphasising how the mirror appears to have 'flipped' each shape over. Demonstrate the 'flipping' process with some actual shapes.

Set the children, in pairs or small groups, to do the worksheet activities. Suggest that they check their work by using an actual mirror to look at the reflection of the original shape.

Differentiation
Less able children will probably need considerable assistance to draw the reflections.

More able children could use a computer to create shapes and generate their reflections by using the 'flip' options in a drawing package.

Plenary
Review the children's worksheet answers as a class. Use a mirror to check their drawings.

The answers are:

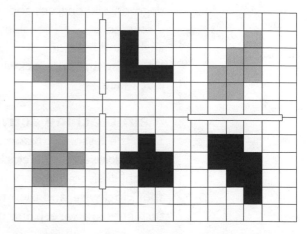

Linked to
P E

8 Make a turn

Objectives

Numeracy

Make and measure clockwise and anticlockwise turns.

Begin to know that angles are measured in degrees and that: one whole turn is 360 degrees or 4 right angles; a quarter turn is 90 degrees or 1 right angle; half a right angle is 45 degrees.

PE

Perform actions and skills with consistent control and quality.

Include variations in direction in gymnastic sequences.

Links to QCA PE Unit 4: Gymnastic activities.

Resources

School hall or playground for a PE lesson; an analogue clock face.

Vocabulary

turn
clockwise
anticlockwise
degree
whole turn
half turn
quarter turn
rotate
angle
right angle

Background

The first statements about angular measures that will become familiar to the children are that: 90 degrees make a right angle; 180 degrees make a straight line; 360 degrees make a full circle or turn. These angles are readily demonstrated using the hands of an analogue clock. The clock can also be used to demonstrate the meaning of 'clockwise' and 'anticlockwise' turns. This maths session should take place as part of a PE lesson in which the children develop their understanding of the vocabulary of turning and angular measure through their own movements.

quarter turn anticlockwise, and so on.

Develop the activity by introducing the vocabulary of right angles and degrees as you give turning instructions. Play a game in which the children must shut their eyes and follow your commands. After each turn, they open their eyes to see whether they are facing the right direction. The children facing the wrong direction are 'out'.

Set the children to work in small groups to play the game among themselves. They should take turns to be the direction 'caller'.

Preparation

Prepare the class for a PE lesson according to your normal practice. The lesson should build on previous maths lessons in which you have: worked with right angles; introduced the basic angular measures 90 degrees, 180 degrees, 360 degrees and 45 degrees; discussed the relationships between these angles and fractions of a turn; demonstrated clockwise and anticlockwise turns with a clock face.

Main teaching activity

Start the lesson with some activities based on clockwise and anticlockwise turns. Ask the children to make a whole turn on the spot clockwise, and then to make a whole turn anticlockwise, half a turn clockwise, a

Differentiation

Make sure that less able children use the basic vocabulary of quarter turn, 90 degrees, right angle, clockwise and anticlockwise correctly.

More able children should be incorporating half-right angle or 45-degree turns into their games.

Plenary

Conclude the lesson with a final whole-class turning game. Has the children's knowledge of turning vocabulary improved?

2 Timeline

Objectives

Numeracy
Read whole numbers to at least 10 000 and know what each digit represents.
Order a set of whole numbers less than 10 000.

History
Place events and objects in a chronological order.
Use common words and phrases relating to the passing of time.

Resources

A roll of frieze paper; felt-tipped pens; metre rulers; cards to make labels; a staple gun; coloured threads and pinboard pins.

Vocabulary

decade
century
millennium
AD
BC
thousand

Background

The periods covered in history in the primary school range from the ancient Egyptians, through the Greeks and Romans to the Vikings, Saxons, Normans, Tudors, Victorians, to the 20th-century wars and the present day. This represents a timeline of some 7000 years, from about 5000BC to AD2000. The children should now be able to read and write numbers in this range, and the making of a timeline in the form of a frieze extending around the classroom should be within their capabilities. In history at KS2, the children are expected to use the conventional forms for dates, including the abbreviations related to the Christian calendar: BC and AD. Understanding the convention for writing dates in this way – decreasing to a fixed reference point, then increasing again – is a useful step on the way to understanding negative numbers.

Preparation

This lesson should build on previous maths lessons in which the children have worked with numbers to 10 000. Collect together the resources needed for making the frieze.

Main teaching activity

Introduce the lesson by explaining that you are going to produce a time line covering a period of 7000 years! Ask questions relating to the historical periods that the class have studied. How long ago was it when the ancient Egyptians/Greeks were building their

pyramids and temples? (5000/2500 years.) Discuss how dates in history are written using the BC/AD convention. Sketch the diagram shown below to make the connection between the number of years ago and the historical date. Highlight how the numbers get bigger in both directions from zero (this will help the children in later work with negative numbers).

Discuss how the timeline should be prepared. If there is enough wall space, it is convenient to represent one millennium by 1m on the timeline. Each millimetre then represents one year, one centimetre is a decade and ten centimetres is a century.

Divide the class into seven groups to prepare a millennium section of the timeline each. Give each group about 1.5m of frieze paper. Ask them to rule a 1m line and mark divisions at 10cm intervals to be labelled with centuries. They could subdivide one or more centuries into decades. Help them to label their timeline.

Differentiation

Less able children could be asked to prepare the timeline from AD1 to AD1000.

Challenge more able children to divide their segments of the timeline into decades and (for a short interval) individual years.

Plenary

Assemble the timeline on the wall, linking the millennia in sequence. Dates relevant to history the children have studied can be written on cards and linked to the appropriate points on the timeline with coloured pins and threads. Ask the children to show you where to position the pins.
2900BC Great Pyramid of Giza built
AD43 Roman army invades Britain
AD1066 Norman Conquest of England
AD1666 Great Fire of London

10 How far is it to Bethlehem?

Objectives

Numeracy
Order a set of whole numbers less than 10 000.
Use, read and write some imperial units (a mile).
Know the relationship between familiar units of length.
Religious education
Links to QCA Religious Education Unit 4B: Celebrations – Christmas journeys.
Geography
Use atlases and globes, and maps and plans at a range of scales.

Resources

A copy of photocopiable page 152 for each child; a large map of the world showing the principal cities; coloured threads, pinboard pins, a pinboard.

Vocabulary

mile
kilometre
distance
apart
furthest
between
to... from

Background

This lesson could be used in the build-up to Christmas. The children locate Bethlehem on a world map. They then locate some principal cities in the five continents and order them according to their distance from Bethlehem. The activity thus links work in mathematics with work in religious education and geography. Clearly, this activity could be adapted according to your cultural setting or the season of the year – for example, to focus on Mecca and Moslem festivals.

used in European countries other than the UK). Do the children know the relationship between miles and kilometres? A mile is just over one and half kilometres, so a distance given in kilometres is always a bigger number than a distance given in miles.

Set the children to work in pairs on the worksheets.

Differentiation

Less able children should complete the basic activity. Show them how to work through the distances systematically, finding the smallest number, then the next smallest and so on, in order to place them in sequence.

Challenge more able children to convert their table of distances into an appropriate bar chart. They could also use the Internet to look up the distances between other world cities – for example, using www.indo.com

Plenary

Work through the sequence of cities and distances, checking that the children have placed them in the correct order. Conclude the lesson by singing the carol *How far is it to Bethlehem?*

The answers are:
Paris, London, Lagos, Tokyo, New York, Sao Paulo, Sydney
Paris, France, Europe
London, England, Europe
Lagos, Nigeria, Africa
Tokyo, Japan, Asia
New York, USA, North America
Sao Paulo, Brazil, South America
Sydney, Australia, Australasia

Preparation

Make and distribute copies of the photocopiable sheet. Set up the world map on a pinboard where all the class can see it.

Main teaching activity

Introduce the lesson by reminding the children of the story of Christmas. *Where exactly is Bethlehem?* Locate Bethlehem on the world map. Identify some principal cities in the five continents and link them to Bethlehem with coloured threads and pins. Explain that the children's task is to use information on the worksheet to place the cities shown in order of distance from Bethlehem.

Discuss whether the distances should be given in miles or kilometres (miles are usually used for journey distances in the UK and the USA, but kilometres are commonly

11 Counting grid

Objectives

Numeracy
Recognise and extend number sequences formed by counting on and back in steps of constant size, extending beyond zero when counting back.
Recognise multiples of 2, 3, 4, 5 and 10, up to the 10th multiple.

ICT
Use a variety of ICT tools.
Organise and reorganise text and tables.

Resources
Computers running software with table/spreadsheet capabilities, for example *Microsoft Word* or *Textease*; printers and paper; a large 1–100 square.

Vocabulary
count
grid
cell
column
row

Background
A hundred square is a valuable resource for counting practice and for exploring number patterns. The production of a hundred (1–100) square from scratch on the computer is an enjoyable activity in which the children develop ICT skills as they work with numbers.

Preparation
Set up the computers running your chosen software package, and check that you can use it confidently to produce a 10 × 10 array of cells. This can be achieved in a number of ways – for example, by creating a table with ten rows and ten columns, by generating a spreadsheet with ten rows and ten columns, or by copying and pasting text boxes repeatedly. The text box approach may be the easiest for many children. In *Microsoft Word*, select the Text Box icon from the Drawing toolbar. Use the mouse to draw a square text box approximately 1cm × 1cm. Enter a number in the box. Select the box, copy it and paste it repeatedly to make a row of ten cells. Line up the cells horizontally and group them. Copy the grouped row and paste it repeatedly until you have ten rows. Align the rows vertically, without gaps, to produce a 10 × 10 grid. The numbers can be highlighted and edited as you wish.

Main teaching activity
Introduce the lesson with some counting practice supported by the 1–100 square display. As a class, count on and back in twos, threes, fours, fives and other intervals, starting from any number on the grid. Point to the numbers as you count.

Discuss the features of the grid with the whole class. Note that it is a 10 × 10 array and thus contains 100 cells altogether. Look at how the numbers are sequenced and identify patterns (for example, multiples of 10 and how the tens and units digits increase going down or across the grid). Explain that the children are going to make their own number grids on the computers. Set them to work in small groups to produce and print their grids.

Differentiation
Less able children may need considerable support to produce a grid. Show them the text box method. You may want to suggest that they start with a 5 × 5 grid.

Children with more advanced ICT skills can explore different methods of producing the grid. Can they generate a 10 × 10 table? Can they produce the grid as a spreadsheet? Can they use the spreadsheet tools to fill the cells automatically? What are the advantages and disadvantages of different techniques? The children should print their completed grids.

Plenary
As a class, look at the grids the children have produced and discuss the ICT techniques they used to generate them. Conclude the lesson by using the grids for some more counting practice.

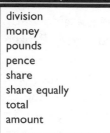

12 Fair shares

Objectives

Numeracy
Use all four operations to solve word problems involving numbers in 'real life' and money, using one or more steps including converting pounds to pence and vice versa.

English
Talk effectively as members of the group. Consider alternatives and draw others into reaching agreement.

Resources

A copy of photocopiable page 153 for each group; coins and notes to represent the amounts on the worksheet.

Vocabulary

division
money
pounds
pence
share
share equally
total
amount

Background

In this activity, the children tackle story problems set in the context of money. They debate how money should be shared 'fairly' between people in a variety of situations. Reaching a collective conclusion requires using mathematical skills with the numbers involved and language skills to argue and explain their reasoning.

Preparation

Make copies of the photocopiable sheet and distribute them with the coins and notes in preparation for group work.

Main teaching activity

Introduce the activity to the class by talking about sharing money. *Suppose I had £25 to buy presents for my four nephews and nieces. How much should I spend on each to be fair?* Review the process of sharing and the idea of equal shares. Develop the theme with some similar questions, including some that produce remainders. Discuss what should be done with the money 'left over'.

Set the children to work in groups on the worksheet problems. They should make notes or jottings to record their ideas and answers. The children can use the coins and notes to help them with their calculations.

Differentiation

Problems 1 to 3 are straightforward, and all the children should solve them.

Problems 4 to 6 are more challenging, involving remainders or unequal distributions.

Problems 7 and 8 are more open-ended, and should lead to more debate on what is a fair system for distributing the money.

Plenary

Ask representatives from the groups to report their decisions on sharing the money and the methods they used to reach their conclusions. Ask for different views on the way the money should be shared in problems 7 and 8.

The answers are:
1. 4p each
2. £2.00 each
3. 40p each
4. 18p and 17p
5. £1, £1 and 95p
6. 20p each and 2p left over
7 and 8. answers will vary

13 Checking results

Objectives

Numeracy
Check with the inverse operation.
Check the sum of several numbers by adding in reverse order.
Check with an equivalent calculation.
Estimate and check by approximating (round to the nearest 10 or 100).
Use knowledge of sums and differences of odd and even numbers.

Literacy
Write notes linked to work in other subjects.
Write clear instructions...

Resources

A flip chart or board; pencils and paper.

Vocabulary

calculation
check
method
even
odd

Background

Children should be encouraged to check all the calculations they make. This is particularly important as they progress to using calculators. The ability to judge whether the result of a calculation is first reasonable, and second accurate, is essential when a misplaced keystroke could produce an absurd result. A complaint often heard in secondary schools is that the children use calculators without considering whether the results obtained are sensible or not.

This lesson is presented as an idea-sharing exercise in which the children consider different methods of checking the results of calculations using the four operations. They compile a checklist in note form and translate it into formally written instructions, developing their writing skills.

Preparation

Prepare a list of addition, subtraction, multiplication and division problems appropriate to the abilities of your class.

Main teaching activity

Introduce the lesson by writing an addition problem such as 28 + 36 on the board. Write up some alternative answers: 68, 640, 63, 64. Say that four different children gave these answers. Explain that you want the class to check the answers, but without doing the original calculation. Lead the children to make statements such as
'68 must be wrong because 68 – 28 = 40, not 36'; '640 must be wrong because it is

about ten times too big'; '28 + 36 is going to be a bit less than 30 + 40, which is 70'; '63 must be wrong because it is an odd number, and when you add two even numbers the answer is another even number',; '64 is correct – if we do the calculation backwards, 64 – 28 = 36.'

Develop the lesson by asking the class to suggest a list of methods for checking calculations. Compile the list in note form on the board as ideas are suggested:

Do calculation 'backwards'.
Do calculation in a different order.
Do calculation a different way.
Check by rounding to make sure calculation is approximately right.
even +/– even = even
odd +/– odd = even
even +/– odd = odd

Set the children the task of expanding these notes into a numbered list of instructions, illustrated with examples. For example:
1. Check by doing the calculation backwards.
For example:
37 + 18 = 55
Check: 55 – 18 = 37

Differentiation

Less able children could concentrate on producing a simple example of each of the methods listed.

Challenge more able children to create examples with three- and four-digit numbers.

Plenary

Read out good examples of the children's writing. As a class, use the methods described to check some of the examples the children have produced.

Linked to
M u s i c

14 Half as long, twice as many

Objectives

Numeracy
Use doubling and halving, starting from known facts.
To multiply by 4, double then double again.
Find quarters by halving halves.
Music
Be taught how music is described through established and invented notations.
Links to QCA Music Unit 10: Play it again.

Resources

A flip chart or board, a marker pen; guitars or other stringed instruments; notebooks.

Vocabulary

half
quarter
eighth
double

Background

Repeated halving is a convenient way of subdividing intervals. On a ruler graduated in inches, the inch units are subdivided into $\frac{1}{2}$, $\frac{1}{4}$, $\frac{1}{8}$, $\frac{1}{16}$ and perhaps $\frac{1}{32}$. The children are not expected to work with these fractions of an inch, but it is worth pointing out this use of halving. In music, the duration of notes is specified by the repeated halving of a full note or 'semibreve'. A half note is a minim, a quarter note a crotchet, an eighth note a quaver and a 16th note a semiquaver. In this lesson, the children explore the halving and doubling of the duration of a sound.

Preparation

Set out some chairs near the board where the children can sit with guitars.

Main teaching activity

Introduce the lesson by asking: *Who can read music?* There will probably be some children in the class who are taking instrument lessons. Ask them how they know from the music how long a note should be played. Discuss long notes such as semibreves and short notes such as quavers. Develop the lesson by saying: *Did you know that in music the lengths of notes are all connected by halving and doubling?*

On the board, draw a horizontal line with a vertical bar towards the left-hand side. Explain that the line represents the length of a musical sound. Ask the guitarists to prepare to play a single note. You should run your pen from the left-hand end of the line at a constant speed along it. The guitarists should pluck the string as your pen passes under

the vertical bar, and let the note continue until your pen reaches the end of the line.

Now divide the line in two with a second vertical bar. Run the pen at the same speed along the line. The guitarists should play two notes, each with half the duration of the original. Describe these as half notes. Now divide the halves into quarters with two more vertical bars. Run your pen again at the same speed – the guitarists should play four quarter notes. Finally, divide the line into eighths and repeat.

Draw up a table like the one below and set the children to copy and complete it in their notebooks.

half	number	double
$\frac{1}{2}$	1	2
1	2	4
2	4	
	8	

Differentiation

Less able children should concentrate on filling in the doubles and halves in the table correctly.

Challenge more able children to research the musical names given to whole, half, quarter and eighth notes. Can anyone discover the name of a 1/64th note? (A hemidemisemiquaver.)

Plenary

Review the completed tables, then repeat the practical exercise with the whole class, clapping the notes as the guitarists sound them.

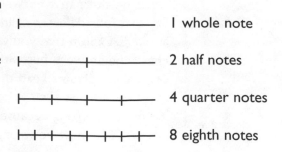

|—————————————————| 1 whole note

|————————|————————| 2 half notes

|————|————|————|————| 4 quarter notes

|——|——|——|——|——|——|——|——| 8 eighth notes

15 Explain yourself – to 100

Objectives

Numeracy
Explain methods and reasoning about numbers orally and in writing.
Use informal pencil and paper methods to support, record or explain additions/subtractions/multiplications/divisions.

English
Speak audibly and clearly, using spoken standard English in formal contexts.
Use vocabulary and syntax that enables them to communicate more complex meanings.

Resources

Sets of number cards, sorted to provide a pack with two each of the numbers 1–10 for each group, and a pack with the numbers 20–100 for each group; a flip chart or board and marker pen; paper and pencils.

Vocabulary

addition
subtraction
multiplication
division
calculate
method
jotting
answer
How did you work it out?

Background

In the popular television quiz programme *Countdown*, the contestants select numbers at random from a pack of cards. They are then given a target number and must combine their selections using the four basic operations to match, or get as close as possible to, the target. This game is readily adapted for use in the classroom. The children work mentally or use jottings to calculate a target number. They then use their speaking skills to explain their calculation with the appropriate vocabulary.

children that they must choose any two or three numbers from those dealt out and combine them using addition, multiplication, subtraction and/or division to calculate the target. Give them a minute or two to jot down their answers. Ask a volunteer to explain how he or she reached the target to the rest of the class. As the volunteer describes the calculations, jot them on the board. Reinforce the use of the correct vocabulary to describe the calculation.

Now take away the numbers the first volunteer used and challenge the children to calculate the target again using two, three or more of the remaining numbers. A second volunteer can explain his or her method. Continue, taking away numbers, until it is no longer possible to hit the target.

Set the children to play the game in groups, taking it in turns to act as quiz master or scribe. Make sure that every child has an opportunity to explain his or her calculations to the group.

Preparation

Collect the number cards and sort them into appropriate packs.

Main teaching activity

Introduce the lesson by asking the children whether they have seen any number puzzles in television quiz programmes. Some children may have seen *Countdown*. Explain the basic principle of the game and say that the children are going to play their own version.

Proceed to play the game with the whole class. Deal out a pack of cards containing two each of the numbers 1–10 so that the children can see them. Ask a child to select a card at random from the pack containing the numbers 20–100. Write this number on the board and state that this is the target. Tell the

Differentiation

Less able children could play one round of the game at a time, without removing any number cards before selecting a new target.

Challenge more able children to find as many ways of calculating a given target as possible from the 20 original numbers.

Plenary

Ask representatives from the groups to talk about some of the calculation strategies they used. For example, ask: *How do you produce a large number with two smaller numbers? Which was the most difficult target to calculate? Which targets were easy to reach in a number of different ways?*

16 Number games

Objectives

Numeracy
Add or subtract 1, 10, 100 or 1000 to or from any integer.
Multiply or divide any integer up to 1000 by 10.
Begin to multiply by 100.
Use doubling and halving, starting from known facts.

ICT
Use a variety of ICT tools.

Design and technology
Evaluate a range of familiar products, thinking about how they work, and how they are used.
Develop ideas and explain them clearly.

Resources

Four packs of number cards 0–9 per game; craft materials for making spinners or dice (card, scissors, glue, felt-tipped pens, cocktail sticks, cubic wooden building blocks); water-filled 500ml plastic bottles; a computer running word-processing software; a printer, card.

Vocabulary

add
double
halve
too many
tens
hundreds
thousands
score

Background

In this activity, the children design and make a number game to practise their calculation skills. The basic design can be adapted for different mathematical activities. The children consider different ways of selecting items at random, for example dice, hexagonal spinners and spinning pointers, and choose which is best suited to their version of the game. The computer is used to produce cards and other printed items.

Preparation

Distribute the craft materials and number cards on tables. Set up the computer running the word-processing software.

Main teaching activity

Set up the basic arrangement for a simple number game as follows. A water-filled plastic bottle on its side serves as a spinner. When it is spun it comes to rest, pointing to one of the six stacks of cards arranged around it in a circle. The cards give calculation instructions – two examples of sets of six instructions are shown above.

Two teams play the game. They keep their score using the packs of number cards 0–9 arranged to represent units, tens, hundreds and thousands.

The teams take turns to spin the bottle, read the instruction on the card it points to,

calculate their new score and adjust the display. The instruction card is then placed at the bottom of the pack. If the calculation takes the score below 0, the score becomes 0. If the instruction is to halve an odd number, the new score is rounded up to the nearest whole number. The first team to score 9999 or more wins the game.

Demonstrate the game and play a few rounds together. Explain that the children's task is to make their own version of the game. They should create and print instruction cards using the computer. Can they think of alternative ways of selecting the cards? They might consider making a hexagonal spinner, or making a dice by labelling the faces of a building block.

Set the children to work in small groups to make and play the games.

> plus 1
> plus 10
> plus 100
> plus 1000
> subtract 1
> subtract 10
>
> subtract 100
> multiply by 10
> multiply by 100
> multiply by 5
> double
> halve

Differentiation

Less able children should reproduce the basic game. They should print several copies of each of the calculation instructions to produce six stacks of cards.

More able children can adapt the game by using dice, spinners or other means to select calculation instructions. They may wish to extend the range of instructions to include multiplications and divisions by other numbers. Ask them to explore how this affects the outcome.

Plenary

Conclude the lesson by asking representatives from the groups to demonstrate their games. Discuss the advantages and disadvantages of spinners and dice for selecting things at random. Play a few rounds of selected games as a class.

17 Assessment 1

Preparation

Make copies of the assessment sheet. If you feel that the sheet is too 'busy', the three activities could be separated and enlarged on individual sheets.

Lesson introduction

Begin the assessment lesson by reviewing the relevant cross-curricular topics covered during the term. Remind the children of some of the projects and investigations they have undertaken, and ask them to recall and recount their work. Emphasise the mathematical content – for example, *Do you remember how we calculated milometer readings from the distances travelled?*

Main assessment activity

Distribute the sheets and ask the children to work on them individually. Guide the whole class through the questions one at a time, reading the text with them and prompting them to work out and fill in their answers. Try to make the whole activity enjoyable!

Practical activity

Set out a row of five parallel pencils.

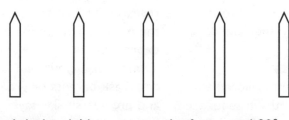

Ask the children to turn the first pencil 90° clockwise, the second pencil 90° anticlockwise, the third pencil 45° clockwise, the fourth pencil 180° clockwise and the fifth pencil 360° clockwise.

The correct solutions are:

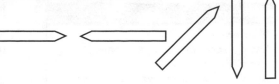

Plenary

Review the answers to the questions as a class. Collect the completed question sheets to use as an aid to judging individual children's progress, and to include in your records. The answers are:

1. 50, 110, 320, 820
2. 200, 900, 400, 600
3. 5:30, 7:15, 3:24, 6:58
4.

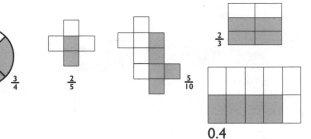

Linked to
L i t e r a c y

 **Through the seasons**

Objectives

Numeracy
Use the vocabulary related to time.
Use this year's calendar.
Know the number of days in each month.

Literacy
Compare and contrast poems on similar themes, particularly their form and language.

Resources

A flip chart or board; copies of the current year's calendar on a single sheet; a selection of poems about the months and seasons reproduced as photocopiable sheets or OHTs. Suitable poems include:
'Windy Nights' by Robert Louis Stevenson
'The Days are Clear' by Christina Rossetti
'Ladybird! Ladybird!' by Emily Brontë
'Autumn Fires' by Robert Louis Stevenson
'Winter' by William Shakespeare

Vocabulary

January, February...
month
calendar
season

Background

Much fascinating research can be undertaken on the history of our calendar. For example, when the decision was made in 1752 to move from the Julian to the Gregorian calendar, the date changed from 2 September to 14 September overnight. There were riots in the streets as people demanded their missing days back! In this lesson, the children examine the calendar to determine how many days there are in each month. The lesson is linked to work in literacy as the children read and compare poems about the passing months and seasons. They also practise the well-known rhyme:

month	number of days
January	31
February	28 or 29
March	31
April	30
May	31
June	30
July	31
August	31
September	30
October	31
November	30
December	31

> *30 days hath September,*
> *April, June and November.*
> *All the rest have 31,*
> *except February alone*
> *which has but 28 days clear*
> *and 29 in each leap year.*

Preparation

Collect and copy the poems (using your CLA licence). Copy and distribute the calendars.

Main teaching activity

Begin the lesson by asking the children to recite the names of the months in sequence. Write the month names on the board. *Do you know how many days there are in a month? Do all the months have the same number of days?* Set the children to work in small groups to compile a list of the months and

use the calendar to find out how many days each month has. They should produce a table like the one shown above.

When the children have completed their tables, discuss them as a class. Talk about February and leap years. Every fourth year, February has 29 days. (The reason for this is that the Earth actually takes $365\frac{1}{4}$ days to circle the Sun. If we did not allow for this, the seasons would gradually move out of step with the calendar.) Display the *30 days hath September* poem and recite it with the class. Suggest that they memorise it.

Develop the lesson by comparing and contrasting some of the poems you have selected. *How do the poems describe the features of the months? How does the weather differ from month to month?*

Differentiation

Less able children should concentrate on completing the calendar activity and learning the '30 days hath September' poem.

Challenge more able children to research further sayings and poems about the months. For example, have they heard expressions such as 'April showers', or 'Don't cast a clout 'till May is out'? They could ask parents or grandparents to explain and provide similar sayings.

Plenary

Conclude the lesson with some quick-fire questions on the months: *What month comes after April? How many days are there in August?*

19 Shoe styles

Objectives

Numeracy
Solve a problem by collecting quickly, organising, representing and interpreting data in tables, charts, graphs and diagrams including those generated by a computer, for example:
tally charts and frequency tables,
pictograms,
bar charts.

Design and technology
Investigate and evaluate a range of familiar products, thinking about how they work, how they are used and the views of the people who use them.

Resources

A copy of photocopiable page 155 for each child; a computer running software with graphics and database capabilities, such as *Textease* or *Microsoft Excel*.

Vocabulary

survey
pictogram
tally
frequency table
most popular, most common
least popular, least common

Background
Which is the most popular method of fastening shoes? Which is the most effective fastener? In this lesson, the children conduct a survey of different styles of shoe fastenings. They investigate the popularity of the different styles and make judgements of their effectiveness. The activity links work in technology on products and the children's opinions of them to work on data handling in mathematics and ICT.

Preparation
Make and distribute copies of the photocopiable sheet. Set up the computer with your chosen software and make sure that you can use it confidently to enter data and produce bar charts.

Main teaching activity
Introduce the lesson by asking the children to look at their shoes. *How are they fastened? Do they have laces, buckles, Velcro or zips, or are they slip-ons? What are the advantages and disadvantages of each type of fastening? Which type is most secure? Which is easiest to use? Which looks best?*

Develop the lesson by explaining that the children are going to conduct a survey of the different shoe fastenings in the class. Discuss the worksheets and remind the children how to collect data by recording a tally to compile a frequency chart. As a class, conduct a show of hands to enable the children to complete tallies of the different

shoe fastenings being worn. Once the data are recorded, discuss different ways of presenting them. The second chart on the worksheet is for the children to record their survey results in the form of a pictogram. Discuss how a pictogram icon represents a number, for example 2, 5, 10 or 20 units. Discuss the choice of a suitable icon for a shoe survey and the number of items it should represent. If the children decide that each shoe icon should stand for two units, ask them how they would represent one unit in their table (with half a shoe).

Set the children to work in pairs to complete their pictogram.

Differentiation
Less able children should concentrate on the basic shoe survey.

More able children can extend the activity in a number of ways. They could survey opinions of the effectiveness and style of the different fasteners. They could extend the survey to other classes. They could transfer their data to a computer database, displaying a frequency table and bar chart using the facilities of the program.

Plenary
Review the children's findings. Which is the most common fastening? Why do the children think this is? Have any children extended the survey? What have they discovered? Can the children design a shoe with the most popular fastening? What else might they want to know to help them make their designs?

Linked to
I C T

20 Missing digits and signs

Objectives

Numeracy
Choose and use appropriate number operations.
Solve mathematical problems or puzzles and explain patterns and relationships.
ICT
Use a variety of ICT tools.

Resources

A copy of photocopiable page 156 for each child; computers running word-processing software.

Vocabulary

puzzle
problem
pattern
calculate
method
How did you work it out?
number sentence
sign
operation
symbol

Background

Missing-sign problems such as 45 * 29 = 16 and missing-digit problems such as *4 + 5* = 120 develop the children's number skills in an enjoyable puzzle-solving context. In this lesson, the children solve a series of these problems and discuss the patterns they observe and the best strategies for finding solutions. They then use their ICT skills to manipulate and edit text in order to create a set of similar problems for their friends to solve.

Preparation

Make and distribute copies of the photocopiable sheet. Set up the computers running word-processing software.

Main teaching activity

Introduce the lesson by looking at the worksheet as a class. A spider has blotted the ink over some of the digits and signs. The children's task is to decide what the missing numbers and signs are. Set them to work in small groups on the first five problems. After 10 minutes or so, gather the class together to discuss the methods they have used. Some ideas that should be drawn out in the discussion include:

● *If the result of the calculation is less than either or both of the original numbers, the calculation must be a subtraction or a division.*

● *If the result is more than double the larger of the original numbers, the calculation must be a multiplication.*

● *You can find missing digits in addition and subtraction sums by reversing the calculation using the digits you have – but be careful:*

sometimes you may need to regroup the tens and units.

● *Some multiplication and division missing-digit problems have more than one possible answer.*

Set the children to complete the remaining problems on the worksheet.

The children who have completed the worksheet exercise could be set the task of writing their own problems. Creating missing-sign or missing-digit problems is generally simpler than solving them. Demonstrate the technique: write down a number sentence, then replace the sign or selected digits with question marks or blobs.

Differentiation

Less able children could be set to create a sheet of these problems on the computer, using the editing facilities of the software package.

More able children could be challenged to explore problems with three- and four-digit numbers. How many digits can be left out before the problem becomes impossible to solve?

Plenary

Review the answers to the worksheet as a whole class. Ask selected children to present some of the problems they have created for the whole class to solve. The children's problems could be printed out and exchanged around the class as a homework activity. Remind the creators of the sheets that they will need to provide you with the answers, so that you can mark the homework!

The answers are:

1. 12 + 12 = 24	2. 25 + 18 = 43
3. 59 − 19 = 40	4. 6 × 5 = 30
5. 200 ÷ 10 = 20	6. 295 + 10 = 305
7. 97 − 69 = 28	8. 7 × 4 = 28
9. 35 ÷ 7 = 5	10. 4300 ÷ 100 = 43
11. 160 ÷ 2 = 80	12. 12 × 9 =108
13. 100 ÷ 4 = 25	

21 What temperature?

Objectives

Numeracy
Recognise negative numbers in context, for example, on a temperature scale.
Science
Be taught that temperature is a measure of how hot or cold things are.
Use simple equipment to make measurements.

Resources

A digital thermometer and an alcohol liquid-in-glass thermometer; ice cubes; salt; plastic dishes; a copy of photocopiable page 157 for each child; a cup of warm tea.

Vocabulary

above/below zero
negative number
minus

Background

The abstract concept of negative numbers is difficult for children to grasp. However, negative numbers can be understood in particular contexts. Zero degrees Celsius is the temperature at which water freezes to ice. It is not difficult to imagine a temperature colder than ice and therefore a temperature that is less than zero on the Celcius scale. Negative numbers can also be introduced in the context of a number line, or of direction (for example, distance above and below ground). In this lesson, the children read temperatures from a temperature scale. The process both introduces them to negative quantities and develops scale-reading skills.

Preparation

Make and distribute copies of the photocopiable sheet. Make sure that the digital thermometer is working satisfactorily. Make some ice cubes and a cup of warm tea.

Main teaching activity

Introduce the lesson by explaining that you are going to measure some temperatures with a digital thermometer. Start by turning on the thermometer and recording the temperature of the room. Dip the thermometer probe in the tea and observe how the temperature rises. Record the temperature of the tea. Next, push the probe into some ice on a tray. Observe how the temperature falls to near 0°C. Ask the children whether they think it is possible to have temperatures lower than zero.

Now explain that you are going to make the temperature fall below zero. Sprinkle some salt around the tip of the thermometer probe in contact with the ice. Observe how the temperature drops to a negative value. Explain the significance of the minus sign that precedes the digits. (The temperature falls below zero because a water and salt mixture freezes at less than 0°C. When the salt is added, the ice melts. The melting process uses heat energy and cools the salt-water mixture below zero. This explanation will be detailed enough for most children at this stage, though they should be familiar with mixtures and 'freezing' temperatures.) Remove the thermometer probe from the ice and observe how the temperature gradually rises through zero back towards room temperature.

Having established that negative temperatures exist, set the children to work in small groups on the worksheet. Compare the temperature scale to a number line. Explain that the scale is just a vertical number line related to the position of the liquid in the thermometer tube. The children should read and record temperatures from the scale to the nearest division.

Differentiation

Less able children should read temperatures to the nearest labelled division.

More able children should read to the nearest marked division. Challenge them to make up and calculate some more temperature differences.

Plenary

Review the worksheet answers as a class. Can the children think of any other uses for negative numbers? For example, in a quiz where you loose points for wrong answers, your score could become negative if you gave more wrong answers than correct ones.

The answers are:
1. 100°C, 55°C, 37°C, 22°C, 0°C, –10°C, –20°C 2. 100°C 3. –30°C 4. 100°C, 18°C, 32°C, 20°C, 120°C, 10°C

Linked to
I C T

22 Attendances

Objectives

Numeracy
Read and write whole numbers to at least 10 000 in figures and words, and know what each digit represents.
Order a set of whole numbers less than 10 000.
ICT
Talk about what information they need and how they can find and use it.
Prepare information for development using ICT, including selecting suitable sources, finding information and classifying it.
Links to QCA Information Technology Unit 4D.

Resources

A copy of photocopiable page 158 for each child; sports pages from newspapers giving tables of results and statistics.

Vocabulary

count on
order
sequence
greater than
fewer than
most
least

Background

Newspapers are a valuable source of numbers for placing mathematics in real-life contexts. The sports pages in particular are packed with tables of statistics. Attendances at football grounds are a source of real numbers to 10 000 and beyond. In this lesson, the children interpret a table of attendance figures to develop ordering and calculation skills with numbers to 10 000. The activity can be developed into an ICT investigation by asking the children to research attendances at their favourite football grounds, or other appropriate sporting statistics, and then to produce charts and tables on the computer.

Preparation

Collect appropriate sporting statistics from newspapers. Make and distribute copies of the photocopiable sheet in preparation for small-group work.

Main teaching activity

Introduce the lesson by examining some of the sporting statistics published in the week's newspapers. Which football team had the biggest crowd at its ground? How many more people were at this game than at a rival team's game? How did the size of the football crowds compare with the numbers attending the Grand Prix or a pop concert? What other numerical information is available in the paper?

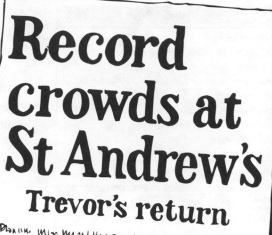

Develop the lesson by showing the children the worksheet and setting them to answer the questions. Answer the first two questions as a class. Discuss the technique of counting on to find the difference between two similar large numbers.

Differentiation

Less able children should concentrate on answering the problems on the worksheet.

When more able children have completed the basic problems, suggest that they research attendances at actual football matches or other events. Direct them to extract the information from newspaper reports of the games, or from the Internet. They could compile a table of attendances similar to the one on the worksheet (preferably on the computer) and write similar questions for others to answer.

Plenary

Review the answers to the worksheet as a class, discussing the counting-on techniques used by the children to find the answers to questions involving differences. Ask selected children to present their findings on attendances at real events.

The answers are:
1. Athletic 2. Town 3. 5998, 6005, 8515, 8995, 9003, 9297, 9302 4. 5 5. 7 6. 8

23 Roman home

Objectives

Numeracy
Measure and calculate the perimeter and area of rectangles and other simple shapes, using counting methods and standard units.
History
Learn about the Romans in Britain and their culture.
Links to QCA History Unit 6A.

Resources

A copy of photocopiable page 159 for each child; paper and pencils; books with illustrations of Roman homes; a tape measure; a flip chart or board.

Vocabulary

area
perimeter
surface
covers

Background

Perimeter and area are distinct features of a shape which the children may confuse. The perimeter is the distance all the way around the shape. (See Lesson 6.) The area is the amount of surface the shape occupies. The units of perimeter are those of length (cm or m), but those of area are length squared (cm^2 or m^2). The distinction between the two measures is best introduced by dividing a rectangle into unit squares, as illustrated below. Explain that the length of each side of a unit square is 1 unit, and its area is 1 square unit. The perimeter of the rectangle can be found by counting the number of unit sides around its edge, the area by counting the total number of unit squares. In this lesson, the children find the perimeters and areas of the various rooms in a Roman house. In the process, they learn the names and uses of the different rooms.

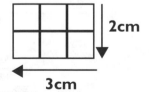

perimeter = 3 + 2 + 3 + 2 = 10cm
area = 3 × 2 = 6cm²

Preparation

Make and distribute copies of the photocopiable sheet. Collect books with illustrations of Roman homes. This lesson should build on a previous numeracy session in which you have used counting methods to find the perimeters and areas of rectangles.

Main teaching activity

Introduce the lesson by showing the children some pictures of Roman homes. Discuss their features, the different rooms inside and their purposes. *Who lived in these homes? Did everyone in Roman times have a beautiful villa? How did the homes of wealthy Romans compare with the homes we have today? How large were the rooms? How many rooms were there in a house?*

Develop the lesson by showing the children the floor plan of a Roman house on the worksheet. Talk about the names and purposes of the rooms labelled. Explain that the plan has been drawn on a grid of unit squares (1m × 1m) Remind them how to find perimeters and areas using a grid, and set them to complete the table.

Differentiation

Less able children could concentrate on finding the area and the perimeter of two smaller rooms.

Challenge more able children to find the area and perimeter of the whole house.

Plenary

Review the children's findings. The answers are shown below. *How do these sizes compare with modern rooms?* Use the tape measure to find the length and width of the classroom. Sketch a plan of it on the board and divide it into unit squares to find the room's area and perimeter. Suggest that the children repeat the exercise on their bedroom to compare it with a Roman bedroom.

room	perimeter in metres	area in square metres
C	12	9
Cu	14	12
V	14	10
T	18	20
Tri	14	12
A	26	36
P	32	63

24 Give the co-ordinates

Objectives

Numeracy
Describe and find the position of a point on a grid of squares where the lines are numbered. Recognise simple examples of horizontal and vertical lines.
Geography
Use maps and plans at a range of scales.
History
Study the Anglo-Saxons in Britain.
Links to QCA History Unit 6B: An Anglo-Saxon case study.

Resources

A copy of photocopiable page 160 for each child; a flip chart or board.

Vocabulary

co-ordinate
horizontal
vertical
grid

Background

On street maps, grid squares are often identified with numbers and letters. For example, Castle Street might be listed as being in map square D6. This square can be found on the map at the intersection of the column of squares labelled D and the row of squares labelled 6. For more accurate work on graphs and detailed plans, it is more usual to number the lines that form the grid rather than the squares. The position of a point is then given as a pair of numbers or 'co-ordinates' that give the horizontal and vertical locations of the point. The children should be familiar with both systems. In this lesson, the children use co-ordinates to locate finds in a hypothetical excavation of an Anglo-Saxon site. The activity can be linked to a case study on the discoveries at the Sutton Hoo site. Further information about Sutton Hoo may be found at the website www.suttonhoo.org

Preparation

Make and distribute copies of the photocopiable sheet.

Main teaching activity

Introduce the lesson by sketching a simple grid on the board and explaining that it is a map of an Anglo-Saxon archaeological site. Ask the children to suggest some finds that might appear on the map – for example, a house, pottery, a sword, a fireplace, a burial chamber, a rubbish tip. Sketch the features so that each coincides with the intersection of a horizontal and a vertical grid line. Explain how the position of each feature can be described by numbering the horizontal and vertical lines and giving a pair of co-ordinates. With the children's help, write down the co-ordinates of each of the features drawn. Emphasise the importance of always giving the horizontal co-ordinate first to avoid confusion. For example, if the house is at (1, 5) and the rubbish tip is at (5, 1), giving the vertical co-ordinate first will lead someone into the rubbish tip instead of to the house!

Set the children to work in pairs or small groups on the worksheet activity. Explain that it is a plan of an Anglo-Saxon site, and they should imagine they are archaeologists who must record the co-ordinates of their finds.

Differentiation

Make sure that less able children give the co-ordinates correctly.

Challenge more able children to write a treasure hunt story, with mathematical clues that can be used to find the co-ordinates of buried treasure.

Plenary

Review the answers to the worksheet. If any children have written a treasure hunt story, try to find the treasure by solving their clues.

The answers are:

find	co-ordinates
brooch	(3, 8)
sword	(4, 1)
helmet	(8, 9)
fireplace	(1, 9)
pottery	(6, 6)
arrow head	(2, 3)
burial chamber	(5, 4)
necklace	(8, 3)

Linked to
I C T
S c i e n c e

25 Shape keys

Objectives

Numeracy
Describe and visualise 3-D and 2-D shapes.
Recognise equilateral and isosceles triangles.
Classify polygons using criteria such as number of right angles, whether or not they are regular, symmetry properties.
ICT
How to prepare information for development using ICT, including classifying information and checking it for accuracy.
Links to QCA Information Technology Unit 4C: Branching databases.
Science
Make and use keys.

Resources

A copy of photocopiable page 161 for each child; boxes of 2-D and 3-D shape models; paper and pencils.

Vocabulary

triangle
isosceles triangle
equilateral triangle
scalene triangle
polygon
side
corner
angle
equal

Background

A branching database uses a series of yes/no questions to identify items uniquely. In science, this type of database is used to identify living things and known as a 'key'. Branching databases are used frequently in ICT applications, and several educational programs are available for creating one on the computer (for example, *Decision Tree*).

This activity as presented is paper-based, but could be developed on the computer as an ICT project. The children are first introduced to a branching database for identifying triangle types; they then develop a key of their own for distinguishing a selection of different shapes. This links to work in science on plant and animal groups. You could, for example, set the children to work on a computer minibeast identification key such as the one included in the CD-ROM *Science Explorer II* (Granada Learning).

Preparation

Copy the photocopiable sheet and distribute the copies with the boxes of shapes. This lesson should build on previous numeracy lessons in which the properties of 2-D and 3-D shapes have been described and discussed.

Main teaching activity

Use drawings or plastic shapes to remind the children of the different types of triangle. An equilateral triangle has three equal sides and angles. An isosceles triangle has two equal sides and angles. A right-angled triangle has one right angle. A triangle with all three sides different lengths is called a scalene triangle.

Look at the triangle key on the worksheet and explain how it is used to identify triangles. Starting at the top, questions must be answered 'yes' or 'no' and branches followed until the shape has been identified. Let the children work in pairs or small groups for a few minutes, selecting shapes and identifying them as a particular triangle type or as 'not triangles'.

Develop the lesson by setting the children to produce their own keys for sorting shapes. Start by selecting three or four different shapes to give to a group. Ask them to write a series of yes/no questions in the form of a branching database, using the triangle example as a model. Emphasise the importance of selecting questions that can be answered with 'Yes' or 'No' for each shape.

Differentiation

Less able children should concentrate on producing a branching database for three or four distinct shapes – for example, square, rectangle, triangle, circle.

More able children can develop more general databases – for example, to identify a wider range of 2-D regular and irregular polygons.

Plenary

Conclude the lesson by working through the shape keys the children have produced to check that they correctly identify the shapes for which they were developed. If time allows, link this to science by demonstrating a minibeast identification key.

26 Interesting numbers

Numeracy
Recognise odd and even numbers up to 1000, and some of their properties.
Recognise multiples.
Make and investigate a general statement about familiar numbers.

Literacy
Speak with confidence, choosing material that is relevant to the topic and to listeners.
Make short notes in list form.

Resources

A pack of number cards 1–20; a pack of number cards including all numbers to 100 and selected 'interesting' numbers to 1000 (for example, 144, 180, 270, 360, 365, multiples of 50); pencils and paper.

Vocabulary

number
even
odd
multiple
century

Background
The brilliant self-taught Indian mathematician Srinivasa Ramanujan thought that every number was 'interesting'. He enjoyed explaining mathematical facts about the numbers around him, including the numbers on taxis and buses. Sadly, he died at the age of just 32. In this lesson, the children are challenged to make interesting mathematical statements about numbers drawn at random from a pack of number cards. They start by formulating and explaining their facts orally, then proceed to compile a written list of facts for numbers in a sequence.

Preparation
Assemble the packs of number cards. These can be created on the computer if necessary. Distribute pencils and paper on tables in preparation for group work.

Main teaching activity
Introduce the lesson with Srinivasa Ramanujan's statement that every number is interesting. Explain that the task for today is to find something interesting to say about the numbers on the cards you draw from the pack. Start by drawing numbers at random from the 1–20 pack. Make a statement about the first few numbers drawn, then encourage the children to make similar statements of interest. The children should be prompted to use the correct vocabulary and express themselves clearly. For example:

1 – the smallest whole number
2 – the smallest even number
3 – the number of corners on a triangle, a hat trick!
4 – double 2, my birthday!
5 – the number of fingers of one hand, half of 10

15 – a multiple of 5 and 3
16 – 2 × 2 × 2 × 2
17 – double 8 plus 1
18 – voting age
19 – the last teens number
20 – a multiple of 2, 4, 5 and 10, one 'score'

When the children have understood the activity and are contributing well, introduce the second pack of cards to extend the range of numbers to 100 and beyond.

In the second part of the lesson, set the children to work in groups to record some of the facts they have discussed in writing. Some groups could work at the computer to produce their lists using a word-processing package. Assign a sequence of numbers for each group to compile a list of facts about.

Differentiation
Less able children can be set to record facts about the numbers 1 to 10 or 20.

Challenge more able children to compile fact lists for numbers to 100 and beyond.

Plenary
Create a class display of the facts the children have compiled. Ask some oral questions based on the fact lists: *Which number is the number of degrees in any whole turn? Which number is also called a score? How many runs has a cricketer scored when he has made a half-century?*

27 Sorting materials

Objectives

Numeracy
Solve a problem by collecting, representing and interpreting data in diagrams, for example, a Carroll diagram with two criteria.

Science
Be taught that some materials are better electrical conductors than others.
Construct circuits, incorporating a battery.
Links to QCA Science Unit 4F: Circuits and conductors.

Resources

A copy of photocopiable page 162 for each child;. bulbs, bulb holders, batteries, battery holders and wires to set up the circuit shown on the worksheet; magnets; materials for testing (these could include: metal objects such as paper clips, drinks cans, keys, coins, nails, cutlery; non-metal objects such as a plastic bricks, wooden sticks, glass marbles, corks, fabric, paper, card; two or three non-metal conductors such as a stick of charcoal, a pencil lead, a glass of salt water).

Vocabulary

Carroll diagram
sort
group
set

Background
The Victorian mathematician Charles Dodgson, better known as Lewis Carroll (see page 55), developed diagrams for sorting according to whether or not an item has a particular property. When two criteria are considered, items are sorted into boxes on a 2 × 2 grid. Suppose that the properties considered are A and B. The four boxes are: A, B; A, not B; not A, B; not A, not B – as illustrated in the example on the right (where shapes are sorted). In this lesson, the children use two-criteria Carroll diagrams to record the results of their investigations on the magnetic and electrical properties of materials.

Preparation
Distribute the equipment, materials and photocopied sheets on tables. This lesson should build on science lessons in which electric circuits have been introduced.

Main teaching activity
Introduce the lesson by reminding the children of previous work on electric circuits. They should recall that a complete circuit is needed for an electric current to flow. The parts of the circuit must be made from metal wires or other materials that conduct electricity. Explain that the children are going to test different materials to see whether or not they conduct electricity.

Look at the materials you have selected and discuss whether they are metals or non-metals. What types of materials do they think conduct electricity? Are metals the only materials that conduct electricity? To test their predictions, they should set up the circuit shown on the worksheet. Set the children to work in small groups on the practical activity.

The children should test each sample in turn by touching the two free wire ends to either end of the material. If the material conducts, the bulb will light. The salt water can be tested by dipping the wire ends under the water – make sure the wires do not touch.

Show them how to record their observations by writing the sample names in the correct boxes of the Carroll diagram.

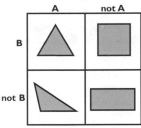

A = triangle
B = regular

	metal	not metal
conducts	paper clip nail coin	pencil lead charcoal salt water
does not conduct		rubber matchstick marble cork

Differentiation
Less able children will need support to identify metals and non-metals and to place them in the correct boxes.

More able children could develop the activity to consider other material properties. For example, they could draw up a Carroll diagram for the criteria metal/not metal, magnetic/not magnetic.

Plenary
Review the children's findings. The answers are shown above. *Do all metals conduct electricity? Do all non-metals not conduct electricity? Are there any materials in the metal/ not conductor box? If not, why not?* If any children have produced a diagram for the criteria metal/not metal, magnetic/not magnetic, discuss it in a similar way. They should have found that all magnetic materials are metals, but not all metals are magnetic.

28 Litter survey

Background

Litter is a problem in many schools. The children are asked to dispose of litter correctly, but it still appears in the playground and elsewhere. A litter survey raises the children's awareness of litter, its damaging effects on the environment and the importance of disposing of litter safely in bins that are regularly emptied. In this lesson, the children survey litter in the school environment, recording their results in a frequency table and presenting their findings using simple icons superimposed on a map.

Preparation

Prepare a large sketch map of the school environment for display. Label the locations that the children will survey for litter – for example, playground, car park, playing field, bicycle sheds, entrance gate and so on. Assemble the materials, including the litter pickers, disposable gloves and plastic bags.

Main teaching activity

Introduce the lesson by talking about the litter problem around the school. Why is it wrong to drop litter? What should be done with waste materials? Explain that the children are going to conduct a litter survey to highlight the problem and to try and encourage everyone in the school to dispose of their litter properly.

Divide the class into small groups. Look at the school map together. Assign each group an area to survey for litter. Issue the groups with plastic bags, disposable gloves and litter pickers. Tell the children not to pick up litter with their hands. Discuss the importance of hygiene and the reasons for using the gloves and litter pickers. The groups should systematically walk their assigned area, collecting and counting the pieces of litter.

When the children have completed the practical part of the survey, draw a frequency table (similar to the one below) on the board and ask representatives from each group to report the number of pieces of litter they have collected.

Ask the children to consider a suitable symbol or icon to represent items of litter. Depending on the amount of litter collected, the icon may need to stand for one, two, five or more items. Discuss the appropriate number as a class. Ask the children to draw icons on the labels. With the children's help, stick appropriate numbers of icons in the different locations on the map to indicate the quantities of litter found.

area	number of pieces of litter collected
playground	4
bike sheds	8
playing field	12
school entrance	5

Differentiation

Less able children can help you count items of litter and stick icons on the map.

Ask the more able children to discuss and formulate a litter policy for the school. *Where are the problem areas? How can the litter be reduced?* They should write a list of their ideas to be included in the display.

Plenary

Plan an assembly in which the class present their findings and their ideas for reducing litter to the whole school.

29 Recycling sums

Objectives

Numeracy
Use all four operations to solve word problems involving numbers in 'real life', using one or more steps.
Interpret data in tables.

Science
Compare everyday materials and objects on the basis of their material properties and relate these properties to everyday uses of materials.

Geography
Collect and record evidence.
Study environmental issues.
Links to QCA Geography Unit 8:
Improving the environment.

Resources

Digital weighing scales; an empty glass bottle, a plastic lemonade bottle, a food can, a newspaper, a cabbage; a copy of photocopiable page 163 for each child; a flip chart or board.

Vocabulary

table
column
row
measure
kg
weigh

Background

Litter, waste and recycling are popular topics that link work in science on materials to work in geography on the local environment. A litter survey (Lesson 28) provides mathematical data for the children to represent and interpret. The children could also undertake surveys of the waste produced at home. Many local authorities now make regular collections of recyclable materials from households. Encourage the children to count and record the items their family puts out: how many bottles, cans, newspapers? In this lesson, the children interpret a table of data about the waste produced by a 'typical' family, answering mathematical story problems based on these numbers.

Preparation

Collect the resources and set them out in view of the whole class. Make and distribute copies of the photocopiable sheet.

Main teaching activity

Introduce the lesson by talking about waste and recycling. *Why is it important to recycle waste materials? Which materials can be used again? How can we help to recycle materials? Does the council collect materials for recycling, or is there a recycling centre nearby?*

Develop the lesson by asking how much waste a typical person or family produces. *How many bottles each week, how many cans,*

how much paper? Look at the worksheet with the children and discuss the information in the table. This gives data for a 'typical' family. The quantities of the different waste materials are given in 'equivalent' units. Explain what this means – for example, the amount of paper thrown away each week is equivalent to 15 newspapers, although not all the paper is in the form of newspapers. Ask the children to list other forms the waste paper might take (junk mail, food packaging and so on). Do the same for plastic, glass and metal.

Set the children to work in small groups to answer the questions on the worksheet.

Differentiation

Less able children should concentrate on answering questions 1–3. These are straightforward calculations.

More able children should proceed to the measurement activity in question 4. They should weigh each of the sample items, and complete the mass column next to each item. Can the children convert their measurements from grams to kg? Can they calculate the number and mass of each item disposed of in a year?

Plenary

Review the worksheet answers as a class. Ask representatives to discuss their findings from the measurement activity. Follow up the activity by making a display of the recyclable waste produced by a family in a week – make sure that all the items displayed have been washed and do not have sharp edges.

The answers are:
1. 1040 2. about 63 3. 390

Linked to Science

30 Matching measures

Objectives

Numeracy
Recognise simple fractions that are several parts of a whole.
Recognise the equivalence of simple fractions.
Know the equivalent of 1/2, 1/4, 3/4 and 1/10 of 1km, 1m, 1kg and 1 litre in m, cm, g and ml.
Convert up to 1000cm to m and vice versa.

Science
Make and compare measurements using standard units.

Resources

A selection of science, maths and technology measuring equipment – this could include rulers, tape measures, digital balance, kitchen scales, measuring jugs and cylinders; a copy of photocopiable page 164 for each child; a flip chart or board.

Vocabulary

measure
measuring scale
length
km, m, cm, mm
weigh
mass
weight
kilogram, gram, kg, g
capacity
litre, millilitre, l, ml

Background

Although our metric measuring system is much simpler than the former imperial system, we still have a number of alternative ways for expressing the same quantity. For example, when buying apples we need to know that 'half a kilo', '500 grams' and '0.5kg' are equivalent measures. The equivalent measures the children should know are summarised in the illustration below. Identifying the equivalence of readings on scales labelled in various ways is important for the use of measuring equipment in science.

Preparation

Make and distribute copies of the photocopiable sheet. Set out the measuring equipment ready for an introductory whole-class discussion.

Main teaching activity

Introduce the lesson by examining the measuring equipment as a class. Discuss the measuring scales and their subdivisions. Use them as a basis for reminding the children of the link between cm and m, ml and l, and g and kg. Introduce the fractional units in the tables above. *Where is* $\frac{1}{10}$ *kg on this scale? What is a quarter of a litre in millilitres?* Use the scales to demonstrate the equivalence of the different measures. Summarise the relationships by reproducing the tables on the board.

Continue the lesson by setting the children to work in pairs or small groups on the worksheet activities. They should record each of the readings from the scales, using the units shown.

Differentiation

Less able children should record each reading in one way.

More able children should be challenged to convert each reading into at least two equivalent forms.

Plenary

Review the answers to the worksheet as a class. Conclude the lesson with some rapid unit conversions, based on the tables of equivalent units. *What is three quarters of a litre in millilitres?*

$\frac{1}{10}$ kg = 0.1kg = 100g
$\frac{1}{4}$ kg = 0.25kg = 250g
$\frac{1}{2}$ kg = 0.5kg = 500g
$\frac{3}{4}$ kg = 0.75kg = 750g

$\frac{1}{10}$ l = 100ml
$\frac{1}{4}$ l = 250ml
$\frac{1}{2}$ l = 500ml
$\frac{3}{4}$ l = 750ml

$\frac{1}{10}$ m = 10cm = 100mm
$\frac{1}{4}$ m = 25cm = 250mm
$\frac{1}{2}$ m = 50cm = 500mm
$\frac{3}{4}$ m = 75cm = 750mm

The answers are:
1. 1.5m, 150cm, 1500mm
2. 0.6l, 600ml
3. 2.5kg, 2500g
4. 0.75m, 75cm, 750mm

31 Explain yourself – to 1000

Objectives

Numeracy
Explain methods and reasoning about numbers orally and in writing.
Use informal pencil and paper methods to support, record or explain additions/subtractions/multiplications/divisions.

English
Speak audibly and clearly, using spoken standard English in formal contexts.
Use vocabulary and syntax that enables communication of more complex meanings.

Resources

Sets of number cards, sorted to provide a pack containing two each of the numbers 1–10 plus 50 and 100 for each group, and a pack of 20 or more cards containing selected numbers in the range 100–1000; a flip chart or board; paper and pencils.

Vocabulary

addition
subtraction
multiplication
division
calculate
method
jotting
answer
How did you work it out?

Background

This lesson builds on Lesson 15, in which the children played a version of the game *Countdown*. In this game, they select numbers from a pack of cards. They are given a target number and must combine their selections using the four basic operations to match, or get as close as possible to, the target. The children can work mentally or use jottings. In this lesson, the target number is in the range 100–1000. The children must use their speaking skills to explain their calculations with the appropriate vocabulary.

them using addition, multiplication, subtraction and/or division, to calculate the target. Give them a minute or two to jot down their answers. Ask for a volunteer to explain to the class how he or she reached the target. As the volunteer describes his or her calculations, jot them on the board for the class to follow. Reinforce the use of the correct vocabulary.

You can develop the game by taking away the numbers the first volunteer used and challenging the children to calculate the target using any of the remaining numbers. A second volunteer can explain his or her new method. Continue playing, taking away numbers, until it is no longer possible to reach the target.

Set the children to play the game in groups, taking it in turns to act as scribe. Make sure that every child has an opportunity to explain his or her calculations to the group.

Preparation

Collect together the packs of number cards.

Main teaching activity

Introduce the lesson by reminding the children about the target number game they played in Lesson 15. Explain that in this lesson they will play the game with target numbers up to 1000.

Proceed to play the game with the whole class. Deal out a pack of cards containing the numbers 1–10, 50 and 100 so that the children can see them. Ask a child to select a card at random from the pack containing the numbers 100–1000. Write this number on the board and state that this is the target. Tell the children that they must choose any five numbers from those dealt out and combine

Differentiation

Less able children could be given target numbers that are multiples of 50.

Challenge more able children to find as many ways as possible of calculating a given target from the original numbers.

Plenary

Ask representatives from the groups to talk about some of the calculation strategies they have used. For example, why is it nearly always helpful to choose the 100 card and a single-digit card to start? (By multiplying these cards, the nearest 100 to the target number can be made.)

Linked to
S c i e n c e

32 Decimal scales

Objectives

Numeracy
Understand decimal notation and place value for tenths and hundredths, and use them in context.
Record readings from scales to a suitable degree of accuracy.

Science
To make and compare measurements using standard units.

Resources

Rulers graduated in cm and mm; measuring sticks graduated in m and cm; papers and pencils; a flip chart or board; various tape measures, measuring sticks and rulers.

Vocabulary

m
cm
mm
decimal point
unit
tenth
hundredth

Background

The use of measuring sticks and rulers graduated in m, cm and mm is a useful practical context in which to introduce and develop decimal notation. 1mm is $\frac{1}{10}$ of 1cm, so a measurement in cm to the nearest mm has one place of decimals (for example, 5.7cm). 1cm is $\frac{1}{100}$ of 1m, so a measurement in m to the nearest cm has two places of decimals (for example, 1.65m). In this lesson, the children choose appropriate units to measure and compare the length of the top joint of their thumb and their height, developing measuring skills that are important in many areas of the curriculum – particularly in science.

Preparation

Distribute measuring sticks and rulers on tables.

Main teaching activity

Introduce the lesson by discussing the graduations on the length-measuring equipment. Ask the children to remind you about the connection between mm and cm. Look at a ruler graduated in mm and cm and discuss how it is used correctly to make a measurement to the nearest mm. How should this measurement be written in cm? Write some examples on the board, using the decimal point notation. Explain that the decimal point separates the units (cm) from the tenth units (mm). Let the children take turns to make measurements and record lengths to the nearest mm on the board –

for example, the lengths of pencils.

Develop the lesson by looking at the measuring stick. Ask the children to recall the connection between cm and m. With their help, make a measurement in m to the nearest 0.01m (for example, the height of a door) and record it on the board. Explain that this measurement has two places of decimals: the tenths (10cm) and the hundredths (1cm).

Set the children to work in small groups to make two measurements: the length of the top joint of each child's thumb and the height of each child. The children should discuss the appropriate level of accuracy for making these measurements, and select suitable measuring equipment. They should then consider the best way of using the equipment accurately. For example, to measure heights a child could stand with his or her back to the board, then a ruler could be placed horizontally on his or her head, and a mark made on the board. The height of this mark from the floor can then be measured with care. Lead the children to measure thumb lengths to the nearest mm and heights to the nearest cm.

Differentiation

Less able children could work in pairs to make the measurements.

Challenge more able children to make a wider range of measurements, such as the circumference (perimeter) of the head and the separation of the eyes. They should select equipment and record measurements to an appropriate level of accuracy.

Plenary

Review the children's findings as a class. Discuss why it would not be appropriate to measure height to the nearest m (not accurate enough) or the nearest mm (too precise to be meaningful). Reinforce the decimal notation by writing some measurements on the board and asking the children to say how many m, cm or mm they represent – for example, 1.65m is 1m and 65cm; 3.2cm is 3cm and 2mm.

Linked to
Geography
Science

33 Highest and lowest

Objectives

Numeracy
Read and write the vocabulary of comparing and ordering numbers.
Use symbols correctly, including less than (<) and greater than (>).
Understand decimal notation in context.
Recognise negative numbers in context.
Geography
Explain what places are like.
Use secondary sources of information.
Know the locations of significant places.
Builds on QCA Geography Unit 7: Weather around the world.
Science
Know that temperature is a measure of how hot or cold things are.

Resources

A copy of photocopiable page 165 for each child; a world map; a globe; a flip chart or board; a large demonstration thermometer.

Vocabulary

negative number
positive number
greater than
less than

Background

Daily newspapers publish tables of weather data from around the world. The statistics include temperatures in major cities. In this lesson, the children interpret tables of temperatures in some major cities of the world on typical days in January and July. They compare both positive and negative temperatures, using the greater than (>) and less than (<) signs. They find the cities on a world map, and consider the seasonal temperature differences between North and South.

Preparation

Make and distribute copies of the photocopiable sheet in advance of the lesson. Set up the map where the whole class can see it.

Main teaching activity

Introduce the lesson by talking about the temperature today. Read the room temperature from the thermometer. Look closely at the scale, discussing the significance of 0°C and negative temperatures. Do the children know the typical temperatures for a warm summer's day in the UK (20 to 25°C); a frosty winter's day (–5 to 0°C); a bright spring day (10 to 20°C)? Have the children experienced much higher or much lower temperatures in other parts of the world? In what parts of the world is it very cold? In what parts is it very hot?

Develop the lesson by introducing the worksheet. Explain that the tables show average temperatures at two times of year in major world cities. As a class, locate the cities on the map. *Which cities are in the northern hemisphere? Which cities are in the southern hemisphere?* Set the children to work in pairs or small groups on the worksheet questions.

Differentiation

Less able children should concentrate on answering the worksheet questions.

More able children can be challenged to research temperatures in more detail using the Internet – for example, at www.worldclimate.com

Plenary

Review the answers to the worksheet questions as a class. Conclude the lesson with a discussion of the seasonal temperature differences between the northern and southern hemispheres. Use the globe to demonstrate that in July the northern hemisphere is tilted towards the Sun and is experiencing summer. In January, the southern hemisphere is tilted towards the Sun and therefore it is summer in the South and winter in the North.

The answers are:
1. Lagos
2. New York
3. New York
4. Lagos
5. >
   <

 Assessment 2

Preparation

Make copies of the assessment. If you feel that the sheet is too 'busy', the three activities could be separated and enlarged on individual sheets.

Lesson introduction

Begin the assessment lesson by reviewing the relevant cross-curricular topics covered during the term. Remind the children of some of the projects and investigations they have undertaken, and ask them to recall and recount their work. Emphasise the mathematical content — for example, *Do you remember how we calculated the perimeters and areas of the rooms in a Roman house, using a plan of the house?*

Main assessment activity

Distribute the worksheets and ask the children to work on them individually. Guide the whole class through the questions one at a time, reading the text with them and prompting them to work out and fill in their answers. Try to make the whole activity enjoyable!

Practical activity

Set out the empty containers by the digital weighing scales. Ask the children to weigh them and record their masses in grams.

Plenary

Review the answers to the questions as a class. Collect the completed question sheets to use as an aid to judging individual children's progress, and to include in your records. The answers are:
1. 10cm, 8 cm^2
16cm, 10 cm^2
16cm, 12 cm^2
2. $25 + 14 = 39$, $98 - 50 = 48$, $8 \times 6 = 48$
$45 \div 5 = 9$, $90 \div 45 = 2$, $12 \times 10 = 120$
$81 - 9 = 72$, $6 \times 6 = 36$, $36 - 19 = 17$
3. See diagram below.

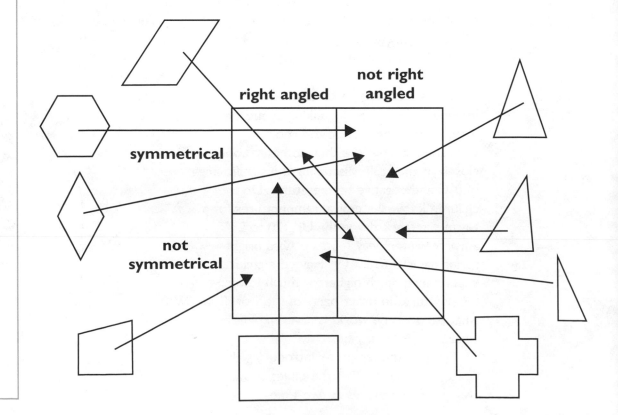

35 Sponsor me

Background

Charity fund-raising
events, including
sponsored 'marathons',
are a regular feature of
life in many schools.
Collecting names for a
sponsorship form,
estimating the number
of lengths that might
be swum or poems
recited in the time
available, and
calculating the
proceeds tests the
children's developing
mathematical skills in a
worthwhile practical
context. A discussion
of the motivation for
fundraising and
charitable work raises
the children's
awareness of moral
and social issues, and
of community life.

appropriate, ask the
children to suggest
different sponsored
'marathons' that the
class could undertake
– for example,
walking, swimming,
poetry reading,
arithmetic, singing and
so on.

Look at the
worksheet with the
children. It contains a
table showing how many 'sums' were done
by a group of children in a sponsored 'maths
marathon'. Discuss the information in the
rows and columns, and explain that the
children's task is to complete the
sponsorship form and calculate the total
raised. Discuss the mathematical operations
they will need to find the various totals.

Set the children to work in pairs or small
groups on the task.

Differentiation

Less able children could concentrate on
calculating and comparing the amounts
raised by the first five children on the form.

More able children should complete the
full task and, if time allows, start to plan a
similar sponsored marathon for the class.

Plenary

Review the completed worksheets as a class.
Discuss a possible class sponsorship activity.
What should the activity be? How long
should it last? What would an appropriate
sponsorship amount be?

The answers are:

Preparation

Make and distribute copies of the
photocopiable sheet.

Main teaching activity

Introduce the lesson with a discussion of
charity and fund-raising events the children
have participated in. Perhaps there is an event
coming up that you plan to support, such as
'Children in Need'. Talk about the motivation
for fund-raising, explaining that the followers
of every major religion, and the vast majority
of people without a particular
religious faith, believe in the
importance of helping those less
fortunate than themselves.

Develop the lesson by
considering different ways of raising
money. Discuss sponsored activities,
considering how they make raising
funds challenging and enjoyable for
everyone who takes part. If

name	money raised in pounds and pence
Simon	£2.50
Laura	£4.00
Sophie	£4.00
Shane	£2.20
Vineeta	£6.00
Zak	£6.00
Russell	£5.60
total	£30.30

36 Choosing chairs

Objectives

Numeracy
Suggest suitable units and measuring equipment to estimate or measure length.
Measure lengths to the nearest half cm.
Solve a problem by collecting, organising, representing and interpreting data in tables.
Design and technology
Evaluate familiar products, thinking about how they are used.
Art
Be taught about the materials used in craft and design and how these can be matched to ideas and intentions.
Links to QCA Art Unit 4B: Take a seat.

Resources

An example of each of the different-sized chairs in the school, a copy of photocopiable page 168 for each child; rulers and tape measures for measuring to the nearest half cm.

Vocabulary

measurement
height
cm
table
record
survey

Background

Children grow steadily through their primary school years. Within a class, height varies considerably from child to child. Year 4 children are not yet working with averages, and it is therefore difficult to compare height changes from class to class. However, within each class, the chair heights are consistent. In a typical primary school, there will be four or five chair sizes between Foundation and Year 6. The chairs are often colour-coded according to size. In this lesson, the children investigate the design and size of school chairs for different age groups.

Preparation

Collect the chairs and set them out. Copy the photocopiable sheet and distribute copies in preparation for group work.

Main teaching activity

Start the lesson by asking the children to order the set of chairs by size. Discuss the design of the chairs and talk about the reasons for the size difference. Ask the tallest child in the class to try the chairs and select the most comfortable height. Ask the shortest child in the class to do the same. *Did they select different chairs? Why?* Talk about other design features. *Why is it important for a chair to be stable? Why must it be both strong and light? What materials are chosen to give the correct combination of strength and low mass? Why is it helpful if the*

chairs can stack? What features of the chair design allow them to stack?

Develop the lesson by explaining that the children are going to make measurements of the chair seat heights and record them in a table. They will also note the age range of the children who use the different chairs. Set the children to work in small groups to make their measurements and record their data. They should select suitable rulers and tape measures to measure the seat heights to the nearest half cm.

Differentiation

Less able children should make and record the basic measurements.

Most children could extend the investigation in a number of ways. Some could look at table heights; others might transfer their data to the computer to produce a bar chart of chair heights against the children's age. Some children could investigate stacking. *What is the safe limit for stacking chairs?* (No more than four to keep the chairs light enough to lift and stable enough not to topple over.)

More able children could be challenged to investigate whether the chair heights are appropriate to each class. They could plan a survey in which the children in a class are asked to choose the most comfortable chair for them. Do the children's preferences match the chairs that are in the classroom?

Plenary

Discuss the children's findings as a class, confirming that they have all made appropriately accurate measurements of the chairs. How have they extended their investigations? What have they discovered?

37 Compass points

Objectives

Numeracy
Describe and find the position of a point on a grid of squares where the lines are numbered.
Use the eight compass directions N, S, E, W, NE, NW, SE, SW.

Geography
Use appropriate geographical vocabulary.
Use maps at a range of scales.

Resources

A copy of photocopiable page 169 for each child; magnetic compasses; a class set of maps of the UK showing towns and cities, or a larger wall map.

Vocabulary

compass point
co-ordinates
N, S, E, W, NE, NW, SE, SW

Background

In Year 4, the children should extend their understanding of compass directions to include NE, NW, SE, SW. Their work should extend to the use of grids with numbered lines rather than numbered squares. In this activity, the two skills are integrated in a map-reading exercise. The children must locate features on a map and describe the directions between them using the eight compass points.

Preparation

Copy the photocopiable sheet and set copies out in preparation for group work. This lesson should build on a previous mathematics session in which the children have been introduced to, and worked with, co-ordinates.

Main teaching activity

In the first part of the lesson, introduce the children to the compass points. Draw a compass symbol on the board and talk about the convention for naming the intermediate directions between the four principal compass points. The direction 'halfway' between North and West is called North-West or NW. Ask the children to help you name the other intermediate directions.

Continue the lesson by using the UK maps to ask some oral questions about the directions between different locations. *What direction must you travel in when you go from Bristol to London? Why are Plymouth and Exeter*

said to be in the South-West? Which city lies to the South-East of Preston?

Set the children to work in pairs or small groups on the worksheets. Remind them of the use of co-ordinates and ask them to write answers to the problems.

Differentiation

Less able children should concentrate on answering question 1, which involves compass directions only.

Most children should use their knowledge of compass points and co-ordinates to answer question 2.

Challenge more able children to plan a route from one map location to another by writing the starting co-ordinates and compass directions. Can their friends follow the route?

Plenary

Review the worksheet answers as a class. Conclude the lesson with some compass questions based on the map. *What is SE of the church? If you stood at (8, 4) and looked NE, what would you see?*

The answers to the worksheet are:
1. N, E, SE, SW, NW
2. Start at station. Go NW to wood. Go SW to church. Go NW to pond. Go SW to crossroads. Go SE to water tower.

Linked to
I C T

38 Turtle time

Objectives

Numeracy
Begin to know that angles are measured in degrees and start to order angles less than 180°.
Classify polygons using criteria such as number of sides and whether or not they are regular.
Make shapes.

ICT
Know how to create, test, improve and refine sequences of instructions to make things happen.
Links to QCA Information Technology Unit 4E: Modelling effects on screen.

Resources
An analogue clock face; large cut-out paper or card regular polygons (triangle, square, pentagon, hexagon); computers running software with turtle graphics capabilities (for example, LOGO); a floor turtle or other programmable robot, preferably with a drawing pen.

Vocabulary
polygon
triangle
square
pentagon
hexagon
heptagon
octagon
angle
turn
corner
side
regular

Background
The concept of angle is readily developed by considering it as a measure of amount of turn: 360° make a full turn, 180° a half turn, 120° a third of a turn, 90° a quarter turn, 72° a fifth of a turn, 60° a sixth of a turn and so on. In this lesson, the children walk around large polygons set out on the floor. They turn at each corner and, by considering the number of turns needed for a full circuit, deduce the fractions and angles of turn they are making. The investigation is developed by using programmable robots or on-screen 'turtle' graphics to draw polygons with simple repeated commands.

Preparation
Set up the computers and/or floor turtles with your chosen software package.
Make sure that you can program instructions for drawing polygons confidently. For example, a simple program to draw a square would be:

Forward 10
Right 90
Forward 10
Right 90
Forward 10
Right 90
Forward 10
Right 90

The basic instruction to move forwards 10 units and then turn right 90° is repeated four times, and therefore can be programmed more efficiently using:
Repeat 4 [Forward 10, Right 90]
This lesson should build on a previous mathematics lesson in which degree measure has been introduced.

Main teaching activity
Show the children the large polygons. Set them out on the floor and ask a child to walk around a square, turning at each corner until he or she has returned to the starting point. *How many complete turns has his or her body made during one circuit of the square?* (1) *What fraction of a whole turn did he or she make at each corner?* (There are four corners, so the child must have made a quarter of a turn at each corner.) *What are the angles corresponding to a whole turn and a quarter turn in degrees?* (360° and 90°.) Repeat the exercise with the other polygons.

Develop the lesson by moving the children on to the computers or floor robots. Demonstrate how to write a simple program to draw a square. Set the children to investigate how the program should be modified to draw triangles, pentagons and other polygons. What angles should they enter? How many times must they repeat the forward and turn commands to produce the different polygons?

Differentiation
Less able children should concentrate on drawing a square and a triangle.
Challenge more able children to investigate polygons with larger numbers of sides. *Can anyone draw an octagon?*

Plenary
Review the children's programs and drawings. Ask them to describe in their own words how they set about achieving the desired outcome. Did they try things that did not work? How did they work out how to change their programs to produce the correct result?

Linked to
D & T
Art & Design

39 Building blocks

Objectives

Numeracy
Visualise 3-D shapes from 2-D drawings.
Design and technology
Communicate design ideas in different ways.
Art
Be taught about visual elements including form and space.

Resources

A copy of photocopiable page 170 for each child; sets of wooden building cubes; art books containing reproductions of paintings with obvious perspective.

Vocabulary

cube
two-dimensional
three-dimensional

Background

Anyone who has attempted to follow the instructions to assemble furniture delivered as a 'flat pack' is familiar with the problem of visualising a three-dimensional structure from a two-dimensional drawing! Once the structure is put together successfully, the drawing becomes 'obvious'. But it can be a considerable struggle to reach this stage. Practical experience is the best way to develop an understanding of the visual conventions linking a 3-D object to its 2-D representation. As the flat-pack example demonstrates, this is an important skill in design and technology projects. In this lesson, the children use construction blocks to build 3-D structures from 2-D drawings.

Preparation

Make and distribute copies of the photocopiable sheet on tables, together with the building blocks.

Main teaching activity

Introduce the lesson by building an L-shaped structure (like the one illustrated above right) with the wooden blocks. Ask two children to view it from perpendicular directions and sketch what they see on the board. Discuss the problem of representing three-dimensional objects on a two-dimensional page. The appearance of the object depends on the angle from which it is viewed. Explain how a skilled designer or artist can select an angle from which to draw an object so that the three-dimensional shape seems to emerge on

the two-dimensional page. In art this is known as 'perspective'. Look at and discuss some examples of perspective in drawing and painting in art books.

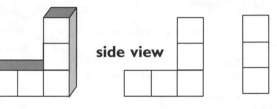

side view

end view

Develop the lesson by showing the children the worksheet. Discuss how the drawings represent three-dimensional stacks of cubes. Explain that the children's task is to reproduce the shapes shown in the drawings by stacking actual cubes. Set the children to work in small groups on the task.

Differentiation

Less able children should concentrate on the construction project, particularly the first two shapes.

Challenge the more able children to attempt the project in reverse. They should make a structure and then try to sketch it (or perhaps draw it using the 3-D shape tools of a software package such as *Microsoft Word*). Can their friends reproduce their structures from their drawings?

Plenary

As a class, inspect the shapes that the children have built using the blocks. How well do they match the drawings on the worksheet?

40 In which year?

Objectives

Numeracy
Use the vocabulary of estimation and approximation; make and justify estimates and approximations of numbers.
History
Use dates and vocabulary relating to the passing of time.
Links to QCA History Unit 9: What was it like for children in the Second World War?

Resources

A copy of photocopiable page 171 for each child; a flip chart or board; history reference books and/or CD-ROMs.

Vocabulary

number line
century
decade
year
estimate

Background

Estimating the position of a number on an undivided number line requires children to develop mental strategies for subdividing the line. For example, to mark 30 on an undivided 0 to 100 line, you might mentally divide the line into quarters, then place the 30 at just beyond one quarter of the distance along the line. To estimate the position of an arrow on a line, you might visualise the line divided into 10 equal parts and judge the position of the arrow against these subdivisions. In this lesson, the children talk about these and similar strategies they use for positioning or estimating the location of numbers on an undivided line. They then apply the strategies to estimating the years of significant events in the 20th century from an unlabelled timeline.

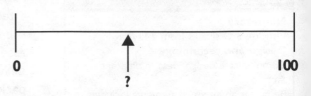

Preparation

Make and distribute copies of the photocopiable sheet. Make a collection of suitable history reference materials for researching 20th-century dates.

Main teaching activity

Introduce the lesson by drawing an undivided 0 to 100 number line on the board. Mark an arrow on the line and ask the children to estimate the number to which it points (see above right).

Ask the children to describe the strategies they used to make their estimate. Did they see the two portions of the line as fractions? Did they mentally subdivide the line into quarters or tenths? Continue the

process by marking several more arrows for the children to estimate. Develop the lesson by asking individual children to mark given numbers on the line. Do the rest of the class think these are correct?

Set the children to work in small groups on the worksheet exercise. They should use estimation skills to deduce the years of the significant 20th-century events marked on the timeline. Explain that the period from the start of 1900 to the start of 2000 is 100 years. Once they have made their estimates, they should check them using the history reference materials provided and make corrections where necessary.

Differentiation

Less able children could be given an undivided 0 to 10 number line and some simple estimation problems based on it to begin to develop their estimation skills.

Challenge more able children to create a worksheet similar to the one on page 171, but covering the 19th century, for their friends to solve.

Plenary

Review the worksheet answers. Ask the children to discuss which years they found easy to estimate. Which years are more difficult to estimate?

The answers are:
first aeroplane flight 1903
start of First World War 1914
discovery of the planet Pluto 1930
end of Second World War 1945
coronation of Queen Elizabeth II 1953
first man on the Moon 1969
decimal coins introduced in UK 1971
explosion at Chernobyl 1986
death of Princess Diana 1997

41 Rivers and mountains

Objectives

Numeracy
Read and write whole numbers to at least 10 000 in figures and words.
Order a set of whole numbers less than 10 000.

Geography
Locational knowledge of the largest mountain ranges and longest rivers in the world, Europe and the United Kingdom. Use atlases and secondary sources, including ICT, to extract geographical information.

Resources

A flip chart or board; a world map showing physical features (mountains and rivers); pinboard pins; research materials, for example atlases, geography books, CD-ROM encyclopaedias, Internet access.

Vocabulary

highest
longest
km
m

Background

The tallest mountain in the world, Mount Everest, is 8848m high. The longest river in the world is the Amazon, length 6750 kilometres – the river Nile has a similar length. Year 4 children should be working with numbers up to 10 000, and can therefore be asked to order and compare mountain heights and river lengths around the world. In this lesson, the children research the locations and names of the world's longest rivers and highest mountains, list them in order, and compile tables of their findings.

Preparation

Assemble the research materials and set them out where the children can access them readily. Pin up the world map to form the focus of a wall display.

Main teaching activity

Introduce the lesson by asking the children: *What is the name of the highest mountain in the world? What is the longest river in the world?* Some children may know the names of these features, but probably will not be able to quote their height and length. Explain that the children's task is to research the names, heights and lengths of some of the highest mountains and longest rivers in the world.

Divide the class into six groups. Set each group a different task. Group 1 could research the world's three highest mountains, Group 2 the three longest rivers in the world, Group 3 the three highest mountains in Europe, and so on. The children should use the research materials provided to find the required information and record it in a table.

Differentiation

Less able children can be assigned the straightforward task of finding the world's highest mountains and longest rivers.

More able children could develop their research to find the highest mountains and longest rivers on each continent.

Plenary

Ask representatives from each group to report their findings. Find the mountains and rivers on the wall map. Use the children's tables to develop the map into a display, marking the highest mountains and longest rivers with coloured pins.

42 Multiplication grids

Objectives

Numeracy
Know by heart multiplication facts for the 2, 3, 4, 5 and 10 times tables.
Begin to know multiplication facts for the 6, 7, 8 and 9 times tables.

ICT
Work with others to explore a variety of ICT tools.
Organise and reorganise text and tables.

Resources

A copy of photocopiable page 172 for each child; computers running software with table or spreadsheet capabilities, for example *Microsoft Word* or *Textease*; a flip chart or board.

Vocabulary

multiplication
table
column
row
pattern

Background
A 10 × 10 multiplication table summarises all the multiplication facts that the children in Year 4 should be committing to memory. Creating your own multiplication table and looking for the patterns it contains is a valuable way of developing and reinforcing multiplication knowledge. Multiplication tables can be filled in on prepared grids or generated using ICT tools. Creating and completing tables on the computer is an important ICT skill and forms the basis for later work with spreadsheets.

Preparation
Make and distribute copies of the photocopiable sheet. Set up computers running suitable software with which you are familiar. Check that you can create tables or spreadsheets confidently in advance of the lesson. Prepare a table for completion on the computer similar to the one on the worksheet. Draw up a blank multiplication table on the flip chart for the numbers 0–5 to introduce the lesson.

Main teaching activity
Introduce the lesson by completing the flip chart table with the whole class. Point out the symmetrical patterns that appear in the table. Ask the children to explain them – for example, the number 20 appears twice in the table, on either side of the diagonal, because 4 × 5 = 5 × 4 = 20
Set the children to work in twos or

threes on the computers to complete their own multiplication tables. If insufficient computers are available for all the children, some children can complete tables in pencil on the photocopiable sheet. The computer-produced tables should be printed for later discussion and display.

Differentiation
Less able children should start by completing the columns and rows corresponding to the 2, 3, 4, 5 and 10 times tables. They could refer to times tables on wall charts to help them.

More able children can be challenged to extend their tables to 12 × 12 and beyond. Children with exceptional ICT skills could be challenged to generate tables automatically, using the spreadsheet facilities of *Textease* or another spreadsheet program.

Plenary
Ask selected children to show their tables to the class and explain the patterns they have discovered in them.

The answers are:

×	0	1	2	3	4	5	6	7	8	9	10
0	0	0	0	0	0	0	0	0	0	0	0
1	0	1	2	3	4	5	6	7	8	9	10
2	0	2	4	6	8	10	12	14	16	18	20
3	0	3	6	9	12	15	18	21	24	27	30
4	0	4	8	12	16	20	24	28	32	36	40
5	0	5	10	15	20	25	30	35	40	45	50
6	0	6	12	18	24	30	36	42	48	54	60
7	0	7	14	21	28	35	42	49	56	63	70
8	0	8	16	24	32	40	48	56	64	72	80
9	0	9	18	27	36	45	54	63	72	81	90
10	0	10	20	30	40	50	60	70	80	90	100

Linked to
I C T

43 One in every...

Objectives

Numeracy
Begin to use ideas of simple proportion, for example, 'one for every...' and 'one in every...'.
ICT
Work with others to use a variety of ICT tools.
Develop and refine ideas by organising and reorganising images.
Links to QCA Information Technology Unit 4B: Developing images using repeating patterns.

Resources

Plastic farm animals; a copy of photocopiable page 173 for each child; computers running software with clip art capabilities – for example, *Textease* or *Microsoft Word*.

Vocabulary

for every...
one in every...

Background

The language of simple proportion is an everyday feature of classroom life. Take the opportunity for some practical maths practice as you organise the children in their activities. *There are 7 computers for 28 children, that's one for every 4, so please sit 4 to a computer. There are 12 pencils for each table, and 4 children per table, so that's 3 pencils each.* In this activity, the children use the language 'for every...' and 'one in every...' to describe the proportions of different animals in the patterns created by the regular repetition of animal clip art. They then proceed to use the computer to create similar designs and pattern for themselves.

Preparation

Make and distribute copies of the photocopiable sheet. Set up the computers running your chosen software package. Make sure that you can use the software to import animal clip art, resize images and copy and paste them repeatedly. Set out a row of 12 farm animals with, for example, 2 sheep, 4 cows and 6 pigs.

Main teaching activity

Introduce the lesson by talking about the row of farm animals. *How many sheep are there altogether? How many cows? How many pigs? How many cows are there for every sheep?* (2) *How many pigs are there for every sheep?* (3) *One in how many animals is a sheep?* (6) *One in how many animals is a cow ?* (3) *One in how many animals is a pig?* (2) Arrange and count the animals to help illustrate the

answers to each of these questions. Set the children to solve the problems on the worksheet.

Review the worksheet answers, then set the children to work in small groups at the computers to create some 'one in every...' and 'one for every...' patterns. Show them how to import clip art of animals, select and copy the images and paste them.

Differentiation

Less able children could work with plastic animals to set up rows using proportions you suggest – for example, *Make a row of cows and pigs with 3 cows for every pig.*

More able children can move quickly to the computer-based activity, developing and describing patterns with three, four or more different animals.

Plenary

Review some of the patterns created by the children. Ask other children to describe the patterns.

The answers to the worksheet are:
1. two
2. three
3. two
4. six
5. three
6. two
7. two
8. ten
9. five
10. five

44 Leftovers

Objectives

Numeracy
Understand the idea of a remainder, and know when to round up or down after division. Derive quickly division facts corresponding to the 2, 3, 4, 5 and 10 times tables.

English
Identify the gist of an account and evaluate what they hear.
Speak for different purposes.

Resources

A set of suitable division problems based on the 2, 3, 4, 5 and 10 times tables; paper and pencils.

Vocabulary

divide
share
remainder

Background

Division with whole numbers is in a different category from addition, subtraction and multiplication. Unlike the other whole-number operations, the answer to a division problem is not always another 'whole' number: sometimes there is a remainder. In practical problems, the remainder may need to be dealt with in different ways. For example, if you ask the question *How many teams of 5 can be made from 22 players?*, the answer is '4 with 2 left over'. In this case, the division is rounded down. However, if you ask *How many cars do we need for 22 people with 5 in each car?*, the answer is '4 full cars, plus a 5th car for the extra 2 people'. In this case, the division must be rounded up to find a practical answer. In this lesson, the children listen carefully as you describe a practical division problem. They then discuss the question and its solution as a group, and report their conclusions to the class orally.

Preparation

Set out paper and pencils in preparation for group work. Prepare a set of suitable practical division problems that you can pose orally to the whole class. For example:

● *How many teams of 5 can be chosen from a class of 28?*
● *How many 5p stickers can you buy with 18p?*

● *How many tables do you need for a class of 27 with 4 children per table?*
● *How many boxes do you need for 98 bottles with 10 per box?*

Adapt these and similar problems by changing the numbers during the lesson.

Main teaching activity

Introduce the lesson by reminding the children about division: pose some division story problems that do not produce remainders, such as *How many teams of 5 can we make with 20 children?*

Develop the lesson by changing the numbers in the initial problems to produce remainders. Discuss with the class what it is appropriate to do with the remainder in each case. For example, in a team problem the children 'left over' do not make up another team; they could take turns to replace members of a full team. But in the case of a filling-cars problem, an extra car is needed to transport the 'remainder'.

Continue the lesson by setting a series of remainder problems for the children to discuss and solve in groups. Ask each problem orally and give the children a few minutes to discuss their answers, making jottings where appropriate; then ask representatives from the groups to report their conclusions.

Differentiation

Set groups of less able children simple problems involving division by 2, 5 or 10.

Challenge more able children with problems in which they must divide by 6, 7, 8 or 9.

Plenary

Conclude the lesson with some rapid division questions – for example: *What is 23 divided by 5?* (Answer: 4 remainder 3.)

45 Slippery slopes

Objectives

Numeracy
Begin to know that angles are measured in degrees.
Start to order a set of angles less than 180°.

Science
Learn about friction as a force that may prevent objects from starting to move.
Compare everyday materials and objects on the basis of their material properties.
Links to QCA Science Unit 4E: Friction.

Resources
Wooden rulers, rubbers, coins, wooden bricks, plastic bricks, ice cubes and other materials for testing; card; pencils; protractors.

Vocabulary
slide
angle
greater angle
smaller angle

Background
When you climb a slope, the force of friction between your shoes and the ground prevents you from slipping. If the slope is muddy or icy, the friction force is reduced and it is more difficult to keep your footing. The steeper the slope, the greater the friction force needed to prevent your shoes from sliding. In this lesson, the children compare the friction between different materials by using a simple test to compare the slope angles at which sliding starts.

Preparation
Assemble the resources and distribute them in preparation for group work.

Main teaching activity
Introduce the lesson with a general discussion of friction and climbing slopes. Talk about climbing slippery slopes that are muddy or icy. Discuss the best materials for making shoe soles to produce good grip or high friction. Sketch slopes with different 'angles' on the board. Discuss how a slope with a steeper angle is more difficult to climb and requires greater friction between your shoes and the surface.

Develop the lesson by describing the friction test illustrated above right. The material to be tested (for example, a rubber eraser) is placed on the ruler. The ruler is tilted gradually to increase the angle of slope up to the point at which the rubber just starts to slip. The slip angle is a measure of the friction force between the rubber and

the ruler. The angle can be recorded by holding a card behind the ruler held at the slip angle, then marking the angle between the table and the ruler.

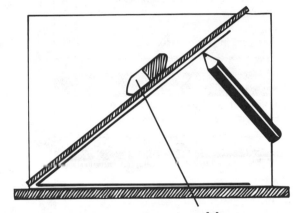
rubber

Set the children to work in groups to record the 'slip angles' for a range of different materials, including ice cubes if available. Suggest that they repeat the slip test several times for each sample. (With ice cubes, they should use a cube fresh from the freezer each time.) For the test to be fair, the children should raise the end of the ruler slowly, then hold it steady while the angle is marked on the card. Each card should be labelled with the material tested.

Differentiation
Less able children should concentrate on making careful relative measurements by recording angles as pencil lines on card.

More able children could begin to measure the angles using protractors.

Plenary
Compare and order the slip angles recorded for the different materials. *Which material has the most friction on the ruler surface? Which has the least?*

46 Choosing presents

Objectives

Numeracy
Use informal pencil-and-paper methods to support, record and explain money calculations.
English
Take part in group discussion.

Resources

A flip chart or board; a selection of gift catalogues; paper and pencils.

Vocabulary

price
spend
total
cost
most expensive
least expensive

Background

Choosing and buying presents for friends and family is enjoyable and rewarding. But you must use your mathematical skills to divide your resources 'fairly'. You should not spend more than you can afford, nor too much on any one item. In this lesson, groups of children are given a budget to select presents from catalogues for an imaginary family. Through discussion, they must identify suitable presents, add up prices and calculate the sum remaining from their initial budget.

Preparation

Collect appropriate gift catalogues and distribute them on tables in preparation for group work.

Main teaching activity

Introduce the lesson by talking about buying birthday and Christmas presents. *What is an appropriate gift for a grandmother, or for a new baby? What could you buy your 12 year-old brother or sister? What could you buy for Mum or Dad?*

Explain that in this lesson the children's task is to work in groups to select appropriate presents for, for example, a 55-year-old grandmother, a 35-year-old mother, a 35-year-old father, a 14-year-old girl, a 12-year-old boy and a 2-year-old toddler. Each group has a budget of £25.

Set the children to work in groups on the task. They should review the presents available in the gift catalogues, and discuss their suitability for the different family members. They should jot down two or three possible alternatives for each person with the prices, and make calculations to check that they are keeping within their budget. Through discussion, they should arrive at the final selection of presents, then calculate the total cost and the money left over from their budget.

Differentiation

Differentiate the difficulty of the task according to the ability level of the children by adjusting the number of family members and the budget.

Less able children should be set to buy fewer presents with a smaller budget.

More able children can work with a larger family and budget.

Plenary

Ask representatives of the groups to list the presents they have chosen and their costs, and to describe some of the issues they discussed as they reached their decision.

47 Plan a journey

Objectives

Numeracy
Use, read and write the vocabulary related to time.
Estimate and check times using minutes and hours.
Use the notation 9:30.
Read simple timetables.
Geography
Use secondary sources of information.
Use maps and plans.
**Builds on QCA Geography Unit 6:
Investigating our local area.**
ICT
Work with others to explore a variety of information sources.

Resources

Maps of the local area at an appropriate scale to include 5–10 railway stations; computers with Internet access.

Vocabulary

time
timetable
table
column
row
hour
minute

Background

Most children love trains and rail journeys. The Railtrack education website at www.discover-railtrack.co.uk provides an excellent range of cross-curricular educational resources based on the railway network, including a number of maths activities. The site links to the interactive rail timetable, which is simple enough for Year 4 children to use for journey planning. The timetable uses a 24-hour clock – but if you restrict the children to planning morning journeys, this need not be a problem.

Preparation

Obtain and reproduce local maps for the children to use (these could be downloaded from the Internet). Make sure you are familiar with the Railtrack website and the use of its interactive rail timetable.

Main teaching activity

Introduce the lesson by talking about railway journeys the children have made. *Where is the nearest railway station? What is its name? Where can you travel locally by rail?* Look at the maps with the children and identify the railway lines and stations.

Explain that the children are going to plan a railway journey. From the map they must choose a starting station and a destination. Explain that they are going to make the journey tomorrow morning and need to check the times of the trains on the Internet. Set them to work in small groups to make their initial plans away from the computer. What time would they like to travel? Discuss the various formats for representing times on timetables, including 9:30, 9.30 and 0930.

Move the children to work in groups at the computers (taking turns if necessary). Show them how to access the interactive rail timetable, enter their departure and destination stations, and select a travel time. From the initial data, the journey planner produces a simple timetable of trains departing near the preferred travel time. The children should print copies of these timetables to interpret later.

Differentiation

Make sure that the less able children plan morning journeys to local stations.

More able children can extend the range of their journeys. This may involve making connections and interpreting the 24-hour clock.

Plenary

Ask representatives of the groups to show the journey plans they have produced. They should talk about their departure station, destination, departure time and journey time, demonstrating how they have established the times from the Internet travel planner.

48 Festivals and holidays

Objectives

Numeracy
Use this year's calendar.
PSHE and citizenship
Respect cultural, ethnic, racial and religious diversity.

Resources

A large current year planner for wall display; a selection of current year calendars and diaries that the children can use to research holiday dates around the world (most diaries contain tables of national and international holidays); paper and pencils; research resources (including books and CD-ROMs) from which the children can research holidays and festivals; pins, coloured wool or ribbon, a pinboard.

Vocabulary

calendar
year
month
day
date

Background

The pattern of the year, with school terms interspersed by holidays, becomes established in the children's thinking as they move through the school. Some holidays are regular breaks for rest and leisure activities. Others are associated with celebrations, festivals or other special occasions, often with a religious basis. In Year 4, children are ready to use this year's calendar to research and record particular dates. Creating a wall year plan marking the dates of religious festivals, school terms and holidays links work on the calendar to discussion of the origins of and the customs associated with festivals and holidays around the world.

Preparation

Pin up the year planner where all the children can see it. Assemble the research materials and set them out in preparation for group work.

Main teaching activity

Introduce the lesson by talking about holidays and festivals. *When are the school holidays? How is holiday time different from school time? Are there any special festivals or celebrations that take place during the holidays? What special festivals do your family celebrate each year? At what times of year do these festivals take place? What are the usual activities on these special days?* Invite children to explain the origins and significance of these festivals to the class.

Develop the lesson by drawing the children's attention to the year planner on the wall. Examine the organisation of months and days in columns and rows. Explain that you are going to use the planner to record the dates of special holiday festivals around the world. Divide the class into groups and assign each group a two-month period to research. They should use diaries and calendars to identify the dates of national or international holidays and festivals during their assigned months. They should then focus on two or three of the festivals they have discovered, and use the research materials to produce a short written account of the beliefs and customs associated with these days.

Differentiation

Guide less able children to research festivals familiar to them from their culture – for example, Easter, Diwali, Hanukkah, Eid or the Chinese New Year.

More able children should be encouraged to research and write about festivals from a range of cultures.

Plenary

Discuss the children's writing as a class. Enter the names of the festivals in the appropriate dates on the wall planner. Create a display, using pins and coloured ribbon or wool to link the highlighted festivals to samples of the children's writing about them.

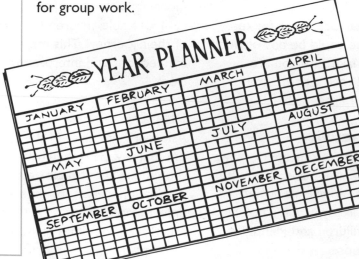

Linked to
S c i e n c e

49 Wildlife survey

Objectives

Numeracy
Solve a problem by collecting quickly, organising, representing and interpreting data in tables, charts, graphs and diagrams, including those generated by a computer.
Science
To identify locally occurring animals.
Links to QCA Science Unit 4B: Habitats.

Resources

Notebooks and pencils; field guides and posters for identifying birds, minibeasts and mammals; materials for creating charts and tables, including suitable computer software such as *Textease* or *Microsoft Excel*; a flip chart or board.

Vocabulary

count
tally
frequency table
bar chart
most common
least common

Background

A survey of wildlife in the different habitats around the school – for example, on the playing field, in trees and bushes, in and around the school pond, under stones, or on the school building – can be an ongoing science investigation throughout the year. Records of birds, insects and other animals spotted can be kept as class wildlife 'logs' on a daily or weekly basis. The children can sketch the animals in their nature notebooks, and identify them with the help of field guides. The records should be reviewed periodically, and the children's data handling skills used to create tables, charts and graphs for display.

Preparation

Earlier in the term, assemble suitable reference materials to create a nature corner in the classroom. In a science lesson, introduce the nature corner to the class and explain that the children should keep a daily record of, for example, birds visiting the bird table outside the window. Discuss an appropriate procedure for keeping this record – for example, by assigning two children per day to put out food and observe for 15 minutes, counting, identifying and recording the birds that come to the table. Similar records could be kept of animals observed in and around the pond, or found under stones.

Main teaching activity

When the children's nature records have accumulated sufficiently to justify preparing tables and charts, devote a maths lesson to creating a display and interpreting the data. For example, if you have been recording birds visiting the bird table, use the daily log to tally and prepare frequency tables of the numbers of birds and the different species observed during the period. Draw up the tables on the board for the children to interpret.

Set the children to work in groups to display the data in various ways. One group, for example, could create a bar chart of total bird numbers day by day or week by week; another could plot total numbers of different species observed during the period. Other groups could work with pictograms instead of bar charts, or use their ICT skills to create tables and charts on the computer. Discuss the various possibilities with the children.

Differentiation

Less able children could produce a simple table of the numbers of birds seen on five successive days.

More able children can explore the potential of software packages for displaying data – for example, producing bar charts and pie charts from the same data set.

Plenary

Use the children's charts and tables to create a display in the wildlife corner. Conclude the lesson with questions based on the display:
● *Which is the most common species visiting the bird table?*
● *What was the greatest number of birds seen on any one day?*

50 Assessment 3

Preparation

Make copies of the worksheets. If you feel that the assessment sheet is too 'busy', the three activities could be separated and enlarged on individual sheets.

Lesson introduction

Begin the lesson by reviewing the relevant cross-curricular topics covered during the term. Remind the children of some of the projects and investigations they have undertaken, and ask them to recall and recount their work. Stress the mathematical content – for example, *Do you remember how we discussed sharing money fairly?*

Main assessment activity

Distribute the assessment sheets and ask the children to work on them individually. Guide the whole class through the questions one at a time, reading the text with them and prompting them to work out and fill in their answers. Try to make the whole activity enjoyable!

Practical activity

Set out the building blocks and copies of page 170. Ask the children to reproduce the shapes on the sheet.

Objectives

The assessment activities in this book are designed to introduce Key Stage 2 children to SAT-style questions. They are set in cross-curricular contexts based on the preceding term's lessons. The questions in Assessment 3 test the children's progress in: recalling facts for the 2, 3, 4, 5 and 10 times tables; using symbols correctly and knowing the relationships between familiar units of length, mass and capacity; deriving quickly division facts corresponding to the 4 and 5 times tables and dealing with remainders; visualising 3-D shapes from 2-D drawings.

Resources

One copy per child of photocopiable pages 174 and 170; pencils; wooden building blocks.

Plenary

Review the answers to the questions as a class. Collect the completed question sheets to use as an aid to judging individual children's progress, and to include in your records. The answers are:
1. See table below.
2. 1kg > 1g, $\frac{1}{2}$ l = 500ml, 0.2m < 25cm, 0.5kg < 700g, $\frac{3}{4}$ cm >5mm, 30mm = 3cm, $\frac{1}{10}$ m = 10cm, 100mm < 1m, 0.1kg = 100g
3. 7p, 3p
4. 9p, 4p

×	0	1	2	3	4	5	6	7	8	9	10
0	0	0	0	0	0	0	0	0	0	0	0
1	0	1	2	3	4	5	6	7	8	9	10
2	0	2	4	6	8	10	12	14	16	18	20
3	0	3	6	9	12	15	18	21	24	27	30
4	0	4	8	12	16	20	24	28	32	36	40
5	0	5	10	15	20	25	30	35	40	45	50
10	0	10	20	30	40	50	60	70	80	90	100

Words and numbers

● Write these numbers in figures.

three thousand two hundred

two thousand one hundred and eighty-three

five thousand three hundred and sixty

seven thousand six hundred and six

four thousand eight hundred and seventy-six

nine thousand and eighteen

● Write these numbers in words.

3001	
2050	
4700	
5018	
5608	
9316	
7854	
9999	

Compare yourself with a gorilla!

Gorilla

arm span = 240cm

height   = 170cm

chest   = 140cm

waist   = 140cm

mass   = 156kg

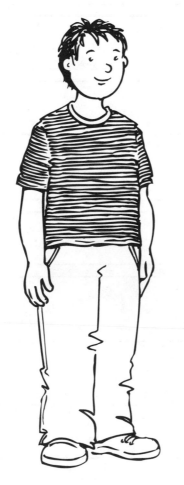

Me

arm span =

height   =

chest   =

waist   =

mass   =

Milometer

● Fill in the new milometer reading at the end of the journey.

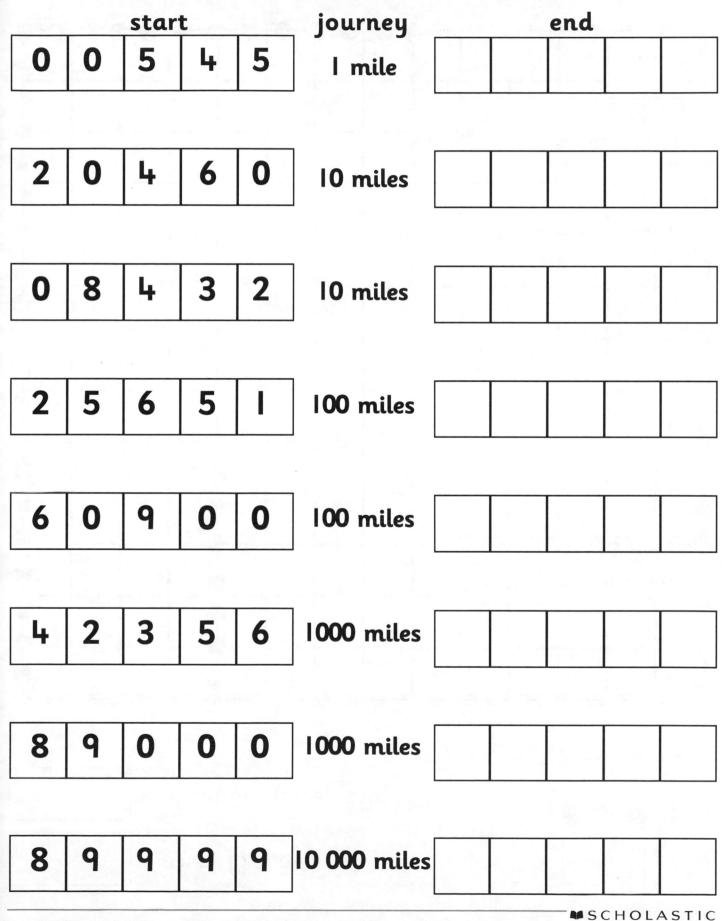

	start				journey		end			
0	0	5	4	5	1 mile					
2	0	4	6	0	10 miles					
0	8	4	3	2	10 miles					
2	5	6	5	1	100 miles					
6	0	9	0	0	100 miles					
4	2	3	5	6	1000 miles					
8	9	0	0	0	1000 miles					
8	9	9	9	9	10 000 miles					

▰SCHOLASTIC

Find the perimeter

● Find the perimeters of the farmer's fields.

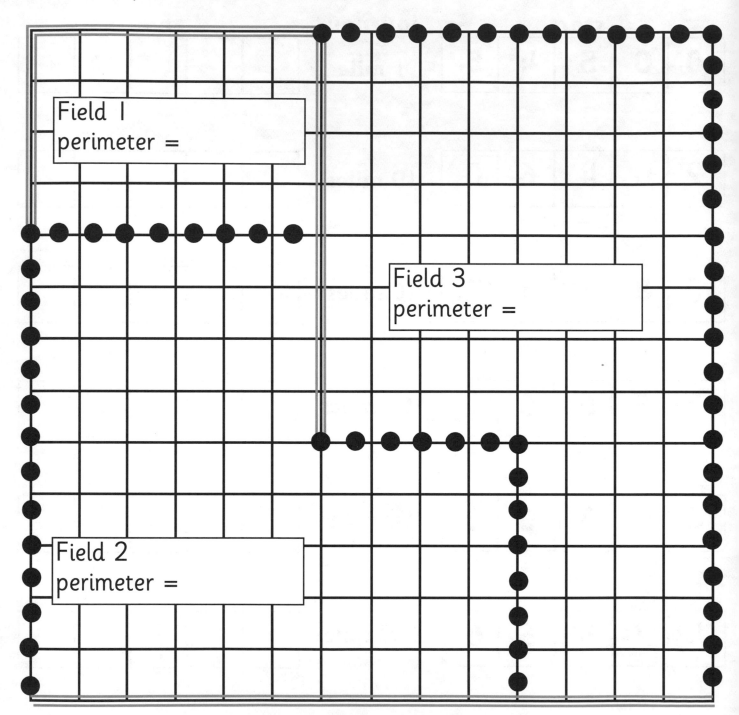

Field 1
perimeter =

Field 3
perimeter =

Field 2
perimeter =

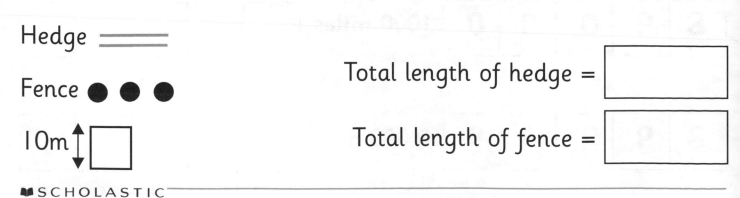

Hedge ═══

Fence ● ● ●

10m ↕ ☐

Total length of hedge = ☐

Total length of fence = ☐

Through the looking glass

● Draw the reflections of the shapes in the mirrors. Use the grid to help.

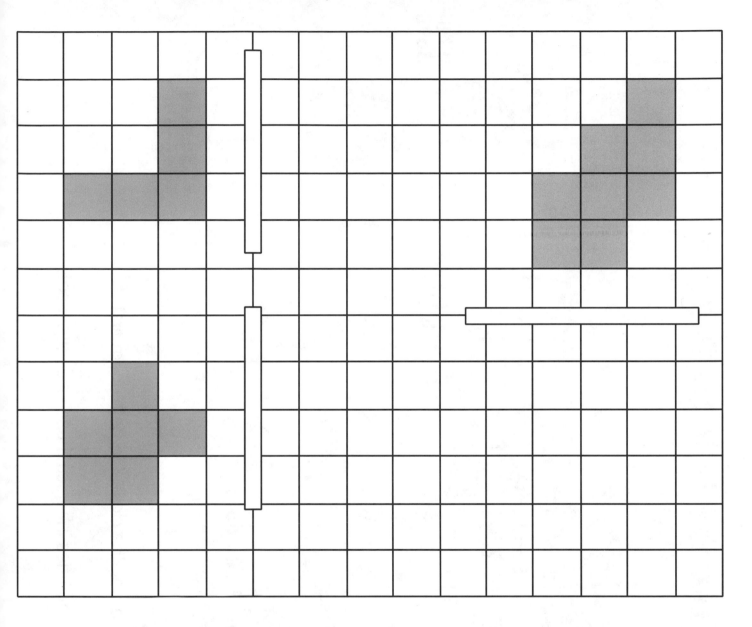

How far is it to Bethlehem?

The distances are shown in miles.

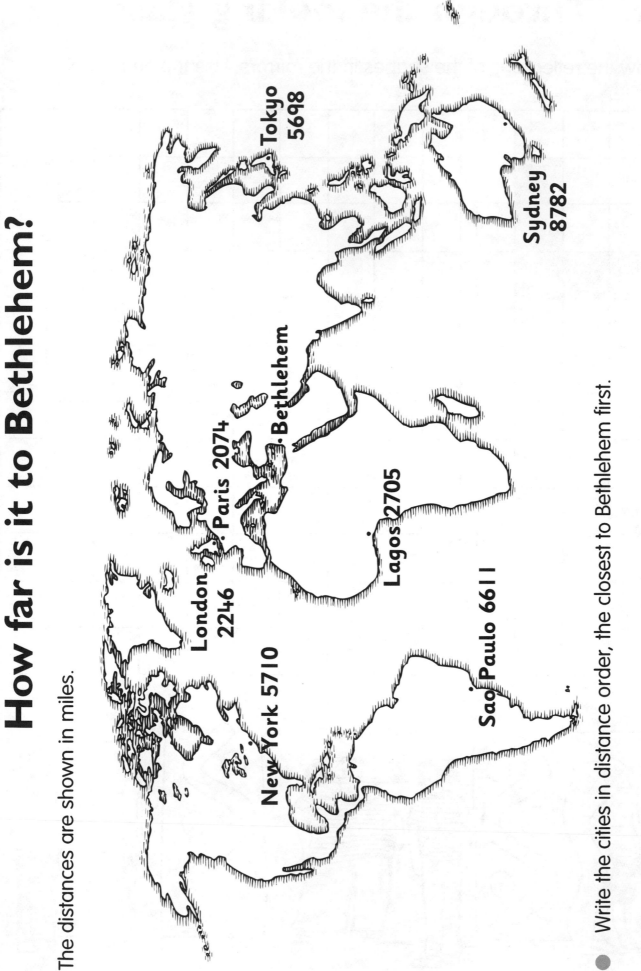

Tokyo 5698

Sydney 8782

Bethlehem

Paris 2074

Lagos 2705

London 2246

New York 5710

Sao Paulo 6611

Write the cities in distance order, the closest to Bethlehem first.

Name the continents and countries in which these cities are located.

Fair shares

- Discuss how to share the money fairly in these problems.

1. Five children share 20p.

2. Three children share £6.00.

3. Four children share £1.60.

4. Two children share five 5p coins and five 2p coins.

5. Three children share one pound coin, three 50p coins, two 20p coins and three 5p coins.

6. Four children share three 10p coins, eight 5p coins and six 2p coins.

7. Simon does a paper round every Sunday. He delivers 40 papers. He is paid £5.00. One Sunday, Simon's younger brother James helps him. James delivers 10 of the papers. How much should Simon give James?

8. Alice is given £10 as a birthday present. She decides to save some of the money, spend some on a book, spend some on sweets and spend some on a present for her sister. Discuss how she should divide up the money.

Name

1. Round these distances to the nearest 10 miles.

54 miles   108 miles   324 miles   815 miles

2. Round these distance to the nearest 100 miles.

220 miles   892 miles   448 miles   550 miles

3. Write these times on the digital clocks.

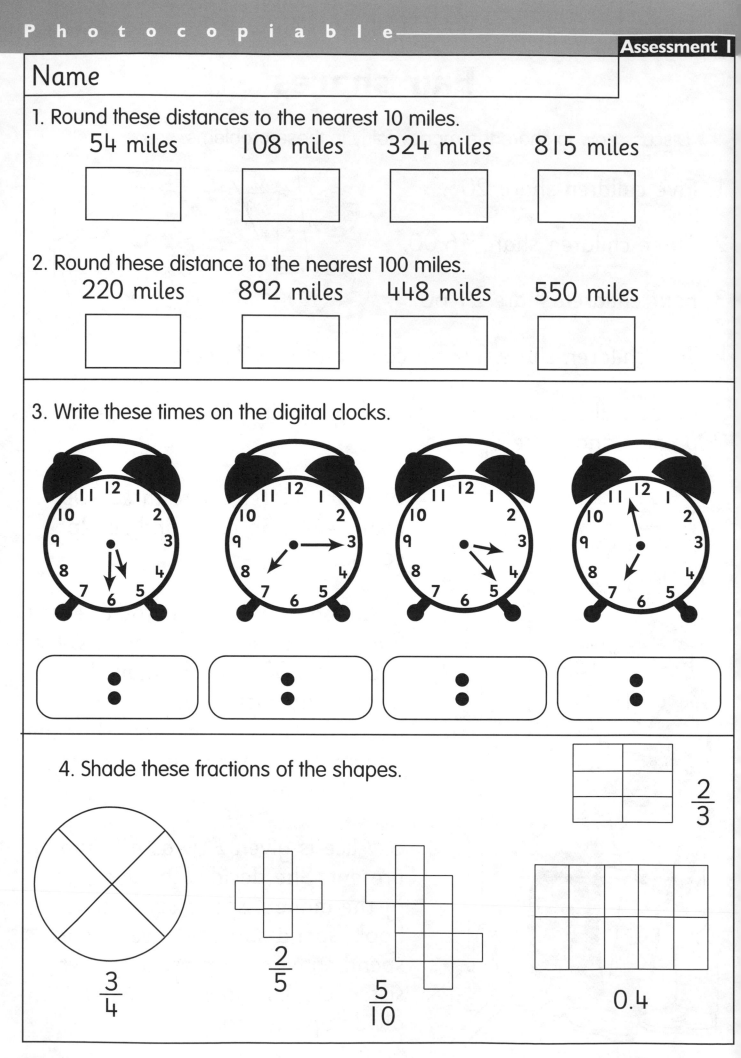

4. Shade these fractions of the shapes.

$\frac{2}{3}$

$\frac{3}{4}$

$\frac{2}{5}$

$\frac{5}{10}$

0.4

Shoe styles

- Conduct a survey of shoe fasteners in your class.

- Use this frequency table.

fastening	tally	frequency
laces		
Velcro		
zips		
buckles		
slip-on		

- Use a pictogram to display your results.

fastening	
laces	
Velcro	
zips	
buckles	
slip-on	

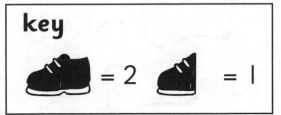

key

= 2   = 1

SCHOLASTIC

Missing digits and signs

● A spider has blotted the ink! Write these number sentences correctly.

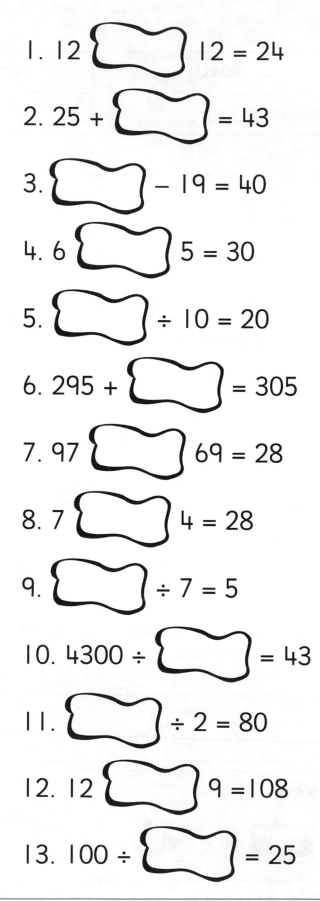

1. 12 ⬡ 12 = 24

2. 25 + ⬡ = 43

3. ⬡ − 19 = 40

4. 6 ⬡ 5 = 30

5. ⬡ ÷ 10 = 20

6. 295 + ⬡ = 305

7. 97 ⬡ 69 = 28

8. 7 ⬡ 4 = 28

9. ⬡ ÷ 7 = 5

10. 4300 ÷ ⬡ = 43

11. ⬡ ÷ 2 = 80

12. 12 ⬡ 9 = 108

13. 100 ÷ ⬡ = 25

What temperature?

● Look at the thermometer and write down the temperatures of:

boiling water ▢   melting ice ▢

a hot bath ▢

the human body ▢   a cold winter's night ▢

a comfortable room ▢   a deep freeze ▢

● What is the highest temperature shown? ▢

● What is the lowest temperature shown? ▢

● What is the temperature difference between:

• boiling water and melting ice? ▢

• a hot bath and the human body? ▢

• a comfortable room and a cold winter night? ▢

• melting ice and a deep freeze? ▢

• boiling water and a deep freeze? ▢

• a cold winter night and a deep freeze? ▢

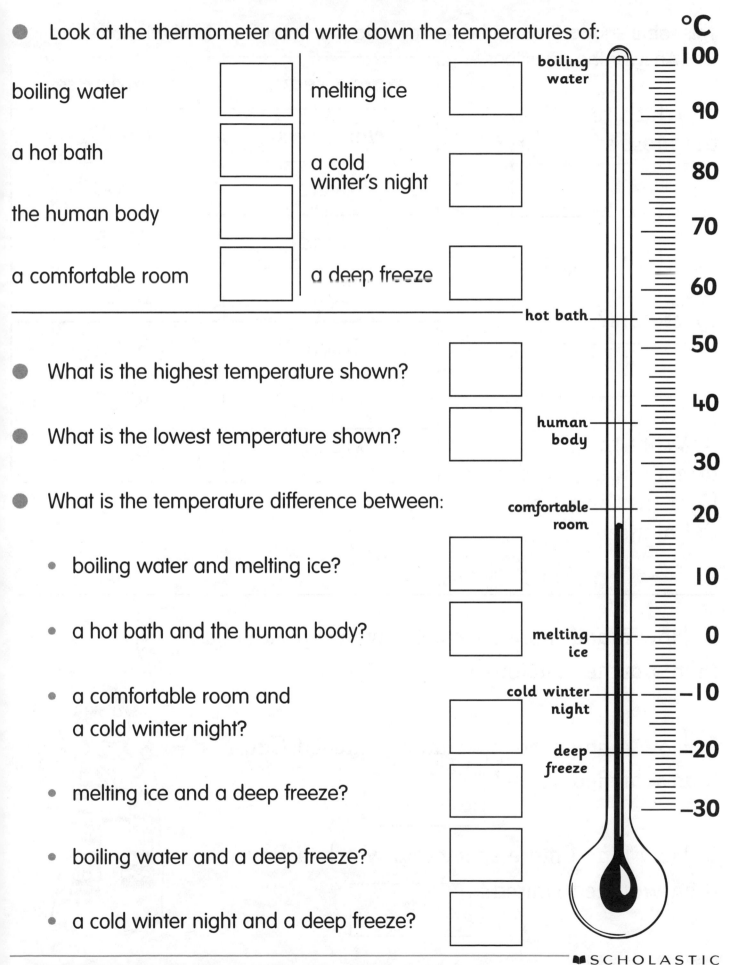

°C

boiling water — 100
— 90
— 80
hot bath — — 50
— 40
human body — — 30
comfortable room — — 20
— 10
melting ice — 0
cold winter night — −10
deep freeze — −20
— −30
— 70
— 60

■ SCHOLASTIC

Attendances

This table shows the number of spectators at Saturday's football matches.

● Answer the questions.

1. Which team had the most spectators?

2. Which team had the fewest spectators?

3. Write the attendances in order, from the lowest to the highest.

home team	attendance
Wanderers	8515
Rovers	9003
United	8995
City	6005
Town	5998
Athletic	9302
Albion	9297

4. How many more spectators watched Athletic than watched Albion?

5. How many more spectators watched City than watched Town?

6. How many more spectators watched Rovers than watched United?

● Complete the table of room sizes.

Roman home

↕1m

	perimeter in metres	area in square metres
room		
C cubiculum (small room/bedroom)		
Cu culina (kitchen)		
V vestibulum (entrance hall)		
T taberna (shop)		
Tri triclinium (dining room)		
A atrium (entrance hall)		
P peristylium (garden)		

◣SCHOLASTIC

Give the co-ordinates

Record the co-ordinates of the finds in this table.

find	co-ordinates
brooch	
sword	
helmet	
fireplace	
pottery	
arrow head	
burial chamber	
necklace	

This map records finds at an archeological dig.

Shape keys

- Use this key to identify triangles.

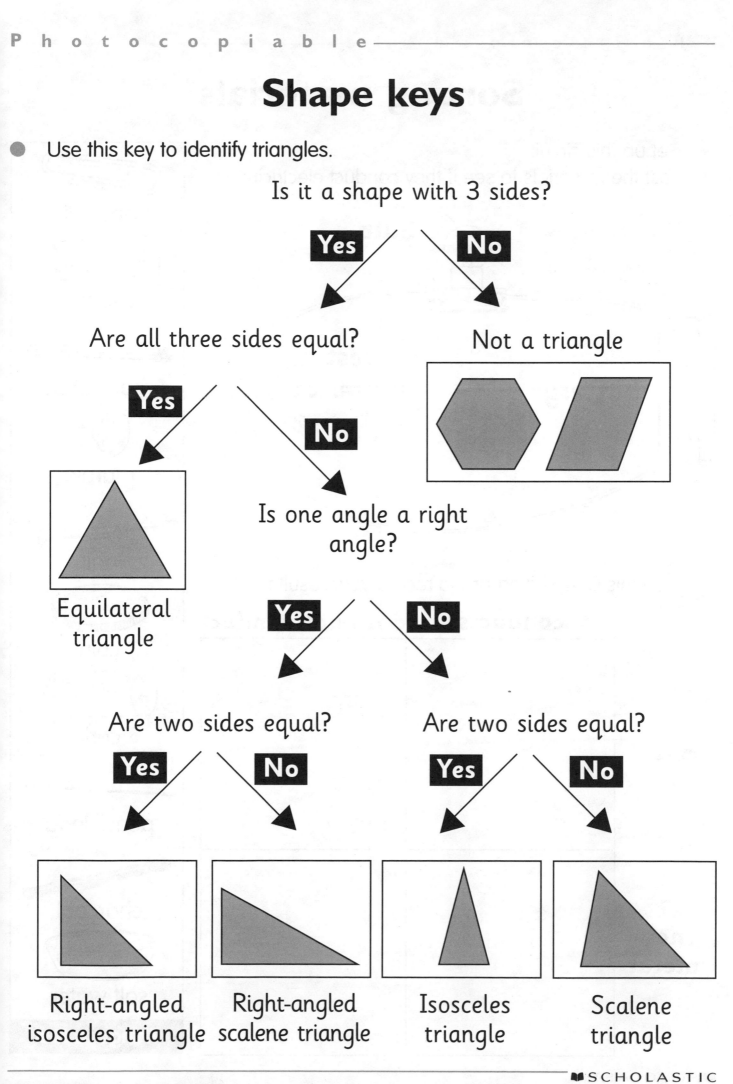

Is it a shape with 3 sides?

Yes / **No**

Are all three sides equal?   Not a triangle

Yes / **No**

Equilateral triangle

Is one angle a right angle?

Yes / **No**

Are two sides equal?   Are two sides equal?

Yes / **No**   **Yes** / **No**

Right-angled isosceles triangle | Right-angled scalene triangle | Isosceles triangle | Scalene triangle

Sorting materials

● Set up this circuit.
● Test the materials to see if they conduct electricity.

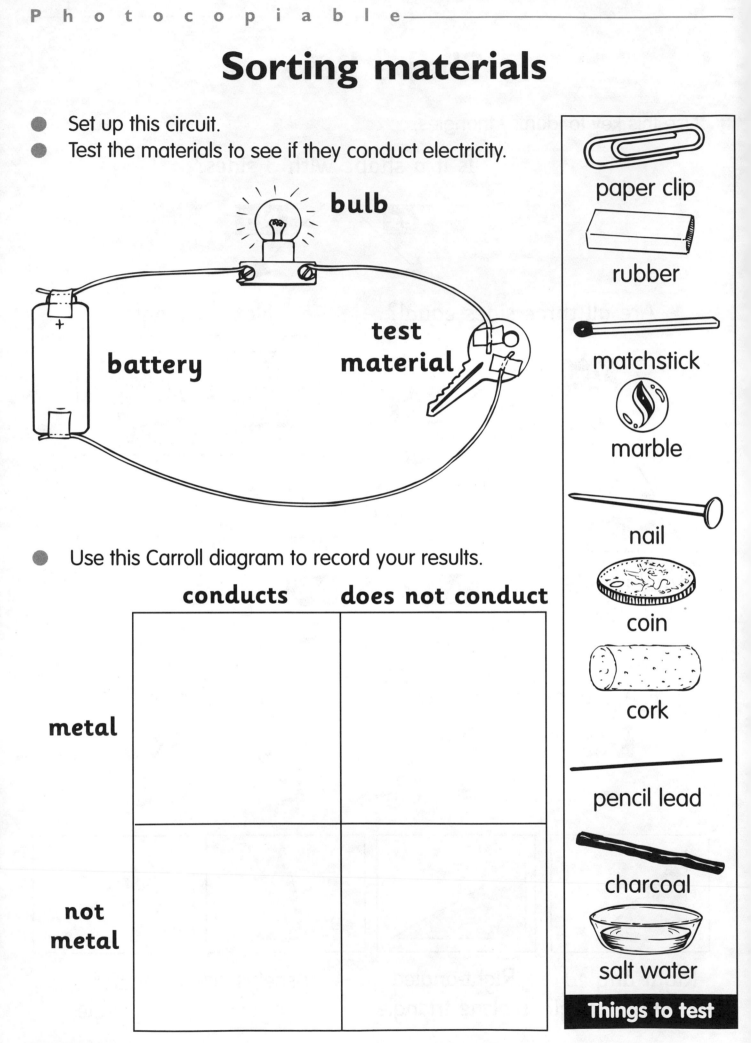

bulb

battery

test material

● Use this Carroll diagram to record your results.

	conducts	does not conduct
metal		
not metal		

Things to test:
- paper clip
- rubber
- matchstick
- marble
- nail
- coin
- cork
- pencil lead
- charcoal
- salt water

Things to test

Recycling sums

This table shows the waste materials thrown away by a family each week.

material	mass equal to	actual mass
metal	20 food cans	
glass	12 jam jars	
plastic	30 lemonade bottles	
paper	15 newspapers	
food waste	8 cabbages	

Answer these questions.

1. How many 'cans worth' of metal does the family throw away in a year?

2. How many 'newspapers worth' of paper does the family throw away in a month?

3. How many 'lemonade bottles worth' of plastic does the family throw away every three months?

4. Use scales to measure the mass of newspapers, cabbages, empty food cans, jam jars and plastic bottles. Calculate the actual mass of each material thrown away each week by the family. Fill in the third column on the table.

Matching measures

● Record these readings.

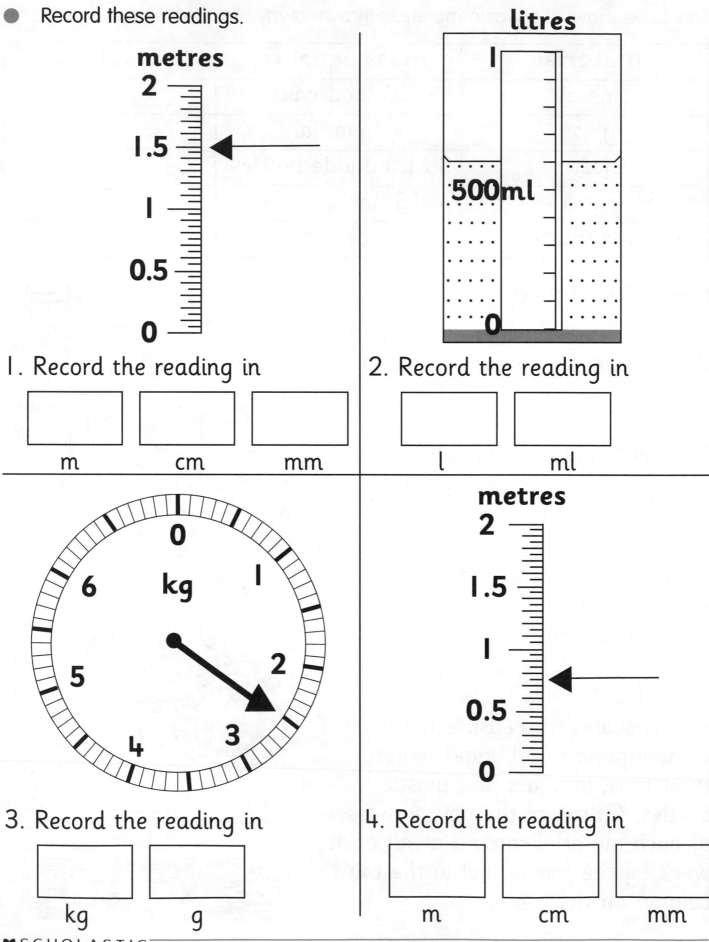

metres
2
1.5
1
0.5
0

litres
l
500ml
0

1. Record the reading in

m	cm	mm

2. Record the reading in

l	ml

kg
0 1 2 3 4 5 6

metres
2
1.5
1
0.5
0

3. Record the reading in

kg	g

4. Record the reading in

m	cm	mm

100 CROSS-CURRICULAR MATHS LESSONS Years 3 & 4/Scottish Primary 4–5

Highest and lowest

This table gives the average temperature in January and July in some major world cities.

● Answer the questions below.

City	Average January temperature in °C	Average July temperature in °C
Lagos	26.8	25.1
London	4.9	18.4
New York	−0.4	24.3
Paris	3.7	19.0
Sao Paulo	21.2	14.8
Sydney	22.1	12.0
Tokyo	3.7	24.7

1. Which city has the highest temperature in July? _____

2. Which city is the coldest in January? _____

3. In which city does the temperature change most between January and July? _____

4. In which city does the temperature change least between January and July? _____

● Use the greater than (>) and less than (<) signs to fill in the gaps in these sentences.

In January the temperature in Sydney is _____ the temperature in Tokyo.

In July the temperature in Tokyo is _____ the temperature in Lagos.

■SCHOLASTIC

Name

1. Find the perimeter and area of each shape.

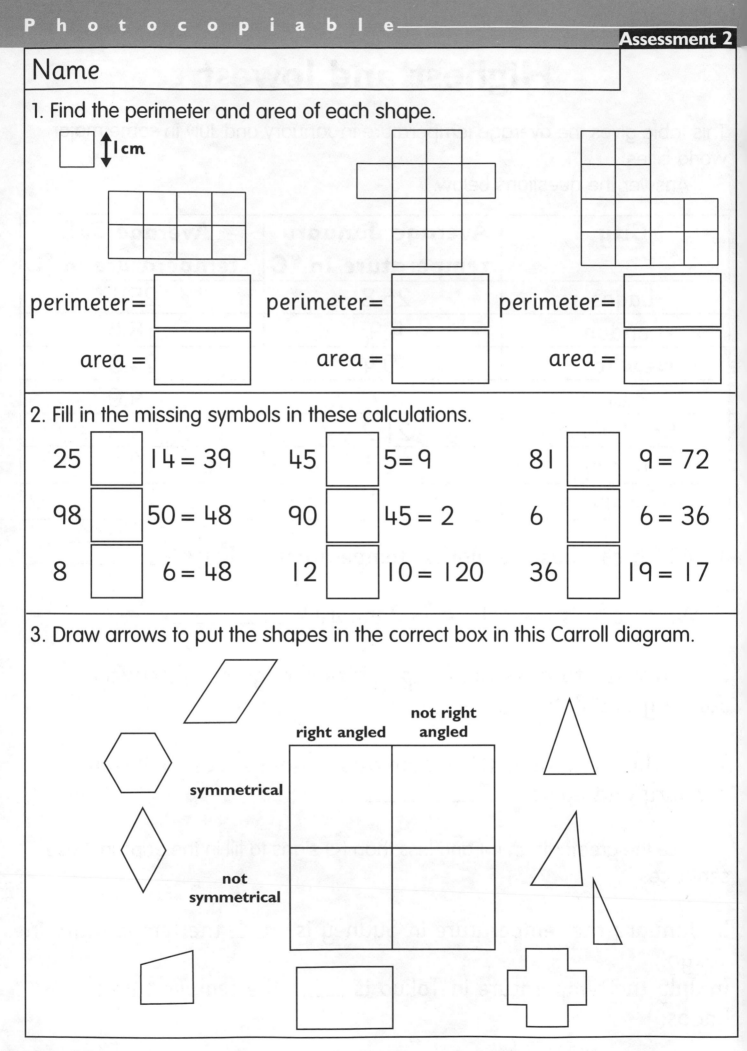

perimeter= [ ]   perimeter= [ ]   perimeter= [ ]

area = [ ]   area = [ ]   area = [ ]

2. Fill in the missing symbols in these calculations.

25 [ ] 14 = 39   45 [ ] 5 = 9   81 [ ] 9 = 72

98 [ ] 50 = 48   90 [ ] 45 = 2   6 [ ] 6 = 36

8 [ ] 6 = 48   12 [ ] 10 = 120   36 [ ] 19 = 17

3. Draw arrows to put the shapes in the correct box in this Carroll diagram.

	right angled	not right angled
symmetrical		
not symmetrical		

Sponsor me

● Some children have run a sponsored 'maths marathon'.

● Complete this form by filling in the totals.

name	amount sponsored per 'sum' in pence	number of 'sums' completed	money raised in pounds and pence
Simon	10p	25	
Laura	5p	80	
Sophie	20p	20	
Shane	2p	110	
Vineeta	15p	40	
Zak	6p	100	
Russell	8p	70	

total money raised =

Choosing chairs

● Use this table to make a survey of chair sizes in your school.

Description of chair	Height of chair seat in cm	Ages of children who use chair

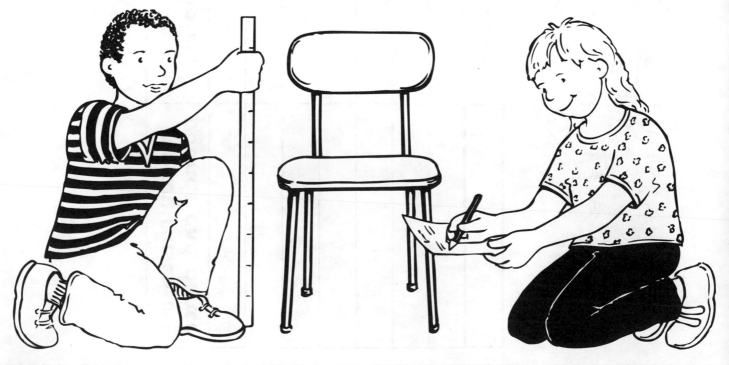

Compass points

1. In which direction must you set off to walk from:

- the pond to the castle? _____

- the crossroads to the church? _____

- the church to the Post Office? _____

- the Post Office to the water tower? _____

- the water tower to the crossroads? _____

2. Some walkers follow a route between these co-ordinates:
(10, 6) to (8, 8) to (5, 5) to (3, 7) to (1, 5) to (5, 1).
Write a description of their journey. List the places they visit and the directions they travel between them.

Building blocks

● Make these shapes with building blocks.

1.

2.

3.

4.

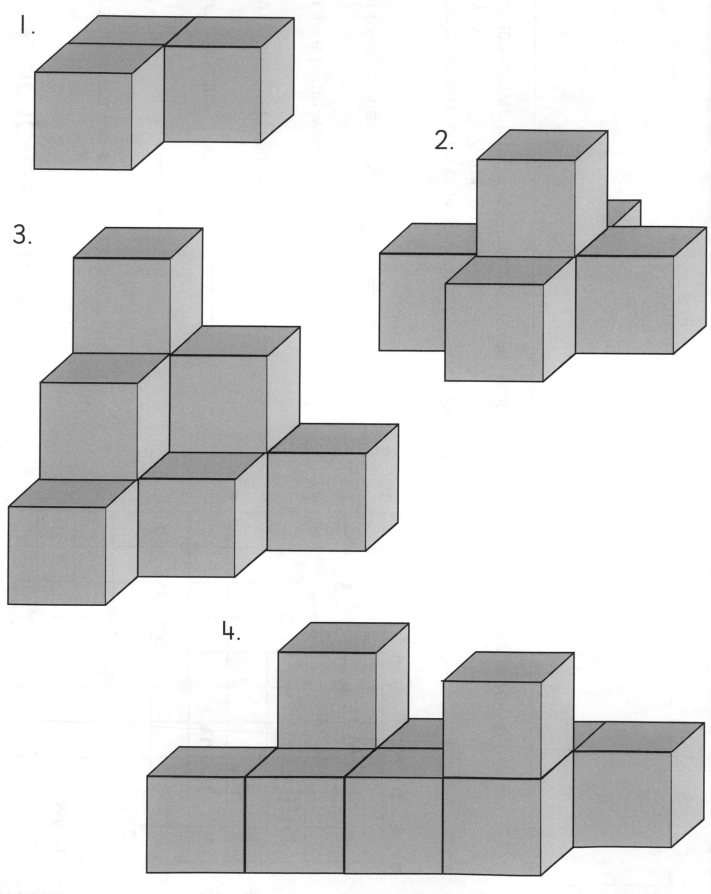

In which year?

● Estimate the dates of these events in the 20th century from the timeline.

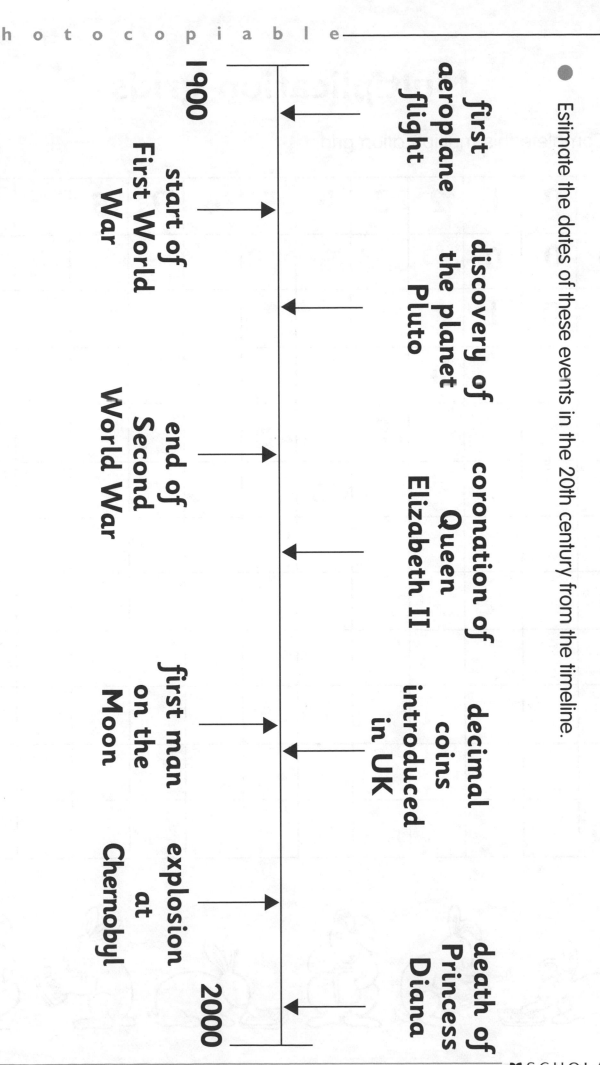

first
aeroplane
flight

discovery of
the planet
Pluto

coronation of
Queen
Elizabeth II

decimal
coins
introduced
in UK

death of
Princess
Diana

1900

start of
First World
War

end of
Second
World War

first man
on the
Moon

explosion
at
Chernobyl

2000

● Use history reference books to check your estimates of the dates.

Multiplication grids

● Complete this multiplication grid.

×	0	1	2	3	4	5	6	7	8	9	10
0	0	0									
1	0	1									
2			4								
3				9							
4					16						
5											
6											
7											
8											
9											
10											

One in every...

● Fill in the missing numbers.

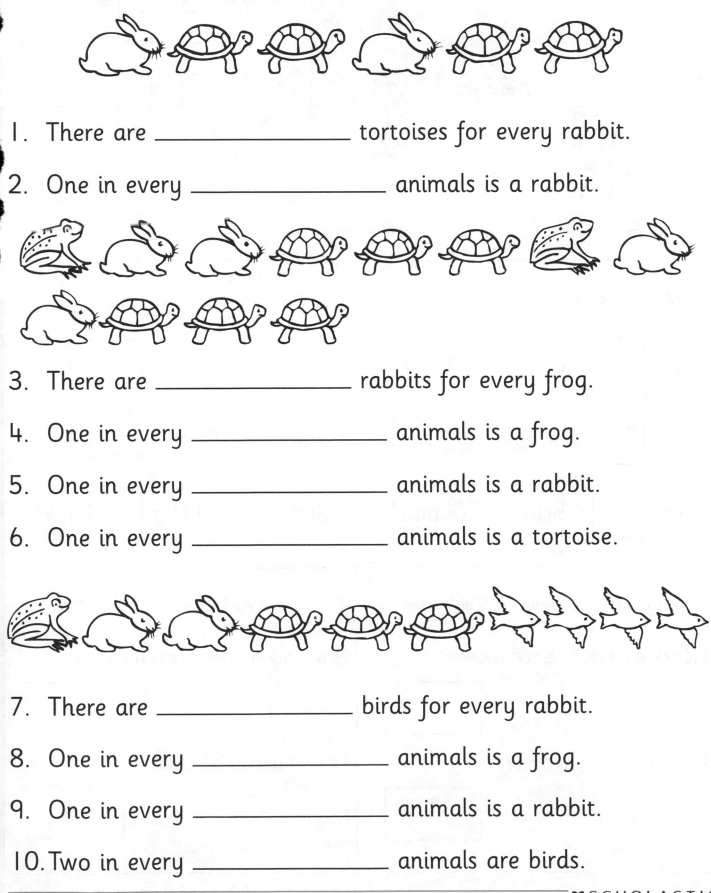

1. There are _____ tortoises for every rabbit.

2. One in every _____ animals is a rabbit.

3. There are _____ rabbits for every frog.

4. One in every _____ animals is a frog.

5. One in every _____ animals is a rabbit.

6. One in every _____ animals is a tortoise.

7. There are _____ birds for every rabbit.

8. One in every _____ animals is a frog.

9. One in every _____ animals is a rabbit.

10. Two in every _____ animals are birds.

Name

Complete this multiplication grid.

×	0	1	2	3	4	5	6	7	8	9	10
0	0	0									
1	0	1									
2			4								
3				9							
4					16						
5											
10											

2. Write >, < or = between these measurements.

1kg ☐ 1g   0.5kg ☐ 700g $\frac{1}{10}$ m ☐ 10cm

$\frac{1}{2}$ l ☐ 500ml $\frac{3}{4}$ cm ☐ 5mm   100mm ☐ 1m

0.2m ☐ 25cm   300mm ☐ 3cm   0.1kg ☐ 100g

3. Share 31p between 4 children.

How much does each receive?

☐

How much is left over?

☐

4. Share 49p between 5 children.

How much does each receive?

☐

How much is left over?

☐

Numeracy index

Cross-curricular index